W9-AHB-123

How to Spot the
Next Starbucks,
Whole Foods,
Walmart, or
McDonald's
Before
Its Shares
Explode

ALSO BY MARK TIER

NONFICTION

Understanding Inflation

The Nature of Market Cycles

How to Get a Second Passport

The Winning Investment Habits of Warren Buffett & George Soros:
Harness the Investment Genius of the World's Richest Investors

When God Speaks for Himself: The Words of God You'll Never Hear
in Church or Sunday School (with George Forrai)

Ayn Rand's 5 Surprising Simple Rules for Judging Political Candidates:
Never be Fooled by a Politician Again

How to Make More Money by Sitting on Your Butt—
and Other Contrarian Conclusions from a Lifetime in the Markets

FICTION

Give Me Liberty (coedited with Martin H. Greenberg)

Visions of Liberty (coedited with Martin H. Greenberg)

Freedom! (coedited with Martin H. Greenberg)

Trust Your Enemies

How to Spot the Next Starbucks, Whole Foods, Walmart, or McDonald's *Before* Its Shares Explode

A Low-Risk Investment You Can Pretty Much "Buy and Forget"— Until You Want to Retire to Florida or the South of France

Mark Tier

St. Martin's Press  New York

HOW TO SPOT THE NEXT STARBUCKS, WHOLE FOODS, WALMART, OR MCDONALD'S *BEFORE* ITS SHARES EXPLODE. Copyright © 2017 by Mark Tier. All rights reserved.
Printed in the United States of America.
For information, address St. Martin's Press, 175 Fifth Avenue, New York, N.Y. 10010.

www.stmartins.com

Photos courtesy of Mark Tier, Shaun Narca, Tim Staermose, Natasha Tier, Henry Newrick, and Alexis Gotladera.

The Library of Congress Cataloging-in-Publication Data is available upon request.

ISBN 978-1-250-07156-9 (hardcover)
ISBN 978-1-250-17132-0 (international; sold outside the U.S., subject to rights availability)
ISBN 978-1-4668-8270-6 (e-book)

Our books may be purchased in bulk for promotional, educational, or business use. Please contact your local bookseller or the Macmillan Corporate and Premium Sales Department at 1-800-221-7945, extension 5442, or by e-mail at MacmillanSpecialMarkets@macmillan.com.

First Edition: August 2017
First International Edition: August 2017

10 9 8 7 6 5 4 3 2 1

CONTENTS

The 5 Clues to Spotting the Next Starbucks

The Differences That Make the Difference

➚ Why does Starbucks have more stores than any other coffee company, and not Peet's (which had a twenty-year head start on Starbucks), Seattle's Best, or someone else?

➚ What turned an "upstart" discounter named Walmart into the world's biggest and most profitable retailer, *and* one of the world's top two companies by sales?* While passing the then much larger Kmart and Target chains to become bigger than both of them combined?

➚ How come Ray Kroc's McDonald's gained the "first mover" advantage to become the world's biggest hamburger chain, while Burger King, which had a two-year head start, lost theirs? And a third burger chain, Burger Chef, which was within shooting distance of taking the number one spot from McDonald's—went out of business instead?

➚ And why was Whole Foods, of the hundreds of specialty grocers in the United States when it opened its doors, the one that grew to dominate its market?

---

*Every year since 2000, Walmart and Exxon have shared the top two spots on the Fortune 500 list, alternating (mostly) with the price of oil.

What, to summarize, are the crucial *differences that make the difference* between a good company and a great growth stock?

These are the questions that we'll be examining—and answering—here. The aim is to give you the tools and the concepts you need to identify the *next* start-up company that could follow in the footsteps of these four.

Tools that can *also* be applied to start the "next Starbucks" yourself.

And with numbers like these, who wouldn't want to get in on the ground floor?

	VALUE OF $1,000 INVESTED AT THE IPO OF			
	McDonald's	Walmart	Whole Foods	Starbucks
IPO date	21 April 1965	1 October 1970	23 January 1992	1 June 1992
$1,000 invested at IPO now worth*	$3,705,110.93	$8,637,595.15	$26,757.65	$201,901.18
Dividends	$6,438,828.27	$1,526,522.10	$3,913.39	$4,023.25
Total return	$10,143,939.20	$10,164,117.26	$30,671.04	$205,924.42
Compounded annual return	19.6%	22.2%	14.8%	24.5%
S&P 500	6.38%	7.27%	6.85%	7.1%

* As of 26 October 2016. S&P comparison over same time period as each company's IPO to present.
Sources: Yahoo! Finance, walmart.com, aboutmcdonalds.com.

By comparing Starbucks' pattern of growth to that of other high-growth companies, we can single out the five significant factors they *all* have in common. The practices that made Starbucks, McDonald's, Walmart, Whole Foods, and their ilk tower above their many competitors.

Once we've identified the "differences that make the difference," they become:

The 5 Clues to Spotting the Next Starbucks

➤ *They* permanently *change people's habits:* McDonald's permanently changed the way we eat—indeed, McDonald's kicked off the fast-food business as we know it today. Walmart and Whole Foods changed the way people shop; and before Starbucks, how many Americans had heard of a $4 latte, let alone drunk one?

➤ *They're copycats:* Ray Kroc duplicated the original McDonald brothers' store worldwide—lock, stock, and barrel.

➤ *Their success is* validated *by competition:* There are thousands of Starbucks, McDonald's, Walmart, and Whole Foods "clones" around the world—with more opening just about every day. Competition proves the founder's concept and demonstrates that the potential size of the market is enormous. A company that does not inspire competition is destined to serve a small market niche.

↗ *They're driven by the founder's vision and passion:* A company whose management doesn't inspire its employees won't inspire—and keep—its customers. The founders of Starbucks (Howard Schultz), Whole Foods (John Mackey), Walmart (Sam Walton), and McDonald's (Ray Kroc) all successfully transmitted their vision and passion throughout their companies, translating it into a unique customer experience.

↗ *They have superb* entrepreneurial *management and execution:* Thousands of good to great businesses share the first four characteristics, but without entrepreneurs at the helm who also have superb management and execution skills, they're destined to remain small, or even one-man bands.

None of these factors is necessarily unique to a growth company. But when you find all five together in *one* company, you can be pretty confident that you've found a great candidate for the next high-growth stock.

But how can you, as an average investor in the street, find such a hot growth stock? Especially when you have no access to top management, no insider information, and no hope of getting any and would rather go to Starbucks than read its annual report?

While it's not easy, it's a lot easier than you probably think.

The first step is to appreciate how and why companies that faithfully practice the five clues inevitably outstrip competitors that don't.

This is the subject of part 1, where we compare Starbucks, McDonald's, Walmart, and Whole Foods with each other—and with their various competitors that fell behind—to see exactly how and why the clues separate a great company from a merely good one.

In part 2, we apply the resulting framework to see how it is possible to identify a great company—when it is still small.

You'll end up with detailed techniques you can apply to spot a high-growth stock—and just as important—strike the "next turkey" off your list.

You'll also discover—

↗ Nine ways to spot the "next Starbucks" by just "walking around."

↗ How you can apply the five clues to dig up hidden gems and beat the Wall Street "experts"—from the comfort of your own home.

↗ Four completely different ways to profit from the next hot growth stock—or the last one.

↗ How to weed out the dross by reading between the lines of a company's annual report—even if the last thing you'd want to do is take Accounting 101.

↗ And—paradoxically—you'll also learn there will be times when you can make more money more easily by investing in the *last* Starbucks (or one of its competitors), not the next one.

Applying the five clues to identify the next growth company has a surprising side effect: identifying the "ingredients" essential for a small business to become a big one becomes a "recipe" for starting a successful business of your own.

Which means, rather than investing in the next Starbucks, you could decide to create it yourself!

1 | Why Aren't There Any Starbucks Stores in Italy?

Starbucks opened its first European store in 1998—in the UK.

As I write these words in mid-2017, the only countries in Western Europe that do *not* have a Starbucks are the small and mostly poorer markets of Albania, Bosnia, Croatia, Liechtenstein, Macedonia, Malta, Serbia, and Slovenia.

And Italy.

Which is where Starbucks, as we know it today, began, back in 1983. As *Businessweek* put it, "If it weren't for Italy, Starbucks might not exist."[1]

The first Starbucks outlet in Italy will open in June 2018, twenty years after Starbucks first crossed the Atlantic.

What took them so long?

This hardly seems like the first question that would come to anyone's mind. Yet the answer is the key to understanding Starbucks' success, some of its failures—and how it has permanently changed people's coffee-drinking habits.

As Howard Schultz relates the story in his book *Pour Your Heart into It: How Starbucks Built a Company One Cup at a Time,* he was in Milan on business. He was the marketing director of Starbucks, at that time a Seattle-based coffee roaster and retailer of coffee beans. There "I discovered the ritual and romance of coffee bars in Italy."[2]

CLUE #1

Permanently Change People's Habits

When you see products such as the computer, which has replaced typewriters, low-cost airlines that attract people who've never before flown (not to mention rich cheapskates), and innovations such as the Tetra Pak, which replaces plastic and glass bottles and containers and has revolutionized the shipping industry, you know you could be onto the next big thing.

Inspired by what he saw, Schultz spent his spare time in Milan wandering through the streets and piazzas, observing customers, baristas, and sampling espressos at a handful of the fifteen-hundred-odd coffee bars in Milan back then:

"It seemed they were on every street corner, and all were packed. . . . My mind started churning. . . .

"As I watched, I had a revelation: Starbucks had missed the point—completely missed it. . . . What we had to do was unlock the romance and mystery of coffee, firsthand, in coffee bars."[3]

Schultz returned to the United States with the vision of what would eventually become Starbucks as we know it today: a fusion of Italian espresso café culture with a McDonald's-style operating model.

Vainly, he tried to persuade his employers to expand into espresso bars. Despite repeated rejection, Schultz was persistent. When Starbucks opened a new store in downtown Seattle, he was offered a small corner for an experimental coffee bar.

It was a success.

Nevertheless, Starbucks' management decided to stick to its knitting and not embark on a brand extension. So Schultz quit to pursue his dream, starting Il Giornale in honor of the Milan espresso bars that inspired his epiphany.

From the beginning, Schultz was aiming high: Il Giornale stores all over the United States, if not the world. When his former employer came up for sale, Schultz had five Il Giornale stores—three in Seattle, plus one in Vancouver and another in Chicago.

Why Vancouver and Chicago when it would have been easier, not to mention more economical, to open stores closer to home? Schultz wanted to prove to his investors (and himself) that his concept would travel, whetting their lips for the profits to be had in a nationwide chain.

In retrospect, Schultz's 1987 purchase of Starbucks was a stroke of genius. After all, Il Giornale was *not* an Italian espresso bar, but an American one. Added to which, for too many Americans Il Giornale was unpronounceable.

Changing the company's name to Starbucks was an unexpected bonus to the obvious fit of having an in-house coffee roaster experienced in sourcing high-quality coffee beans from around the world.

Eleven years later, with 1,412 stores in the United States, Canada, Japan, Singapore, and the Philippines, Starbucks began expanding into Europe. The UK was the first stop, but Italy was one of the countries on the list.[4]

Yet, today, as I write these words, there's not a single Starbucks in Italy.

Why not?

We can find the answer some nine thousand miles away in Australia, almost on the other side of the globe.

In 2008, for the first time since it was founded, Starbucks shrank. It closed underperforming stores all over the world. The most, 661, were in the United States. But the worst-hit country was Australia, where 61 of Starbucks' 84 stores disappeared.

What went wrong in Australia?

To start with, Starbucks was nothing new.

I'm Australian, and I had my first cappuccino as a university student in the late sixties. It was in a coffee shop called Gus' Café in Canberra, Australia's capital.

Started by a Viennese named Gus, he'd fought city hall for the right to place tables outside, on the sidewalk. We students cheered him on, if only to give the local government a bloody nose. It became one of our favorite hangouts.

Gus' Café

The history of Gus' Café (from its Web site, which accords with my memory) sounds rather like the experience of Howard Schultz some sixteen years later:

Canberra's thriving, cosmopolitan café society owes much to the perseverance and vision of one unique individual—Augustin "Gus" Petersilka (1913–94). A Vienna native, Gus brought the concept of the continental-style café with him to [Australia's] capital. His idea was simple, yet radical, for its time—the promotion and cultivation of a relaxed and convivial outdoor dining environment in the heart of the city.

However, turning this dream into reality didn't come easily, and Gus's epic battle with local bureaucrats and council officials (including a petition to the queen) is now legendary. Gus's passion and determination resulted in the opening of Canberra's first open-air, late-night café in 1968.

Gus was one of many European immigrants—from Italy, France, Germany, Greece, and Austria—who brought the continental coffee culture to Australia after World War II.

The result is that today you can get a great cappuccino, espresso, or latte just about anywhere in the country. And I mean *anywhere*. The best cappuccino I've ever had was in some small country town I drove through on the way to somewhere else. I can't recall the name of the town, which was about two hundred miles north of Sydney with a population of a couple of thousand—or the café.

The selection of this café was pure chance: a pleasant-looking place to take a break. The superb (compared to the usual good-to-excellent) cappuccino was a surprise bonus.

Long before Howard Schultz had his epiphany in Milan, Australia was, like Italy, "cappuccino country."

When Starbucks opened up in Australia, it brought nothing new or different. And certainly not better.

But in the United States, the UK, Canada, and many other countries, Starbucks flourished. For espresso, these countries were—

Virgin Territory

In 1976 I went to graduate school at UCLA. (I quickly dropped out, but that's another story.) Back then, the best coffee you could get was the stuff that had been sitting on a hot plate for half an hour. Unless you made drip coffee at home. If there was an espresso available anywhere in Los Angeles back then, I never heard of it.

Returning to Australia from LA, I stopped in London. The coffee there was even worse. (And let's not talk about the service: *execrable* fails to describe how dismal it was.)

Australia's Espresso Culture

The simplest way to understand the hold espresso has on Australian coffee drinkers is to visit the sleepy country town of Armidale, five hundred kilometers north of Sydney. Population: twenty-five thousand.

In Armidale's downtown area—the size of a handful of New York City blocks—are *twenty* coffee cafés. Seven more are in other parts of town—without counting the McCafé!

That's more than one café per thousand people.

Assuming this represents total market saturation, it suggests the maximum limit for espresso cafés is 1,120 per million population—comparable to Milan's 1,154 per million people around the time Howard Schultz had his epiphany.

Compare that to the current 70.3 cafés per million people in the United States, or 160.9 in the UK; even if you cut the high Australian and Italian numbers in half or to a quarter, the espresso revolution obviously has a long way to go in these other countries.

The Aussies are coming. "I often have to explain to people that the best coffee you can get is in Australia," writes Heston Blumenthal in *The Guardian*. "They can't quite believe it. It's starting to happen in the UK, and there's some great emerging coffee in Scandinavia, but they are not inspired by Italy, they are inspired by Australia."

The Wall Street Journal agrees: "While many people think Australia's favorite brew is beer, the country is perhaps equally obsessed with coffee. . . . Specialty cafés are being opened across the city [of New York] by a wave of young Australian entrepreneurs who want to change the way New Yorkers drink coffee."

Neither the United States nor the UK had an "espresso culture."

Howard Schultz's epiphany in Milan was (with the benefit of hindsight) simple: If Italians like sitting around in cafés sipping espressos, so will Americans.

His test with Il Giornale confirmed his insight. And Starbucks' expansion around the world—generating hundreds if not thousands of competitors—proves it conclusively.

But not yet in Italy. Indeed, with the exception of New Zealand and Switzerland, Starbucks has limited penetration in espresso-culture countries, measured by the number of stores per million people:

Country	Number of Starbucks Stores	% of all Starbucks stores	Stores per million people
US	13,327	54.5	41.1
Canada	1,437	5.9	39.6
Singapore	125	0.5	21.9
Hong Kong	154	0.6	20.9
Taiwan	380	1.6	16.2
UK	884	3.89	13.6
Japan	1,191	4.9	9.4
Malaysia	220	0.9	7.1
Thailand	264	1.1	3.9
Philippines	90	0.4	2.8
Saudi Arabia	283	1.2	2.8
China	2,205	9.5	1.7
India	83	0.3	0.1
Espresso culture countries			
Switzerland	63	0.3	7.5
Netherlands	59	0.2	3.5
Austria	18	0.1	2.1
New Zealand	25	0.1	2
Germany	161	0.7	1.9
France	121	0.5	1.9
Australia	23	0.1	1
Italy	0	0	0

As of 28 March 2016. Source: http://www.loxcel.com/sbux-faq.html, Starbucks Hong Kong

Virgin territories are far more profitable. Which explains why Starbucks has the most stores per capita in countries such as the United States, Canada, Hong Kong, Singapore, and Taiwan, where it *changed people's habits*.

Even nonespresso markets such as Malaysia, Thailand, and the Philippines, where per capita incomes range from 21 percent (Malaysia) to a mere 4.9 percent (Philippines) of the United States, can be more profitable than Italy (per capita income: 75 percent of the US). As the table shows, Starbucks has a higher penetration rate in these three countries than it has in any continental European country other than Switzerland and the Netherlands.

And, to come, are the markets with the most long-term potential of all: China and India. Already, Starbucks has more stores in China (2,204) than it has in the whole of continental Europe, *plus Russia* (1,629)! With the same penetration rate as the Philippines (2.9 stores per million people) Starbucks could have around 7,500 stores in China and India, over half the US number. And in the long run, *both* markets could be way bigger than the United States.

Compare that to Italy's potential: with the same penetration as France (1.7 per million), about 102 stores. Easy choice.

Schultz *changed people's habits,* turning drip and instant coffee drinkers into espresso drinkers, by the millions—*when Starbucks entered virgin territory.*

While Starbucks is certainly the most spectacular recent example of this phenomenon, it is merely the latest entrant in what we can term—

The McDonald Brothers' Fast-Food Revolution

The restaurant business before McDonald's was like the car industry before Henry Ford's Model T. Cars were made in small production runs or even hand assembled, one at a time, by skilled craftsmen. They were expensive, often unreliable, and only the wealthy could afford them.

The Model T was the world's first mass-produced automobile. Introduced in 1908, it cost $950, less than half the price of the average auto. It sold ten thousand units in its first year.

By 1920 the price had fallen to $280; as Ford refined his production techniques, he passed his lower costs to his customers. When the last Model T came off the production line, 15 million had been sold, and over half the cars in the United States were Model Ts.

Ford's innovations revolutionized the automobile business and were quickly copied by other manufacturers. As a result, cars became a mass-market consumer good rather than a niche product reserved for the wealthy few.

In 1948—forty years after the Model T's introduction—brothers Richard "Dick" and Maurice "Mac" McDonald set in motion a similar revolution in the restaurant business.

By offering a limited, self-service menu of burgers, fries, soft drinks, and shakes, they made eating out an affordable experience for just about everyone.

Today, we think nothing of taking the kids to McDonald's or one of its many clones. But in 1948, for the majority of people a visit to a restaurant was a special occasion, mainly reserved for birthdays, anniversaries, and the like.

The major change that helped drive the growth of McDonald's and similar chains was the postwar boom that slowly eroded people's "Depression mentality." From conversations I've had with American friends in their late sixties, even when their parents graduated from being poor to middle-class, they continued their Depression-inspired habits of rarely eating out.

The next generation were happier to spend rather than skimp, and this happened at the time the McDonald brothers dramatically cut the price of eating out. Their hamburger cost just 15¢, *half* the price charged by most other vendors.[5] They achieved this dramatic price reduction by—

● Limiting choice to just four items: burgers, fries, soft drinks, and shakes, compared to the standard restaurant menu, which can run to a small book. Rather than holding inventory to make twenty or a hundred different dishes, they needed to stock only for four.

● As a result, they could apply Henry Ford's assembly-line concept to the preparation of food. Instead of cooking one meal at a time, they had special equipment made by a local craftsman that cooked two dozen burgers at once, while another machine prepared the same number of buns. Production was broken down into components—frying the patties, preparing the buns, assembling the burger, preparing the fries and drinks—with countermen to serve the customers. As a result, qualified cooks could be replaced with unskilled workers. And as a self-service restaurant, no waiters were needed.

● They also cut the start-up cost. In the 1950s, a McDonald's-style restaurant could be set up for around $75,000, *including* land and building, compared to $300,000 and up for other restaurants.[6]

● Overall, they dramatically cut the cost of production, passing the savings to their customers. McDonald's 15¢ hamburgers attracted buyers in droves.

Today, we take this for granted. But back then the whole world was virgin territory for their concept.

Other restaurateurs, mostly in California, quickly copied their low-cost production methods. Fast-food chains such as Taco Bell, Kentucky Fried Chicken, and Burger King all had their beginnings in the late 1940s and early '50s—inspired by the McDonald brothers' store.

But most of the copycats strayed from the brothers' concept in one or more ways. Some expanded the menu, others charged higher prices, and few of them reached the McDonald brothers' standard of efficiency and cleanliness.

Until Ray Kroc came along and turned the McDonald brothers' fast-food revolution into a nationwide, and later global, phenomenon.

The McDonald's Revolution, Part II

In 1954, Ray Kroc signed an exclusive nationwide franchise deal with the McDonald brothers and opened his first store in April 1955 in Des Plaines, Illinois. He "cloned" the original store, maintaining (and eventually improving) the brothers' highly efficient production methods, limited menu, and affordable prices.

Stretched for capital, he developed a highly profitable franchising method that was also affordable to the franchisee, as we'll see in chapter 5. It also enabled him to maintain a tight control on the quality of franchisees' operations, resulting in a high standard of consistency across different stores. A consistency we now take for granted that was unusual at the time.

Thus, he invented the franchising model that's virtually universal today. When Kroc started out, franchisors made their money from *selling* franchises; few of them paid much attention to whether franchisees maintained standards, flourished—or went out of business. To Kroc, his franchisees were his business *partners:* they swam or sank together. Kroc's profits came from the same source as his partners': *customers.*

McDonald's took off: by 1972 it was the world's biggest restaurant chain by sales, a position it has held every year to this day.*

To appreciate the magnitude of the "McDonald's revolution," imagine for a moment a world with no McDonald's, no Burger King, no Pizza Hut, no Kentucky Fried Chicken, no Taco Bell, none of their many competitors, and no other fast-food chain inspired by the McDonald's model. Not even a Starbucks!

If you want a hamburger, you head to a Greasy Louie's and wait for it to be prepared—praying the cook isn't having a bad day. Or, you could go to a hot-dog stand or a diner such as Denny's. Or to plenty of other sit-down restaurants—which cost two, three, or many more times the price of a McDonald's Happy Meal.

On top of that, disposable incomes in the 1940s and '50s were a mere quarter of what they are today. We could now afford an occasional Big Mac—except there aren't any to be had.

With rare exceptions, most of us would eat at home—just as our parents and grandparents did.

The McDonald brothers proved this. Their new store was in the working-class area of San Bernardino, California; before long a major part of their business came from families eating out for the first time.

Ray Kroc and the McDonald brothers changed the way people eat—and revolutionized the restaurant business. Fast food, as we know it today, simply did not exist on any scale before McDonald's restaurants—and their countless copycats—began appearing across the United States.

Whole Foods and "the Law of Attraction"

Whole Foods was not the world's first organic, environmentally friendly health food store—yet *it* was the one that changed people's habits.

Founder John Mackey's genius—as we'll see in more detail in chapter 4—

---

*Subway has the most outlets—but with lower sales per store.

was to create a unique customer experience in the supermarket space. We go to other supermarkets to restock the refrigerator; a Whole Foods store is actually a pleasure to visit, a place to have lunch or to just hang out as well as load up your trolley with goodies.

Other health food stores existed to serve the niche market of people who were already sold on eating "whole foods."

Mackey reached out to "nonfoodies" by applying the "law of attraction." Though an evangelist on the subject of eating well (Mackey himself is a vegetarian), by offering a close to full range of foods, including many that a strict health food addict would reject, Whole Foods' "soft sell" approach creates many loyal customers who come for the range, product quality, and ambience—but start to change their diets nonetheless, even if minimally to begin with, thanks to the ease of selecting more healthful foods.

As a result, Whole Foods' success has forced other supermarkets, from Safeway and Kroger (and even Walmart), to the corner health food store to alter their product lines.

Which Comes First: the Chicken or the Egg?

Total sales of food products in the United States have been rising at around 2 percent per year. But Whole Foods' organic foods niche between 1996 and 2011 expanded at 18 percent a year.[7] Is this because Whole Foods and its competitors persuaded people to adopt healthier diets? Or did changing consumer demands drive their growth?

The answer is rarely simple.

Steve Jobs built Apple by producing products such as the iPod, iPhone, and iPad, that no one knew they wanted until Jobs and his team created them. Yet, that latent demand had to be there or those product launches would have failed.

The only way to be certain that latent demand exists is to dip your toe in the market. Howard Schultz tested his concept with a small espresso counter in a corner of a Starbucks store when Starbucks was just a coffee roaster. Its success enabled him to gather enough investors to launch Il Giornale.

McDonald's originated when Dick and Mac McDonald decided to close their previous business, a carhop they started in 1937. It had become a hangout for teenagers, giving it an unsavory reputation with the adult and family market.

Analyzing their business, they discovered that 80 percent of their sales were hamburgers, which spurred them to refurbish their store as a hamburger-only restaurant. Sales and profits were lower to begin with; only after a year did they recover to previous levels—and then accelerate to new heights.

By the time of Ray Kroc's visit, the McDonald brothers had thoroughly tested, refined, and *proven* their concept.

Had that latent consumer demand for Schultz's and the McDonald brothers' tests failed to exist, we would never have heard of them.

Only in the case of Walmart does the answer appear clear-cut: few people in this world will turn down the offer of a lower price.

If this is such an obvious business proposition, why didn't stores like Walmart, Kmart, and Target emerge years, if not decades, earlier?

To be profitable, a discount store must compensate for lower margins with a *much* higher volume. That necessitates a large retail space and a similarly large inventory, which, in turn, requires *capital.*

Such a high volume of sales can only be supported by a large customer base, which is easily found in big cities.

But low prices can only be offered profitably if a tight lid is kept on costs, which initially ruled out such high-rent city-center locations.

By the 1950s, the combination of the post–World War II boom and the flight to the suburbs set the scene for a dramatic change in America's retail industry.

The automobile, an essential part of suburban living, meant that large pools of customers were no longer limited to locations served by the fixed mass transit lines of buses and subways. Low-cost out-of-town locations now offered the perfect environment for large discount stores—and entrepreneurs were quick to respond.

Early movers included Ann & Hope (Rhode Island, 1953) and FedMart (San Diego, 1954). Their success inspired a number of clones, including Kmart, Target, and Walmart (all started in 1962 within months of each other: March 1, May 1, and July 2, respectively).

In the next chapter we'll see why Walmart, a late-entry "upstart," overtook the first movers in the big-box space, including the better-capitalized Kmart and Target, and changed American shoppers' habits. Walmart lowered the price structure of the American retail industry, saving not just its own customers but also *all* retail shoppers untold billions of dollars.

2 "Most Everything I've Done I Copied from Somebody Else"
—Sam Walton[1]

As we've already seen, Starbucks is a "copycat" company, a fusion of an Italian café with a McDonald's-style operating system.

There's nothing wrong with that: most successful businesses are copycats. They're based on the idea that people are much the same the world over. So if people in one part of the world—say, Italy—like sitting around drinking espressos, so will people in another part of the world. Say, the United States.

Or to go one step farther—as Starbucks has proved, with stores in seventy-three countries and counting—*everywhere.*

CLUE #2

The Copycat Principle

Starbucks, Ray Kroc's McDonald's, Walmart, and Whole Foods are all copycats. None of them were pioneers in their product and market niche; they all took existing practices from their competitors—and perfected them.

So are most of the other recent success stories; Internet Explorer copied Netscape. In turn Explorer was copied by Firefox and Google. Samsung copied the iPhone—wherever you look, you'll find copycats.

And being a first mover can be a disadvantage. Netscape, Burger King, FedMart, Myspace, and Peet's are just a handful of many such examples.

The genesis of both Starbucks and McDonald's lay in the founder's epiphany: an "Aha!" moment that brought the vision of the business into the founder's mind almost fully formed.

Howard Schultz and Ray Kroc had both the experience to recognize the opportunity and the talents to turn their vision into a reality.

Sam Walton and John Mackey, the founders of Walmart and Whole Foods, had those same talents and experience. But the development of the underlying concepts of these businesses, and their equivalent "Aha!" moments, came more slowly. The slowest of all, Sam Walton's concept for Walmart.

Aside from a stint in the army during World War II, Sam Walton spent his life in the retail business, starting as a management trainee in a JCPenney department store in June 1940.

After the war, he bought a Ben Franklin variety—or five-and-dime—store in Newport, Arkansas. Across the street was another five-and-dime, a Sterling store with twice the sales of his Ben Franklin.

Walton haunted the aisles of the Sterling store to figure out what they were doing that he wasn't.

Which is how much of Walton's, and Walmart's, success began—with his continual study of what *other* retailers were doing. Wherever he traveled, he visited retail stores—including, his children recalled, while on vacation. He carried a yellow legal pad (later, a tape recorder as well) and made notes of anything and everything that struck him as a potentially useful idea.

He went to trade association meetings where he picked the brains of other retailers. He visited store owners in other states, who were happy to answer his many questions, as he was not (then) a competitor.

He returned from every trip with one or more new merchandising, pricing, display, or store-design concepts to try out in his own stores.

He would test each idea in a small and cheap way, discarding it if it failed and rolling it out if it succeeded.

Walton turned copycatting into a fine art. His Ben Franklin store soon caught up with and then outsold the Sterling store on the other side of the street.

But one store wasn't enough. By 1960, Walton had grown into the biggest independent store operator in the United States. But "we were doing only $1.4 million [total sales] in fifteen different stores,"[2] most of them Ben Franklins.

He began looking around for something to take him into the next league.

The concept for Walmart developed from a number of sources, including:

- larger stores—then called family centers—which outsold the combined volume of his fifteen stores in a single location; and

- discount chains such as Ann & Hope in New England and FedMart in California, which made up for lower prices with higher volumes.

Walmart was also a *reactive* move on Walton's part. Only when Dallas-based discounter Herb Gibson opened a discount store in Fayetteville, Arkansas, which competed directly with Walton's variety stores, was he spurred into action.

When the first Walmart in Rogers, Arkansas, opened on 2 July 1962, it was the laggard of the industry.

It was *not* the first discount store in the state, let alone the country; it was in no sense a dramatically new idea (even the name, Walmart, was a clone of Sol

Price's FedMart); and Kmart and Target had beaten Walton to the punch b,
and two months, respectively.

No 1962 observer of the retail trade had Walmart on his list of Retailers Most
Likely to Succeed.

So how did Walmart come from behind, if not from last place, to become the
world's number one?

Take the Concept to the Extreme

One reason: with stores in small towns in Arkansas—America's boondocks—nobody noticed them. Walton could hone his concept while flying under everyone's
radar. Even when Walmart went public in 1970, nobody considered it a serious
competitor to the then much bigger Kmart and Target chains.

Far more important, Walton took his focus on low prices to an extreme. He
insisted on a maximum 30 percent markup compared to other discounters' up
to 50 percent.

To offer the lowest prices and make a profit, he had to have the lowest costs. A
major aspect of the resulting Walmart culture is best expressed in Walton's statement to his buyers: "Every time Walmart spends one dollar foolishly, it comes
right out of our customers' pockets. Every time we save them a dollar, that puts us
one more step ahead of the competition—which is where we always plan to be."

Walmart has received a lot of flak for allegedly paying its workers less or giving
them fewer benefits than its competitors. But that's all part of Walmart's overrid-
ing aim: to give every customer the best possible deal by having the lowest-possi-
ble costs, across the board.

Costco: Even More Extreme

Costco's markups are even lower than Walmart's: just 14 percent.[3] Customers make
up the difference with membership fees. As you can see from this extract from Costco's financials, without membership fees the company would suffer a loss:

$ million	2014	2013	2012	2011	2010
Membership fees	2,428	2,286	2,075	1,867	1,691
Net income	2,058	2,039	1,709	1,462	1,303
Membership fees exceed income by	370	247	366	405	388

Source: Costco 2014 Annual Report[4]

"I Have Never Seen Anything to Equal the Potential of This Place of Yours"
—Ray Kroc to the McDonald Brothers[5]

For seventeen years, Ray Kroc sold paper cups for the Lily-Tulip Cup Company, becoming their star salesman, selling 5 million paper cups a year.

In 1938 he quit Lily-Tulip to start a totally new business selling MultiMixers, which made five milk shakes at a time.

Kroc visited thousands of restaurants, soda fountains, dairy bars, and other kitchens across the United States. For most of these customers, one MultiMixer, occasionally two, was more than enough.

But in 1954, he heard of a restaurant in San Bernardino, California, called McDonald's that had not two, not three, but *eight* of his MultiMixers—and had just ordered two more. This was something he had to see.

He visited the store on his next trip to Los Angeles—and was astounded. It was a drive-in restaurant and didn't look impressive—until opening time. Customers parked, ordered from windows, and took their purchases back to their cars. There was no seating. Yet, within minutes of the store's 11:00 a.m. opening, the parking lot was nearly full, and long, but fast-moving lines of eager customers were at the windows.

Kroc could see immediately why they needed eight of his MultiMixers: they *had* to make up to forty milk shakes at a time to keep up with demand.

Kroc was impressed with everything he heard and saw. When he went to bed that evening "visions of McDonald's restaurants dotting crossroads all over the country paraded through my brain,"[6] each, of course, with eight of his Multi-Mixers churning out forty shakes at a time.

At dinner with the McDonald brothers the following evening, he said to them:

> "I have never seen anything to equal the potential of this place of yours. Why don't you open a series of units like this? It would be a gold mine for you and for me, too, because every one would boost my MultiMixer sales. What do you say?"

> Silence.

The brothers weren't interested.

> "It would be a lot of trouble," Dick McDonald objected. "Who could we get to open them for us?"

> I sat there feeling a sense of certitude begin to envelop me. Then I leaned forward and said: "Well, what about me?"[7]

Kroc was then fifty-two years old, an age when most people are looking for-
to retirement. He suffered from diabetes and arthritis, had no gallbladder
t much of his thyroid gland. He returned to Chicago, mulled it over for a
nd returned a week later to sign a franchise deal.

By 1972, McDonald's, with 2,155 stores, was the world's number one burger chain, a position it has retained, without interruption, to the present day.

Burger King

Ray Kroc was not the only person directly inspired by the McDonald brothers.

In 1953—the year *before* Ray Kroc's visit—two men from Jacksonville, Florida, Keith Kramer and Matthew Burns, visited the McDonald brothers' original store.

When they returned home, they opened their own copycat named Burger King (initially Insta-Burger King). It was purchased by its Miami franchisees in 1961.[8]

The Virtues of Being a Copycat

Being a copycat rather than a pioneer has many virtues. To start with, you know the concept *works*. You don't need to prove that; only whether *you* can make it work in your market.

It's Easier to Raise Capital

The true pioneer must persuade investors that he has the skills, talents, and management team to produce this totally new, untried, and unproven idea at a profit—*and* that consumers will *love* it so much it will fly off the shelves. Easy enough to do in periods such as the dot-com boom of the late nineties; not so easy when investors are more rational.

The founder of a copycat company only has to convince investors that he can make money with a *proven* concept.

You Can Benefit from the Pioneers' Experience

One virtue of being a follower is that you don't have to reinvent the wheel. You can (and *should*) learn from other people's successes and mistakes,* just as Sam Walton did for his entire professional life.

Or, like Ray Kroc, you can take a proven operating system and duplicate it worldwide—with, in Kroc's case, starting further along the learning curve by *not* having to repeat all the McDonald brothers' mistakes.

Or, like Howard Schultz and John Mackey, a combination of both.

You Can Start with a Clean Slate

Any company that's been operating for a while establishes a particular way of doing business. Such an institutional legacy—especially when it develops on a

---

*In school, that's called cheating and gets you into trouble. In the real world, it's called market research.

catch-as-catch-can basis—can be resistant to change, a perilous attitude in a changing market and when the competition heats up.

With sufficient thought and experiment, you can establish your company's culture and style from day one so that every part of the business meshes with your vision for the company and its primary purpose.

So in Australia you'll find Starbucks clones such as Gloria Jeans, Hudsons, and Coffee Club; in Hong Kong, Pacific Coffee, Uncle Ben's, and Habitu; in the Philippines, Bo's and Figaro; in Vietnam, Highlands Coffee; in Thailand, Coffee World . . . to name just a few. Starbucks clones, each and every one.

Then there's Krispy Kreme and Dunkin' Donuts (US), Tim Hortons (Canada), McDonald's with its McCafés, and hundreds of other restaurant, café, and hotel chains that have added espresso-based drinks to their menus.

And that doesn't count tens of thousands of independent, single-store coffee cafés that didn't exist before Starbucks' success—or the countless numbers of other restaurants that now, thanks to Starbucks, offer espresso.

Why do they exist?

For three reasons:

1. Starbucks proved there's a worldwide market for espresso-café culture, that people prefer espresso to drip coffee that's been sitting on a hot plate since God knows when. And are prepared to pay more for it.
2. Starbucks (unlike Google) cannot be everywhere at once.
3. Starbucks could not (and still cannot) provide for every taste or pocket.

Having educated drip- and instant-coffee drinkers to prefer espressos, some wanted *better* espressos than Starbucks'. Others wanted cheaper ones. Today, thanks to its success, Starbucks is being squeezed from two directions at once in its home market. And outside the United States, only in a few countries—Hong Kong and the Philippines, for example—is Starbucks the leading brand.

The McCafé

A hamburger chain serving cappuccinos? Not an intuitively obvious success story.

Yet McDonald's is rolling out its McCafé concept worldwide.

A brand extension, McCafé was started in 1993 in Melbourne, Australia, where it turned out to be a natural fit for Australia's espresso culture—and is now that country's largest espresso chain.

The McCafé comes in three varieties: as stand-alone stores, as a separate counter in a McDonald's where the coffees are made by hand, or as a press-button machine next to the racks of Big Macs and apple pies in a regular McDonald's. As a result, the quality and consistency of the coffee can differ quite dramatically from one store (and one country) to another.

Nevertheless, if you're one of the millions of people who—thanks to Starbucks—prefer espresso to brewed coffee, you can now satisfy your craving with your morning McMuffin in over fifteen hundred locations (so far) worldwide.

The success of McDonald's also spawned a host of fast-food chains. Direct competitors such as Burger King and Hardee's. And even more indirect competitors competing for the fast-food dollar: Taco Bell, Pizza Hut, Domino's, Kentucky Fried Chicken—just to mention a few of the major American chains.

Whole Foods' success went hand in hand with the expansion of Trader Joe's (founded 1967), the Fresh Market (1982), and Sprouts (2001), to name its three major domestic competitors. And while Walmart has overtaken Target and Kmart, there's no dearth of competition in Walmart's market space.

Outside the originator's home territory, the competition is even fiercer. Starbucks, McDonald's, Whole Foods, and Walmart all have first-mover advantage, but primarily in their home turf, the United States.

Entrepreneurs in other countries, spying the success of Starbucks or McDonald's in the United States, set up their own clones before the much-bigger American company can come to town.

So the largest hamburger chain in the Philippines is not McDonald's (460 stores) but the local Jollibee (916 locations). What's more, by honing its product to local tastes, Jollibee forced McDonald's to change the taste of *its* products to compete for Filipino customers.

A Jollibee store in Manila: a McDonald's copycat in more ways than one.

In Finland, McDonald's plays second fiddle to the local chain, Hesburger (founded in 1980), which has 281 stores compared to 72 for McDonald's.

Interestingly, both these companies are McDonald's copycats in more ways than one. Hesburger has expanded beyond its home base into neighboring Estonia, Latvia, Germany, Russia, and Ukraine.

And McDonald's foray into the Philippine market forced Jollibee to upgrade its operations. In 1981, learning that McDonald's was coming to town, a Jollibee management team went to the United States for an intensive study of McDonald's operations. They found that McDonald's "excelled over us in all aspects—except product taste [for the Philippine market]," said Jollibee's founder, Tony Tan.[4]

By upgrading their promotion, store design, service, and other facets of their operations, they more than held their own against the American giant.

Like McDonald's, Starbucks often enters markets where another originator or copycat already has the . . .

First-Mover Advantage . . .

. . . in the UK: Costa Coffee: In 1971, two Italian brothers, Sergio and Bruno Costa, opened a coffee roaster, Costa Coffee, to service the country's then mostly Italian espresso bars. It opened its first retail store in 1978—five years *before* Howard Schultz had his epiphany.

Twenty years later, when Starbucks came to the UK, it had some 700 branded espresso cafés (the market leader being Costa Coffee), plus 4,100 independents.

By the end of 2012, that number had more than doubled. Costa Coffee remains the market leader, with 40.4 percent of the 5,246 branded outlets (Starbucks is number two at 30.7 percent), plus 5,633 independent cafés and 4,831 other places serving espressos.[5] As *The Guardian* reported: "Today [2012], the coffee shop market in the UK is worth 10 times what it was in 1997, with 15,273 outlets currently estimated to be doing business."[6]

> **India's Coffee (and Copycat) King**
>
> "More than my intelligence, I can pick up ideas and copy them better and faster than others,"
>
> —V. G. Siddhartha —also known as India's Coffee King— told *Forbes India*.
>
> Like Sam Walton, everywhere he goes he sees what others are doing and tests the ideas he picks up in his various businesses.

That number doesn't include the nine hundred Costa Express outlets, which are self-service coffee-vending machines.

While Starbucks can't claim to have introduced the espresso revolution to the UK, it was indubitably a significant force in the dramatic expansion of the UK's café culture.

Costa Coffee has also expanded into twenty-eight other countries, mainly in Eastern Europe and the Middle East. With a total of 2,203 stores,[7] Costa Coffee is the world's number two café chain after Starbucks.

. . . in India: Café Coffee Day: "A chance meeting with the owners of Germany's largest café chain, Tchibo, in 1994," reports *Forbes India,*[8] inspired V. G. Siddhartha, CEO and majority shareholder of India's largest grower of arabica coffee beans, Amalgamated Bean Coffee Trading Co., "to set up Café Coffee Day in India."

The first outlet opened in Bangalore in August 1996.

With 1,556 outlets,[9] and a new one opening just about every day, Café Coffee Day dominates the Indian market. With 75 percent of the branded café outlets, it looks destined to maintain its first mover advantage in a business where location is almost everything.

But there are no guarantees. The competition is fierce, including Barista (majority owned by Italian coffee roaster Lavazza), Costa Coffee, Gloria Jeans, Coffee Bean & Tea Leaf, Au Bon Pain—and Starbucks, which opened up in India in 2012, in partnership with Tata.

And now, there's espresso everywhere...

KFC Coffee

Kentucky Fried Chicken . . .

...Thai restaurants!...

JATUJAK — THAI FOOD THAI ICED COFFEE

Thai iced coffee? Does that come with chili?

While not exactly virgin territory, with just 1.2 cafés per million population, India's espresso revolution has barely begun.

. . . in Germany: Tchibo: Tchibo was established by Carl Tchilinghiryan and Max Herz in 1949. Its original business: selling coffee by mail order. Its first coffee shop opened in 1955; today it has 750 in Germany and 300 in seven other countries, plus thousands of other outlets in bakeries, supermarkets, and the like. It claims to be the biggest purveyor of roasted coffee (by value) in several European countries, including Germany, Austria, Poland, the Czech Republic, and Hungary.[10]

In 1973, in a unique move, it began selling nonfood consumer goods in its cafés, from table sets and breadboards to lingerie and cell phones. Every week, a new nonfood special appears.

. . . in Vietnam: Highlands Coffee: Vietnamese American David Thai started Highlands Coffee in 1998, inspired by the success of Starbucks . . . and is now franchising across Asia.

. . . in Colombia: Juan Valdez Café: Started in December 2002 by Colombia's National Federation of Coffee Growers, the Juan Valdez Café chain had 170 outlets in Colombia and 68 in 12 other countries at the end of 2003. Starbucks opened its first Colombian store in July 2014, planning to open 49 more. Interestingly, although Colombia is a major coffee exporter, per capita coffee consumption is low compared to the United States and Western Europe, so there's plenty of room to grow.

. . . in Hong Kong: Pacific Coffee: Pacific Coffee was started by Thomas Neir, from Starbucks' hometown of Seattle, in 1993, because he "couldn't find a decent coffee" anywhere in town. Walk into a Pacific Coffee outlet and you'll think you're in

. . . even at 7-Eleven!

Espresso: just $1 in a Manila 7-Eleven

Starbucks . . . themed red instead of green. Hong Kong is one of the few markets where Starbucks has overtaken the first mover.

. . . *and in Greece, coming from behind: Mikel Coffee Company:* Starbucks came to Greece in September 2002—but today Greece's biggest coffee chain is the Mikel Coffee Company, started by Eleftherios Kyriakakis in 2008. A Starbucks copycat, it soon took away Starbucks' first-mover advantage; today, it has ninety-seven stores compared to Starbucks' twenty-five and is opening new stores at a faster pace.

Ironically, one reason for its success: in the evenings you can buy alcoholic drinks as well as coffee, an innovation that Starbucks is now rolling out in the United States.

Will Starbucks Succeed in Italy?

Though Starbucks only entered Italy in early 2017, the Starbucks' *concept* already has: Starbucks copycats are flourishing.

In a prime location in the Milan piazza where Schultz had his epiphany stands a McDonald's, complete with a McCafé. One of Italy's 122 McCafés,[11] which makes McDonald's the biggest café chain in the home of espresso!

Half a block away is a four-story Arnold Coffee, an intentional Starbucks clone down to its original logo, which brought a warning letter from Starbucks' lawyers.

As befits Starbucks' Americanized Italian espresso café concept, Arnolds (and McCafés) occupy a completely different market niche from the 140,000-odd Italian espresso bars. They're a place to hang out, whether with your laptop or your friends. And, incidentally, you can buy a cappuccino, too.

As a result, "when the other bars are empty," says one of Arnold's two partners, "that's when we're full."[12]

In Milan's Piazza del Duomo where Howard Schultz had his epiphany, a McDonald's McCafé!

More More-Expensive Gadgets

Starbucks' espresso revolution has moved into the home, with an increasing range of coffee-making widgets and gadgets available. Aside from filter coffeemakers and the French press, which have been on the market for years, the coffee drinker at home can now choose from—

- Consumer versions of espresso machines, priced from a hundred-odd dollars to many thousands.

- Milk foamers, for when your espresso machine just makes espresso.

Just pods: a Nescafé Nespresso store in a premium-rent Hong Kong mall.

- Coffee-pod systems. Based on the Gillette model of locking the customer into your brand of razor blades, Nestlé (Nespresso), Coffee Bean & Tea Leaf, Starbucks, and many others now sell pod systems. They're simple and quick to use: slap in the "pod"—a small plastic "bucket" filled with the coffee of your choice—press a button, and Bob's your uncle.

- The AeroPress, a $30, one-person-powered almost-espresso-maker; small enough that you can take it with you wherever you go.

Meanwhile, the once-popular coffee percolator—if you're under fifty, you've probably never seen one—has all but disappeared.

You can even roast your own green coffee beans and grind them at home.

All these suggest trouble for the most convenient form of coffee at home: instant. Starbucks' VIA brand, made from high-quality arabica beans, not the cheaper robusta beans other brands use, demonstrates the market's growing preference for better coffee. Even so, the instant-coffee category is bound to lose market share over time.

A few other indicators of espresso's growing popularity:

- In one department store I saw this sign: BUY AN AIR CONDITIONER: GET AN ESPRESSO MAKER FREE!

- Premier customers at "select" HSBC banks can use free press-button espresso machines . . . while they wait.

- Those same press-button do-it-yourself espresso makers are appearing in more and more places, such as at the breakfast buffet in a hotel I stayed at once in Singapore.

From Labor- to Capital-Intensive

Another indicator of an expanding market is automation. "Handcrafted" coffees are labor-intensive. When the market is small, there's no profit in making expensive gadgets to automate the process.

Today, automation is taking over in the coffee café business. The most extreme example is the $11,000 Clover, which brews you a perfect cup of freshly ground coffee, from the beans of your choice, at the touch of a button.

Starbucks thought it was such a great product it bought the company in 2008.

Big-Box Stores: Fewer Competitors— but Just as Much Competition

Whole Foods and Walmart face fewer players internationally, as at home, than Starbucks and McDonald's. The reason is straightforward: far more capital is required to open a Whole Foods supermarket or a Walmart big-box store.

Nevertheless, the competition is just as fierce.

Walmart's major international competitors include France's Carrefour, the world's number two retailer by sales, and Britain's Tesco, the world's number two by profits.

All three companies are now head-to-head in China and Japan, while two of them meet in Argentina, Brazil, India, Malaysia, Poland, Slovakia, and Turkey. In addition, Tesco invaded Walmart's home turf by opening up in the United States. Walmart returned the favor by setting up in Britain.*

Tesco, founded in 1919, opened its first supermarket in 1929 and had a hundred across the UK in 1939. Today—copying the success of other retailers—it has expanded its footprint into other areas from hypermarts to smaller 7-Eleven–style convenience stores, while also diversifying from food into books, clothing, electronics, gasoline, and banking.[13]

Intriguingly, the origin of Carrefour lies in the United States, not as a direct copycat but via Bernardo Trujillo, a sales representative for the National Cash Register Company (NCR) in the 1950s.

To educate customers of the value of using cash registers, then new and revolutionary high-tech tools, NCR organized Modern Merchandising Methods (MMM) clubs and offered weeklong seminars in Dayton, Ohio, and Paris, France.

Bernardo Trujillo, chief of NCR's merchandising seminars and fluent in French as well as English, hosted the seminars.† Over time, he became known as the Pope of Merchandising, teaching such now-obvious but then-revolutionary principles as "no parking, no business," "islands of loss [i.e., loss leaders], oceans of profit," and "stack them high and sell them cheap."

MMM became known as Modern Merchandising Method. Move More Merchandise, or Make More Money.

Retail chiefs who attended Trujillo's seminars and then applied his principles

---

*As of 2013, Tesco was planning to exit the American and Japanese markets: http://www.tescoplc.com/index.asp?pageid=544.
†It seems Trujillo's lasting influence was more in Europe than in the United States. Google *Bernardo Trujillo* and you'll find that he has a Wikipedia page . . . in *French,* but none in English.

included Emile Bernheim (department stores and the Priba food chain, Belgium), Gustave Ackerman (Pick 'n Pay, South Africa), and Carrefour's founders, Marcel Fournier, Denis Defforey, and Jacques Defforey.

The first Carrefour store opened on 1 January 1958, in Annecy; in June 1963, the company opened Europe's first hypermart. Today, Carrefour has over 15,500 stores,[14] including 1,395 hypermarts.[15]

By comparison, Walmart has over 10,800 retail units,[16] including 3,188 Supercenters in the United States and 261 in other countries.[17] Specializing in big-box stores, the average Walmart store is significantly larger than Carrefour's.

These companies are hardly alone in the hypermart space. Competitors and copycats include RT-Mart (Taiwan and China, where it's the market leader, ahead of Walmart[18]), Auchan (France), Aeon (Japan), Shinsegae (South Korea), Acucar (Brazil), Big Bazaar (India), and SM (Philippines), to name just a few.[19]

There's Always Room for More

Years ago, a friend of mine in Chicago told me the following story. One of his employees resigned to work in his uncle's small business, a three-store "chain" of sidewalk hot-dog stands.

"The last thing Chicago needs," my friend responded, "is another hot-dog stand."

Five years later, that company had grown from three stands to sixty!

Even when a market is saturated and there's no apparent demand for *another* hot-dog stand, an entrepreneur can still invade that market, replacing existing hot-dog stands with ones that are cheaper or provide better products, better service, a better customer experience, or in some other way take customers away from existing sellers—and possibly expanding the market.

In this way, "there's *always* room for more" in every existing market.

4 How John Mackey's *Vision* Saved Whole Foods from Drowning

On Sunday, 24 May 1981, Austin, Texas, was hit by a severe flood: the first, and at that time only, Whole Foods store was eight feet underwater.

Overnight, the company went from being profitable, loved by its customers and employees alike, to $400,000 in the red.

There was no insurance, no off-site inventory, no backup of any kind.

Would the business survive?

At the time, the obvious answer was "No."

The day after the flood was the Memorial Day holiday. Management and team members were despondent. As Whole Foods' founder, John Mackey, relates the story in his book *Conscious Capitalism*, it was "the end of a dream" and "the end of the best job we ever had."[1]

As they began to see what they could salvage, an amazing thing happened: "Dozens of our customers and neighbors started showing up at the store . . . bringing buckets and mops and whatever else they thought might be useful. They said to us, in effect, 'Come on, guys; let's get to work. Let's clean it up and get this place back on its feet.' "[2]

Such customer reactions lifted the spirits of the entire Whole Foods team, founders and employees alike. It's hard to imagine many other businesses so inspiring their customers.

CLUE #4

Driven by the Founder's Vision and Passion

Every new company is driven by its founder's vision for the company and passion for achieving its goals.

When, and only when, the founder *communicates* his vision to all company members, *inspires* them to make it their own, and *creates a system* that enables frontline employees to communicate that same vision to customers and other stakeholders *through action*, which in turn creates a high degree of customer involvement and loyalty, will that vision drive the company's

culture and provide a solid foundation for a great company that has a chance of surviving the founder's retirement or death.

That's just the beginning of this Whole Foods story. In addition to the customers who rallied around:

- Employees worked to clean up the store without pay. Of course, they would draw pay when Whole Foods was back on its feet—but would that ever happen? At the time, no one could know for sure.

- Suppliers extended credit "because they cared about our business and trusted us to reopen and repay them."[3]

- Whole Foods' shareholders came up with additional investments—and the company's banks even loaned the company more money!

To understand the magnitude of Mackey's achievement, imagine for a moment that *your* business was eight feet and $400,000 underwater.

Would *your* employees rally around? Would *your* neighbors and customers show up to help clean up the mess?

Even if they did, what's likely to happen if you go down to *your* bank, red-inked balance sheet in hand, and ask your "friendly" banker to lend you *more* money? Which response would you expect:

1. "Sure, here's another four hundred thousand dollars on top of what you already owe us, plus a line of credit to tide you over."

2. Uncontrollable laughter—and the moment you've walked out the door, the lawyers are called in to initiate bankruptcy proceedings so the bank can grab whatever leftovers it can ahead of your other creditors.

Then you call your suppliers and ask them to replace, *on credit,* the ruined stock that you still haven't paid for. The most likely result: a race between your bankers and your suppliers to see who'll be first in line at the bankruptcy court.

Whole Foods' suppliers *and* banks both chose the *first* option.

Why?

The "Counterculture Capitalist"

John Mackey fully embraced the counterculture movement of the sixties and seventies, studying ecology and Eastern philosophy, embracing yoga and meditation, becoming a vegetarian, topped off with a beard and long hair. He became involved in the food co-op movement, agreeing with their motto: "food for people, not for profit." [4] But he soon discovered that co-ops were dominated by internal politics, the "most politically active members" focusing more on "which companies to boycott" than on serving their customers. He concluded he could do better and "became an entrepreneur to prove it." [5]

Immediately he was transformed in the eyes of his former associates into another "evil, exploiting businessmen" and came under fire for charging too-high prices and paying too-low wages.

Yet Mackey persevered, discovering that business is the opposite of the counterculture myth of venality and greed: that a business can only succeed with the *voluntary cooperation* of everyone it deals with—customers, employees, investors, and suppliers. [6]

John Mackey's Vision: A Business Based on Love and Caring

Just one thing changed in Mackey's transition from co-ops to a for-profit corporation: his preferred *method* of executing his vision. He saw for-profit as a better *way* to create an organization that truly cares for everyone it deals with—customers, employees, suppliers, and investors—*and* fulfill his (and the co-ops') counterculture mission of persuading people to adopt a healthier lifestyle by eating "whole foods."

Underlying Mackey's vision is the insight that all businesses—indeed, all organizations—depend upon *relationships.*

The nature of those relationships, both within the company and without, determines the nature and culture of the company, the employee and the customer experience, and ultimately the health of the business, profit being just one measure of that health.

Whole Foods' bankers and other suppliers, like its employees and customers, cared about the business because Mackey and his associates cared about *them.* They were partners in Whole Foods—not because of any equity or legal claim, but due to the nature of their relationship with the people at Whole Foods.

So when Whole Foods was eight feet underwater, its bankers and suppliers were *ready to listen.* What's more, they *wanted* to be able to help—in the same way that you would wish to help a friend in trouble.

That doesn't mean they opened their checkbooks the moment Mackey walked in the door. But they *did* want to hear what Mackey had to say and were willing, if not eager, to be persuaded. As Mackey could demonstrate that—despite the red ink—the flood was a onetime event unrelated to the underlying health of the company, they pitched in.

From this experience Mackey concluded, "What more proof did we need that stakeholders matter, that they embody the heart, soul, and lifeblood of an enterprise?" [7]

I doubt any other company founder has had his or her vision fully verified in such a dramatic manner.

The core of Mackey's vision for Whole Foods is his belief that *stakeholders matter*.

Stakeholders Matter

Mackey's stakeholder concept includes everybody who has a stake in your business, no matter how small or indirect: customers, employees, investors, *and* suppliers (including banks and other financiers), governments, neighbors, and the community at large—extending to the environment. While that stake may be emotional rather than financial, Mackey believes it's just as real and just as significant to the health of the business.

Operationally, that means that all relationships, both within the company and without, must be based on the bottom-up partnership model, the opposite of the traditional top-down command-and-obey culture.

Investors or Creditors: Who Has the Greater "Stake"?

Legally, only investors have an ownership stake in a business. But—also, legally—creditors' claims against a company's assets rank ahead of investors'. Indeed, in a bankruptcy court, investors come dead last.

Creditors include bondholders, banks, suppliers, employees, and governments: everyone a business deals with daily except investors and customers.

All creditors' financial well-being is tied, in part or—in the case of most employees, in whole—to the company's financial health. So they clearly have a stake in the business's future.

True, investors stand to lose more than creditors; but the creditors' return on *their* investment is fixed, while the investors' return is potentially unlimited.

We can argue about who has *most* at stake—but to do so is to accept the premise that they all have *something* at stake.

What About Customers?

Do customers have a financial stake in a business? Indirectly, yes. After all, they shop there because it's cheaper and/or a better experience in some other way.

More important, every business has a crucial *financial* stake in its customers. No customers, no business.

"Love your customers" may sound like a counterculture mantra from the sixties—but given what *you* have at stake, why *wouldn't* you love your customers?

And Your Neighbors?

Some of your new customers didn't come to visit you: they came to shop at the store next door. You were just an afterthought.

So the healthier your neighbors are, the healthier you are, and vice versa.

For example, where's the best place to open a secondhand bookshop? Somewhere you *know* you'll find lots of book buyers—and where better than right next door to a Barnes & Noble or similar popular bookstore?

The last thing you want to happen is to see that store close down.

"Employee" or "Partner"?

It's become fashionable to refer to employees as "partners" or "associates." But is this change in terminology meaningful?

"Partnership" implies equality. This is certainly true in an incorporated partnership, where a majority or even unanimous vote is required for any significant change.

An employer-employee relationship is clearly not equal in this sense.

But it can be equal *relationally,* when owners and managers refuse to exercise their "employer" prerogatives and *relate* to employees as partners. This must include giving employees an effective veto power over management decisions.

A powerful example comes from Starbucks' Philippines affiliate. In 2011, the management decided to ban smoking in the outdoor seating areas of all Starbucks stores. The result was a dramatic loss of business: stores that had been packed were suddenly half—or sometimes three-quarters—empty.

In one meeting with store managers, the central management proposed laying off probationary employees to cut costs. The store managers said, "You can't do that; you'll be breaking your agreements."

The management agreed and realized it also had to listen to its customers and reinstitute the smoking areas to get them to come back.

What makes this example *doubly* powerful is that Filipino culture—like that of many other Asian and non-Western countries—encourages *subservience, dis*couraging the development of self-confidence and self-esteem. Speaking up (especially to superiors) is actively frowned upon.

The ultimate test of whether a business is following the partnership model is:

- Do employees feel they are *important?*

- Are they encouraged to express their opinions and suggestions?

- Are they *heard* when they do?

- Do they have the sense they can make a positive, even transformative contribution to the business, beyond just punching the clock every day?

Richard Branson could be unpredictably generous—or stingy. In 1970, he gave Nik Powell, his childhood friend and partner in the mail-order record business that was the foundation of Branson's fortune, 40 percent of the company that became Virgin Music. Simon Draper, another early hire, received 20 percent of Virgin Music, also without payment. When Branson personally received a settlement of £500,000 from his lawsuit against British Airways in 1995, he distributed the entire amount to Virgin Atlantic staff.

So when Branson sold Virgin Music to Thorn EMI in 1992, for £560 million ($1 billion), most employees "had just taken it for granted that [they] would all share in the benefits that they had helped Richard, Ken, and Simon to build." This expectation was one factor in Virgin employees' willingness to work long hours for lower wages than they could have received elsewhere.

For example, Steven Lewis, who had walked in the door of Virgin Records when there were only six employees, had received several far richer offers from other record companies—and turned them all down. He and Simon Draper were the two people responsible for building Virgin Music into a billion-dollar company.

Lewis was in charge of Virgin's music-publishing division, which accounted for 20 percent of the group's profits—but only 10 percent of its revenues. Lewis

When treated as partners, employees are excited to come to work, and that excitement transforms the customer experience.

Working with suppliers on the same basis has similar results. As Mackey notes, most of the suppliers who stood by Whole Foods when it was underwater are still suppliers today, thirty-six years later.[8] Loyalty is a two-way street.

A Culture of Fear

Most businesses, says Mackey—indeed, most organizations—are based on the opposite model of "carrot and the stick." That is, incentives—and fear.

He claims a business such as Whole Foods that "loves its customers" (and other stakeholders) has a competitive advantage over that traditional business model.

Is he right?

Fear is an inefficient method of motivation. It results in masters who tell their servants what to do—and a servant's job is *not* to "reason why." Creativity is thus restricted to the higher levels of the organization. The lowly employee whose hands-on experience could result in an improvement saving or making thousands or even millions of dollars is hardly encouraged to open his mouth.

had also been given equity, not in Virgin Music but the company that managed Virgin artists—which had been shut down several years before. So while Draper walked home with £112 million ($200 million) for his 20 percent share of the purchase price, Lewis received nothing.

As did Virgin's employees. Despite their expectations, this time around Branson didn't share the wealth.

At the time, Virgin was under considerable financial pressure. The 1991 Gulf War resulted in a dramatic decline in air travel and a spike in oil prices. To save Virgin Atlantic, Branson had to reduce debt—otherwise he would never have sold the group's "jewel in the crown."

But Branson's stated business philosophy is to put employees (whom he calls "associates") first, customers second, and shareholders last. When employees and customers are looked after, he says, the return to shareholders will take care of itself.

The lesson is clear: for the partnership model to work smoothly, for an employee to be a real partner in the business, the arrangement must be unambiguously defined—and top management must be emotionally committed to making the deal work as originally agreed, come hell or high water.

A fear-driven business inevitably alienates its employees, who turn to unions when they feel there's no other way to protect their interests. As the 2009 Chapter 11 bankruptcy of General Motors all too clearly demonstrates, such a relationship can bring a company to its knees.

The overall differences between businesses driven by love or fear are shown in this table of *extremes:* there will inevitably be days when Whole Foods' partners are bored on the job—or someone in a fear-driven company will challenge the boss and win.

	A Business Based on Love	A Business Based on Fear
Leadership by	Inspiration and persuasion	Command
Employee / Management relationships	Egalitarian / Cooperative	Hierarchic / Dictation from high to low
Primary accountability	To team members and customers	To superiors
Availability of company information	Transparent to all stakeholders	Secretive; on need-to-know basis

Motivation	Company's values, mission, and service to others	Profit / bonuses / fear of losing job / missing promotion
Primary attitude toward others in company	Trust	Mistrust
Loyalty	To team / mission / values	To paycheck / self / family
Employee experience	Involvement / excitement / creativity	Variable
Customer experience	Welcomed as a person and a friend	Variable

The difference becomes startlingly obvious at the customer interface. The business based on love—or, as Howard Schultz phrases it, on creating an emotional connection with customers—results in a superior customer experience.

That, in turn, results in increased *customer loyalty*, which increases repeat business and reduces customer turnover, ultimately producing higher profits and a superior return on investment compared to businesses structured on the top-down, carrot-and-stick approach.

In other words—

Love Works

If your first reaction was "What's love got to do with business and investing?," you're not alone. That was my attitude when I first learned about John Mackey's unique approach to business.

Cynical me's immediate thought: "Good marketing." I certainly didn't buy Mackey's argument that his "stakeholder" approach should replace the traditional model where the primary, if not sole, purpose of a business is to make money for its owners.

When Mackey *debated* this issue with Nobel Prize–winning economist Milton Friedman, I was firmly in the Friedman camp.[9]

But the experience of a good friend of mine dramatically confirmed the accuracy of Mackey's approach in a way that studies of large enterprises—including Whole Foods itself—never can.

Ramona is one of those lucky people who discover why they were born early in life. She lives to teach.

She could have worked anywhere but chose a small kindergarten where she was free to experiment, exercise her creativity, innovate, and create and refine her own teaching methods.

> Love what you do—but your company should love you back.
>
> — Howard Schultz

Ramona is one of those people who care "too much." She cared about the students, cared about her assistants, and cared about the parents. She had never heard of John Mackey, yet her approach to management could have come right out of Mackey's *Conscious Capitalism*.

Because she cared, she loved, demonstrated in this exchange between one of her students and a substitute teacher:

Student: "Do you love us?"

Teacher: "Of course!"

Student: "You're lying. We know teacher Ramona loves us. We feel it. She doesn't have to tell us. With you, we don't feel it."

Ramona enlisted the support and creativity of the assistants by always asking for their input, eager for any improvement regardless of whom or where it came from. Her management style was not to give orders but to make suggestions like "How about doing it this way? What do you think?"

The Results

The kids eagerly looked forward to going to school every day; the thought of playing hooky never occurred to them.

Parents were delighted with their children's progress. When Ramona's students went to "the big school," they read at a grade two (and sometimes three or four) level, had a basic grounding in math and science, and were the kind of students some teachers love to hate. The ones with inquiring minds who are never afraid to point out teachers' mistakes and ask questions adults would prefer not to answer. Self-confident, independent thinkers (and we're talking about six-year-olds and younger in a world of adults, remember).

The Bottom Line

The school's reputation skyrocketed; within eighteen months student numbers zoomed from thirty-five to sixty-one, with more on a waiting list, all by word of mouth.

And the school's profits tripled.

If you employed people who'd tripled your profits, wouldn't you reward them?

Wouldn't you appreciate their efforts, acknowledge their contributions, support them in every way you could . . . in sum, do everything within your power to make sure this person stayed with you indefinitely?

Doesn't that sound like the logical thing to do?

But Ramona paid a high price for her freedom to teach her way.

The school's owner was a penny-pinching control freak: her primary management tool was fear. She got away with paying undermarket wages by capitalizing on her employees' insecurities, especially their fear of losing their jobs. Or, in Ramona's case, by exploiting her passion to teach.

She greeted Ramona's achievement not with appreciation and higher pay, but by accepting new students without apparent limit.

The success of Ramona's approach depended, in part, on reaching every student as a unique individual. So each new student meant more preparation, less play, and even less sleep.

With twice the students and no additional help ("too expensive," according to the owner), Ramona's health suffered; after much agonizing, she quit.

The change in the school after Ramona left was dramatic—and immediate.

The owner stepped back into the saddle, having to give up other remunerative activities to do so. The rule of love was replaced with rule by fear, and the school ceased being a happy place.

In the first week, a dozen kids, 20 percent of the total, simply stopped showing up—a considerable achievement given most had to overcome their parents' objections. The rest were waiting for Ramona to come back.

Ten months later the school's attendance had shrunk to just thirty kids—fewer than the thirty-five students it had when Ramona started working there. The school's owner paid a high price for her management style.

How to Destroy a Brand Name in One Easy Lesson

Van Morrison used to be one of my favorite artists. I still love his music—but I can't listen to it anymore without wincing.

Here's why.

Around 1980—that's *over thirty years ago*, but it *still* sticks in my mind—my wife and I went to the Montreux Jazz Festival. We only had time for one show, so naturally it was Van Morrison's.

Eyes closed, his music was as good as, if not better than, my CDs by him.

Eyes open was the problem.

Morrison sang behind a standing microphone at center stage. On top of the piano, some six feet behind him, was a drink plus an ashtray holding a lit cigarette. Between verses, Morrison would saunter back to the piano, lean on it—turning his back to the audience—take a drag from his cigarette, have a swig from his glass, and maybe chat quietly with the pianist—and get back to the microphone just in time for his next stanza.

To me, his message to the audience was loud and clear: *I don't give a damn about you.*

I left the show feeling that I'd wasted my time and money—and been insulted to boot!

Morrison's disdainful *lack* of engagement demonstrates, by counterexample, the power of *total involvement* with customers.

Why Love Works

Mackey's love-and-caring approach works because *profit is a residual.*

Ramona, for example, had no incentive to increase the school's profits—but she tripled them by attracting new students.

Sales went up.

Increased profits were a *side effect* of loving your customers.

Profits are the difference between income and expenses. As such they are what's "left over" from two other activities: increasing sales and reducing costs.

You can't increase profits by *aiming* to increase profits. You can only increase profits by targeting sales and costs.

Increased profits may be your ultimate aim, but you can only achieve that target by aiming somewhere else.

For example, if you want to drive from Los Angeles to New York, you first have to get onto the freeway. You then aim for, say, Las Vegas or Phoenix, and so on until you finally reach your target. Miss any one of those intermediate aims and you could end up in Miami or Toronto instead.

Arriving in New York is the result of thousands of intermediate aims; you'll never arrive by simply aiming for New York.

So it is with any business.

Walmart's "low, everyday prices" are achieved by, first, reducing its markup across the board and, second, by relentlessly cutting costs to the bone—so further reducing prices. As a consequence, sales' *volume* goes up, as, ultimately, do profits.

Whole Foods' and Walmart's financial results are both a consequence of a narrow focus on somewhere else. In each case, that "somewhere else" is determined by the vision driving the company.

Arguably, though, Starbucks most dramatically demonstrates—

The Power of Vision

In 2000, Starbucks' founder, Howard Schultz, gave up the position of CEO and stepped back from the company's operations, becoming chairman and focusing on international expansion. Seven years later—*despite* the tremendous growth in the number of Starbucks stores, same store sales, revenues, and profits—he'd become convinced that Starbucks in the United States had lost its way and was in danger of losing its position as the "third place"—after home and office—where people gathered, whether to work, surf the Internet, or simply hang out. His concerns included:

Starbucks had ventured into unrelated businesses.[10] CDs, books, even cuddly toys were some of the items offered in Starbucks stores. They added to sales and profits—but what did they (not to mention forays into music and movie production) have to do with coffee or the romance of Italian espresso bars? Absolutely nothing.

But they did increase same store sales, one way the management was—

Giving in to pressure from Wall Street.[11] A rising focus on financial results at the expense of the customer experience was percolating through the company. The top management felt stressed by the need to exceed quarterly profit projections to keep Wall Street analysts happy.

This focus trickled down to dilute the customer experience. In one store, the manager excitedly told Schultz about cuddly toys' high profit margins, and how they added to the store's gross.[12] To Schultz, the man seemed totally oblivious of Starbucks' founding mission.

Starbucks was "no longer celebrating coffee."[13] Coffee beans were no longer ground in-store but delivered ready to brew. The result: the smell of coffee

---

When Maximizing Shareholder Value Is Not Enough

Like profits, maximizing shareholder value is also a residual. A fact dramatically illustrated by Apple's transitions from Steve Jobs to John Sculley (1983) and back to Steve Jobs (1993).

One of Sculley's stated aims as CEO was to maximize shareholder value. Top management received generous stock options—in 1988, Sculley was the highest-paid CEO in the computer business—and to ramp the stock price, $2.218 billion was paid out in dividends and stock buybacks between 1986 and 1996.

Initially, it worked. But the massive "investment" in maximizing shareholder value was money diverted from developing new products and refining current ones. The long-term result: when Sculley became CEO on April 8, 1983, Apple's stock closed at $4.92; when he left the company on October 15, 1993, Apple was at $7.06. A rise of 43.5 percent over his reign, compared to the S&P 500's gain of 207.16 percent over the same period.

Only when Steve Jobs returned to the saddle, with his primary focus of creating beautiful products, did Apple's shareholder value recover—becoming at one point the world's largest company by market value as a side effect.

had all but disappeared from Starbucks stores. All too often replaced by the smell of burning cheese!

Introduced in 2003, sandwiches quickly became popular with customers and were highly profitable, increasing the percentage of the company's revenue from sales of food from 13 percent in 2003 to 17 percent in 2007. But it proved impossible to warm cheese sandwiches without the smell wafting through the stores.

Schultz wanted them banished—and was in no mood to compromise.

This became, symbolically as well as actually, a highly divisive issue within the company. Management split into two camps: those pointing to the immediate financial benefits, which were inarguable; and those who, like Schultz, felt those benefits were short-term, coming at the much-higher long-term price of losing Starbucks' reason for existing.

In February 2007, Schultz shared his concerns in a memo titled "The Commoditization of the Starbucks Experience," which he sent to Starbucks' "most senior leaders."[14] A few extracts illustrate that his primary concern was (and remains) the customer experience:

> *I am not sure people today even know we are roasting coffee.* You certainly can't get the message from being in our stores. . . . Some stores don't have coffee grinders, French presses . . . or even coffee filters. . . .
>
> [We] desperately need to look into the mirror and realize it's time to get back to the core and make the changes necessary to evoke the heritage, the tradition, and the passion that we all have for *the true Starbucks experience.* [Emphasis added.][15]

By the end of that year comparable-store sales "dropped to levels we had not seen in years,"[16] and the financial arguments lost their force; in January 2008, Howard Schultz returned to the position of CEO.

Restoring the Customer Experience

Among Schultz's earliest acts as CEO was to banish those cheese sandwiches. Other ventures unrelated to the "Starbucks experience"—such as selling books, music, toys, and producing movies—were also wound down. But those changes were minor compared to what was to become Schultz's "Transformational Agenda."

Announced the day of Schultz's return in a companywide e-mail titled "The Transformation of Starbucks," his plan rested on three pillars:

● Improve the current state of the US retail business.

● Reignite the emotional attachment with customers.

Own or Starting a Business?
Why You Should Read *Onward*

What could the "Starbucks experience" have to do with a small company or a start-up?

More than you'd think. You can easily apply, with little adaptation, Howard Schultz's plan for the transformation of Starbucks into a design for your own business, whatever it may be.

And if you're starting from zero, his outline enables you to get it right from day one.

What's more, the problems Starbucks faced are a cautionary tale every business owner should take to heart, illustrating the dangers that can arise from losing your focus and succumbing to the hubris of success.

• Make long-term changes to the foundation of Starbucks' business.[17]

Over the following months, the agenda was developed from what Schultz termed "navigational guidelines" into a complete reinstatement of Starbucks' mission and values, and a series of concrete actions that would bring them to life, the first of which was:

Bringing back great coffee. In a bold move, on 26 February 2008, Starbucks stores across the United States closed their doors at 5:30 p.m. The purpose: to retrain baristas in the art of making the perfect espresso and espresso-related drinks. Schultz was concerned that in the name of efficiency, practices such as resteaming milk for cappuccinos (a definite no-no) had devalued the quality of Starbucks' core coffee products.

He also wanted to bring back coffee's romance.

Baristas watched a short film on one of the seventy-one hundred DVDs and DVD players the company had shipped, which went into the intricacies of preparing the perfect espresso. At the end, Schultz made it clear that if a barista felt the drink was less than perfect, "they had my permission to pour it out and begin again."[18]

Reinspiring partners. As a result of the turmoil within the company, store closures, layoffs, and skepticism about Starbucks' future—especially from Wall Street analysts—"Starbucks was losing not just money but also our partners' trust."[19]

Schultz felt the only way to overcome this disquietude, to recover partners' enthusiasm, and to recommit them to Starbucks' underlying vision was in person.

So on Sunday, October 26, 2008, ten thousand Starbucks partners—including eight thousand store managers—arrived in New Orleans for a weeklong conference.

Schultz and the company came under renewed fire for the $30 million cost of this gathering—a touchy-feely investment with no obvious, computable return to number crunchers at a time when the company's US retail operations were in trouble. Schultz admitted that it was risky,[20] and the week before the conference began, Starbucks' stock traded at its lowest-ever price: $7.06—a mere third of the $21 recorded when Starbucks became a public company in 1992.

The leadership conference included workshops and panels, four "huge interactive galleries designed to bring Starbucks' mission, values, operations, and store-management skills to life,"[21] and involvement in the community as Starbucks' partners helped rebuild some of New Orleans's still-devastated neighborhoods. It culminated in a highly emotional general session in which management and partners alike recommitted themselves to the Starbucks mission and values.

At the end of the week, ten thousand partners returned to their posts, galvanized by their experience, and spread the meme companywide.

Devolving authority. Taking a page from John Mackey's (then-yet-to-be-written) book *Conscious Capitalism,* frontline staff were empowered to make more operational decisions without reference to the head office. One example: when in-store partners stepped back to observe themselves from the customer's point of view, they came up with significant organizational improvements that made the stores more efficient—and their job easier. These ideas were readily, if not eagerly, accepted by baristas in other stores, coming as they did from their peers rather than from the top down.

Expanding Starbucks' coffee "footprint" by introducing new products in line with its core mission. Most significant: VIA Ready Brew, introduced in 2009, and Starbucks coffee pod system, the K-Cup, introduced in 2012.

These two new products account for most of the growth in the Consumer Products Group's sales, which—as you can see from the chart that follows—have contributed approximately *half* the growth in the company's US revenues since 2008.

Some other examples include purchasing the Clover company, opening several experimental espresso cafés in Seattle to test different store designs and product offerings, including one serving wine, expanding the Tazo Tea line, and the purchase of premium-tea retailer Teavana Holdings Inc.

These are all components of Schultz's focus on restoring Starbucks' mission, and the customer experience. But he did not ignore—

The Bottom Line

One consequence of the growing focus on pleasing Wall Street: costs had gotten out of control. The problem wasn't obvious until revenues plateaued and began to decline.

A major area of neglect within the company: the supply chain, which had failed to keep up with the helter-skelter expansion of Starbucks stores. This became critical in September 2008 when all stores in the St. Louis area ran out of Ethos water—and the warehouses that supplied them had zero stock!

Two years later, 90 percent of store orders were fulfilled perfectly, compared to 35 percent in 2008, and supply-chain costs had been cut by a cumulative $400 million.

The financial results tell the story—before *and* after.

Margins and Sales Decline

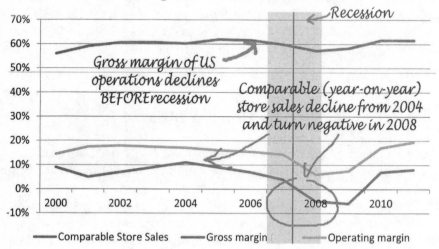

Sources: Starbucks stock price and S&P 500: Yahoo! Finance. All other data: Starbucks annual reports, 2000–2012
(http://investor.starbucks.com/phoenix.zhtml?c=99518&p=irol-reportsannual).

Consumer packaged goods—reported as a separate revenue stream from 2006—includes worldwide sales of products such as VIA Ready Brew, whole beans, and bottled Frappuccinos,

US Store Growth Flattens

← Recession

Dramatic store growth in US flattens from 2008, but continues internationally

Number of stores

US stores — International stores

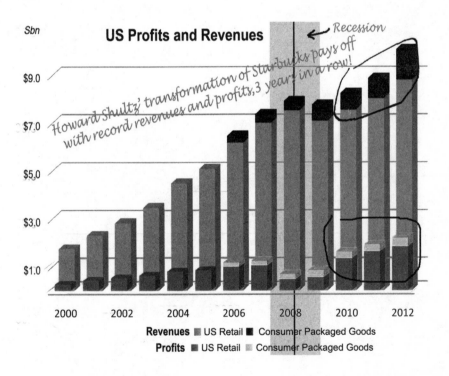

$bn

US Profits and Revenues

← Recession

Howard Shultz' transformation of Starbucks pays off with record revenues and profits, 3 years in a row!

Revenues — US Retail — Consumer Packaged Goods
Profits — US Retail — Consumer Packaged Goods

sold through non-Starbucks outlets such as supermarkets. However, only a small portion of these sales are made outside the United States.

Note: In 2012, Starbucks restructured reporting of retail activities from United States and International to Americas; Europe, Middle East, and Africa (EMEA); and China/Asia Pacific (CAP). So with the exception of store numbers, "US" figures for 2012 are for the "Americas" group. (Courtesy of author)

A powerful example of how a tight focus on a company's underlying vision ultimately flows through to the bottom line.

But successful implementation requires that short-term consequences be ignored in order to achieve long-term results. Although this management strategy has proven successful in companies as diverse as Berkshire Hathaway, Apple, and IBM, such companies are often penalized by Wall Street's insane focus on short-term quarter-to-quarter results.

It's a crying shame that supposed "professional money managers" fail to recognize that the *power of vision* is a fundamental key to long-term business and investment success.

5 How Ray Kroc's McDonald's Trumped Burger King with Superior *Entrepreneurial* Management and Execution

In 1948, brothers Richard "Dick" and Maurice "Mac" McDonald opened a drive-in restaurant in San Bernardino, California, simply named McDonald's, that was destined to revolutionize the world's food business.

Not that that was the McDonald brothers' intention. They lived on a hill overlooking their restaurant and spent a lot of their spare time sitting on the veranda "watching the store." Like Canberra's Augustin Petersilka—who fought city hall and won so he could have *his* café *his* way—they were pioneering innovators in *restaurant operations.* They had no interest in expanding, unlike Howard Schultz, John Mackey, Sam Walton, and Ray Kroc, who are pioneering innovators in business *management.*

But the McDonald brothers were (of course!) happy to take "free money" from visitors who marveled at their operation—initially, a series of neighboring Californians to whom they sold individual franchises; eventually, entrepreneurs who *did* have Schultz-like ambitions:

● Keith J. Kramer and Matthew Burns, who, inspired by what they saw, opened their own copycat, Insta-Burger King, in Jacksonville, Florida, on 28 July 1953.

● James McLamore and David R. Edgerton, who—inspired by the Jacksonville copycat of the McDonald brothers' store—became the Miami, Florida, franchisee for Insta-Burger King (quickly renamed Burger King). Their first store opened in Miami on 1 March 1954—and they bought control of the Jacksonville franchisor in 1961.

● Ray Kroc, who franchised McDonald's and grew it from one store in Des Plaines, Illinois (opened on 15 April 1955), to 34,492 worldwide today.[1]

Today, McDonald's is the world's number one hamburger (and, by sales, restaurant) chain, while Burger King, despite its head start, remains a distant number two.

Along the way, however, *another* hamburger chain you've probably never heard of almost trumped McDonald's: Burger Chef. In 1971 it was less than a hundred restaurants shy of McDonald's almost thirteen hundred—and way ahead of Burger King, which had some eight hundred stores. Burger Chef was adding a new location every forty-eight hours, so it was within shouting distance of wresting the number one slot away from the then-much-slower-growing McDonald's.

But in 1982, shrunken to under half its 1971 size, what was left of Burger Chef was taken over by Hardee's and disappeared from the "hamburger wars." Meanwhile, Burger King's growth almost ground to a halt—leaving the field wide open for McDonald's.

The different fates of these three hamburger chains illustrate the overwhelming significance of the *fifth clue:* superb *entrepreneurial* management and execution.

CLUE #5

Superb Entrepreneurial Management and Execution
Without entrepreneurs at the helm who also have superb management and execution skills, the presence of the previous four clues in a company may signal a profitable and viable operation, but *not* one that could be the next Starbucks, Whole Foods, Walmart, or McDonald's.

White Castle: Creating America's First National Food

Until Walt Anderson and Billy Ingram opened their first White Castle restaurant in Wichita, Kansas, in 1921, products made with ground beef were widely viewed

as being unsafe to eat.

White Castle's featured product was a *square* hamburger, known as a slider, just over half the size of a McDonald's burger, sold for a nickel.

Thanks to White Castle's success, copycats sprang up almost instantly, with "innovative" names such as White Crescent, White Knight, Blue Castle, Royal Castle, Red Barn, Red Lantern, and Klover Kastle.

The affordability of the slider, and White Castle's and its clones' emphasis on pristine cleanliness, changed the unsafe-to-eat perception of the

A White Castle restaurant in New York today.

hamburger. So much so that by the advent of World War II, the hamburger was firmly established as America's first truly national food.

Ironically, though White Castle paved the way for the rapid postwar expansion of McDonald's, Burger King, Burger Chef, Hardee's, Jack in the Box, and other burger chains, in a fate common to most first movers, it didn't benefit itself.

Though White Castle still exists, selling its signature slider, by spurning the franchise model in favor of company-owned stores, it has, today, just 421 locations.

How McDonald's Automated the Food Business— and Created "Fast Food"

In 1937, the McDonald brothers opened a carhop in San Bernardino, California. Carhops, restaurants where you were served in your car, grew rapidly in popularity in the United States during the interwar period, spurred by the dramatic increase in automobile ownership.

Analyzing their business, the brothers discovered that hamburgers were their biggest-selling item, accounting for 80 percent of their sales.

So in 1948 they closed the carhop and replaced it with the world's first self-service, limited-no-choice-menu, fast-food restaurant, slashing the necessary investment in inventory.

They completely redesigned their food-production methods, introducing automation on a scale never before seen in the restaurant business.

They called their new method the Speedee Service System.

By investing capital in production methods, they dramatically lowered their costs. Their new McDonald's was a *self-service* restaurant, eliminating the twenty-plus carhop waiters on roller skates who served customers in their cars.

The machinery they designed, made by a local craftsman, meant they could hire unskilled labor instead of qualified cooks. Most restaurants prepared one meal at a time. By adapting Henry Ford's production-line techniques to food preparation, with just twelve employees—three to cook the burgers, two making milk shakes, two for french fries, two who assembled the burgers, and three men who worked the counter—they could easily serve more than one customer every minute.

The restaurant design was also innovative: their new octagonal store was essentially a kitchen enclosed by glass. Customers could *see* the food being prepared—and, more important, see that the kitchen was kept spotlessly clean, an important selling point.

Selling tenth-of-a-pound hamburgers for 15¢—half the 30¢ charged elsewhere, along with french fries (added in their second year of operation), milk shakes, and soft drinks, the brothers' new store was an almost-instant success. Though profitable from the start, it was a year before their strange new restaurant's profits exceeded the carhop's . . . and kept growing.

Enter the Copycats

Their concept was so innovative it was soon written up in the trade press and attracted a flood of interest, visitors—and copycats.

In 1953, two of those visitors were Keith Kramer and Matthew Burns, who left San Bernardino inspired to create their own McDonald's clone in their hometown of Jacksonville, Florida.

While in California, they met George Read, who'd invented Insta machines that—like the McDonald brothers' innovations—automated the production of hamburgers and milk shakes. Kramer and Burns signed a franchise giving them exclusive use of Read's Insta-Burger and Insta-Shake machines in the state of Florida.

As Kramer and Burns were building their first Insta-Burger store in Jacksonville, they received a visitor: David Edgerton, a former manager of a Howard Johnson restaurant in Miami.

Attracted by the high margins, he was planning to open a Dairy Queen franchise in the Miami area. But when he saw the Insta-Burger store in Jacksonville, he changed direction. Edgerton's Insta-Burger store opened in Miami on 1 March 1954—renamed, at Edgerton's urging, Insta-Burger King.

But his first store got off to a rocky start. Needing capital, Edgerton persuaded James McLamore to join him: on 1 June 1954, they became fifty-fifty partners in Burger King of Miami Inc.

McLamore was also an experienced restaurant operator—and entrepreneur.

He had learned the restaurant business as the director of food service at the YMCA in Wilmington, Delaware. At a mere twenty-one years of age, he revamped the operation so thoroughly it made more money in his first year at the helm than it had in the previous thirty years combined.[2]

Two years later he opened the Colonial Inn, a White Castle copycat.

In February 1951, McLamore visited Miami and was impressed by the number of restaurants offering shoddy service and indifferent food—all with long lines of customers patiently waiting to get a table.

Confident he could do *much* better, McLamore opened a restaurant and put the Colonial Inn up for sale.

His new venture, the Brickell Bridge Restaurant, was a disaster.

As he candidly admitted many years later,[3] his decision was an impetuous mistake. Aside from choosing a poor location, he soon discovered, to his consternation, that February's apparent restaurant boom was *seasonal*. By May, most of those restaurants had shut their doors for the summer and stayed shut till the "snowbirds" returned the following winter.

Searching for a way to fill his almost-empty tables, he hired a twelve-year-old kid named Charlie to walk back and forth in front of his restaurant, wearing a chef's hat and ringing a bell, inviting passersby to come on in.

"Dinner Bell Charlie" attracted a flood of curiosity seekers—but not too many new customers.

> ### McLamore's Impetuous Decisions
>
> One of McLamore's management flaws was a tendency to make impetuous decisions that failed to pay off. This, as we'll see in the following pages, was a major factor that enabled McDonald's to pull ahead of Burger King.
>
> Which is not to say that Ray Kroc and others *never* made such impetuous mistakes. Indeed, Kroc's agreement with the McDonald brothers falls into that same category.
>
> The difference between Kroc and McLamore—a difference essential to growing a business that can become the next Starbucks—is that whenever Kroc recognized he'd made such a mistake, he was willing to pay the price to correct it, even when he couldn't afford it.
>
> Kroc, unlike McLamore, *always* "went the extra mile."

Only when McLamore ran newspaper ads in which Dinner Bell Charlie invited people to a prime sirloin steak dinner for just $1.95 (McLamore's cost) did the Brickell Bridge Restaurant become popular—so popular it had lines of customers waiting outside even during the slow summer months.

McLamore described this marketing idea—the combination of a unique personality for the business with a low price—as "one of the great learning experiences"[4] of his life. A learning experience that would turn Burger King around after several years of far more downs than ups.

How the Whopper Saved Burger King

The Miami market for burgers was owned by Royal Castle, a White Castle copycat, thanks to its sponsorship of Miami's number one children's show.

McLamore and Edgerton's strategy was to scale up stores so they, too, could afford to advertise. But with four money-losing stores, it wasn't working.

In 1956 McLamore met a retired businessman, Harry Fruehauf, who invested $65,000 for 50 percent of the company and became a mentor to McLamore and Edgerton.

Fruehauf's capital injection enabled Burger King to add three more stores, which *also* lost money.

In early 1957, McLamore and Edgerton visited Gainesville, Florida, to see a new Burger King that Kramer and Burns had just opened. It had no customers!

Just a hundred yards down the street was another hamburger store—with a long line of people waiting patiently outside. McLamore wandered over to see what the attraction was.

The restaurant was a ramshackle mess: dirty and dusty from the unpaved parking lot, poorly fitted out, with indifferent service—the opposite of the new and *empty* Burger King store a short walk away.

McLamore joined the slow-moving line to discover that the lure was a quarter-pound hamburger served on a five-inch bun. What's more, he saw some customers come out with bags full of these burgers.

After he bought one for himself and one for Edgerton, a couple of bites proved that the burger was worth the wait.

On the drive back to Miami, unable to get that hamburger out of his mind, McLamore suggested they introduce a copycat burger in their restaurants, call it the Whopper, and change their signage from BURGER KING to BURGER KING: HOME OF THE WHOPPER. Edgerton immediately agreed.

Just a few days later, the Whopper was on sale at all their restaurants.

At 39¢, including tax, it was "a stunning success from the moment it was introduced."[5]

The red ink at their seven money-losing restaurants soon turned black.

Now, McLamore was in his element. With the highly marketable Whopper backed up by new machines that didn't break down and a redesigned operating and ordering system that customers hardly noticed, Burger King began to expand rapidly . . . in South Florida. But not even the Whopper could save Kramer and Burns's northern-Florida operation.

Burger Chef: "The Greatest Might-Have-Been in the History of the Fast Food Business"[6]

Burger Chef had its origin in a prototype store created by an Indianapolis company named General Equipment Inc., a manufacturer of machines for the restaurant trade. The purpose: to showcase their products to potential customers in a real-time environment.

Opened in 1957,[7] the demonstration store, called Burger Chef, quickly filled with local customers who preferred the quality and value of the food produced by the company's machines to that offered by other Indianapolis restaurants.

It also attracted a different kind of interest: entrepreneurs looking for a turnkey franchise operation. The management soon decided to franchise their restaurant concept, partly on the basis—like Ray Kroc and his MultiMixer—that "it *might* be a great way to sell more equipment."[8]

General Equipment was founded by an inventor and entrepreneur, Frank Porter Thomas, who cut his teeth in the amusement-park industry. In 1926 he built the world's first "fun house" ride near Indianapolis. Thanks to its popularity, he was commissioned to build similar rides in New Jersey, Boston, Rhode Island, and Ohio.

Flush with cash, in 1929 he began construction of his own park, which opened in Corpus Christi, Texas, on 4 July 1930.

His timing, in the early months of the Great Depression, could hardly have been worse; it was a disaster.

Thomas returned to Indianapolis broke—down, but not out. A restaurant called the North Pole was serving a new dish: frozen custard. Thomas saw the custard machine and figured he could do better. When he brought his new prototype to the North Pole, the owner promptly bought Thomas's machine and junked the one he'd been using.

Other restaurant owners had similar reactions, and soon Thomas had customers for his EZE-Way frozen-custard maker all over the United States and Canada.

In 1946, Thomas retired, turning the business over to his sons, Frank Porter Thomas Jr., an inventor in his own right, who became president, and Don Thomas, who was in charge of engineering.

That same year, a salesman from California whose customers were feeling the heat from the fast-expanding Dairy Queen chain called to ask, Could they provide a machine that made a similar soft-serve ice cream?

They could and they did. Sales of their new SaniServe, as it was called, mushroomed so fast that in 1950 they had to build a new factory to meet demand.

In 1952, the company added a third product, a modification of the SaniServe, called the SaniShake, which produced a fully completed milk shake with one turn of a spigot, and was a competitor to Ray Kroc's MultiMixer.

In 1956 Frank Jr. was approached by Burger King's Dave Edgerton, who wanted to know if General Equipment would be interested in manufacturing his improved version of the Burger King's flunky Insta-Broiler machine.

The Thomas brothers reengineered and dramatically improved Edgerton's design. With their Sani-Broiler, far superior to the Insta-Broiler, General Equipment now produced an almost-complete lineup of the machines needed to set up a hamburger restaurant, which led to the demonstration store in 1957, and the franchising of Burger Chef a year later.

Burger Chef, in other words, was inspired by Burger King—*and* McDonald's. "Without that phone call [from Dave Edgerton]," Frank Thomas Jr. relates, "we would never have made a broiler, and Burger Chef would never have existed."[9]

When they decided to franchise Burger Chef, they cloned McDonald's method of operation.

Burger Chef's Advantages over McDonald's

Though started three years after Ray Kroc opened his first McDonald's, Burger Chef had several advantages.

1. It was backed by a profitable operation, while Ray Kroc started McDonald's on a shoestring. And it was run by a management team that had already proved its entrepreneurial credentials.

2. Burger Chef wasn't hamstrung by any arrangements like Kroc's deal with

the McDonald brothers (or McLamore and Edgerton's restrictive franchise).

3. Through the serendipity of their prototype store, they had discovered a concept that was highly marketable.

4. Finally, they benefited from the experience—and learned from the mistakes—of Ray Kroc and the many other restaurant franchises that were mushrooming across the United States in the early 1950s.

One spin-off advantage was that they could—and did—invest considerable time, effort, and money in planning the franchising operation before signing up franchisees. Kroc, McLamore, and Edgerton learned the business on the fly; by taking the time to study what worked (and what didn't) from their competitors, Burger Chef opened for business much further down the learning curve.

In other words, like Starbucks, Whole Foods, Walmart, and McDonald's itself, Burger Chef had all the advantages of the second clue, the copycat principle, of *not* being the first—or, indeed, even the second—mover in the hamburger wars.

So had we been applying these principles back in the late 1950s and early '60s, we might well have picked Burger Chef over McDonald's as the hamburger chain that was going to dominate the market.

What's more, Burger Chef almost did!

The first Burger Chef (not counting the prototype store) opened in Indianapolis on 3 May 1958, followed by two more by year's end.

At that time, McDonald's had been in business for three years and had seventy-nine outlets. McLamore and Edgerton had been in business four years and had seven stores.

Burger Chef quickly overtook Burger King with 681 stores by 1967,[10] compared to McDonald's 857, while Burger King was closing in on 300. From a standing start, Burger Chef had become the fastest-growing restaurant chain in the United States and was second, by sales, only to McDonald's.

All three chains were growing fast. Even Burger King, though coming from behind, was adding stores almost as fast as McDonald's. The enormous potential for expansion meant that even Burger King had a realistic opportunity of winning the "hamburger wars." But then . . .

McDonald's Changes the Rules

On 21 April 1965 McDonald's went public and changed the rules of the game. As a listed company, it could now access the bond market and borrow money on more favorable terms than still-private Burger Chef and Burger King and could use its stock as currency.

At that time all three chains could open a new store confident it would be profitable. Just one limitation held back their rate of new-store development: capital. Capital that Burger King and Burger Chef managements felt was now available to McDonald's in relative abundance.

Both managements succumbed to the pressure to seek their own capital injection, afraid that otherwise McDonald's would leave them in the dust.

Little did they know that as a result of its going public, McDonald's expansion rate was about to slow down.

And paradoxically, by succumbing to the fear of being outfinanced, both managements acted in haste, exposing their internal management flaws.

As a result of *finding* new money, all three companies entered a crisis: one chain disappearing; one simply halting dead in its tracks; while the third almost broke in half.

In each case, their fates were self-inflicted, dramatizing the significance of *superb* entrepreneurial management and the consequences of its lack. And, at the same time, the difference between *entrepreneurial* management and *corporate* management.

Ray Kroc: *Always* Going the Extra Mile

The obstacles confronting Ray Kroc's McDonald's were formidable.

To begin with, he was tied hand and foot by the franchise agreement he'd personally negotiated with the McDonald brothers. What he'd thought was a great deal turned into a nightmare that drove him crazy. As he put it later, "A man who represents himself has a fool for a lawyer."[11]

His problems began immediately.

The agreement required him to copy the brothers' San Bernardino store in every excruciating detail. But Kroc's architect's first questions about the plan for his first store in Des Plaines, Illinois, were "Where are you going to put the basement? And the furnace?"

The desert design had to be adapted for Illinois's alternately freezing and hot and humid climate.

But any deviation from the San Bernardino model had to be agreed to by both brothers in a signed letter sent by registered mail. The brothers said "go ahead" over the phone—but refused to send the necessary letter.

While planning his first store Kroc discovered, by accident, *another,* far more serious problem. On a sales call to the Frejlich Ice Cream Company to sell them MultiMixers, he mentioned his deal with the McDonald brothers. Only then did he learn that the Frejlich brothers had bought an exclusive franchise for four McDonald's stores in Cook County just before Kroc signed his agreement.

Cook County was Kroc's home turf, including not only Chicago but also Des Plaines, where he planned to open his first, prototype store!

The brothers had told him of ten other franchises they'd sold in California and Arizona, but neglected to mention the eleventh one, in the Chicago area.

The Frejlich brothers were happy to bank a quick profit, asking $25,000 for their $10,000 purchase. Kroc (after he'd calmed down) persuaded the McDonald brothers to refund the Frejliches' $10,000, but where to find the rest?

He offered a 50 percent interest in his franchising company for $20,000, an investment that would eventually be worth billions. But there were no takers. Ultimately, he arranged a bank loan for the balance.

This action was typical of Ray Kroc. When he faced a problem, he attacked it mercilessly, moving heaven and earth until he'd solved it, paying the necessary price even when he couldn't afford it.

This was just the first of several such seemingly impossible obstacles that Kroc overcame by frontal assault.

Ray Kroc *always* went the extra mile.

Soggy French Fries

Another major problem for Kroc: the french fries in his Des Plaines store were soggy, far below the standard set by the McDonald brothers.

It took Kroc a year of intense research to find the reason: desert air.

The McDonald brothers stored their potatoes in a warehouse behind their restaurant. Open to the dry desert air—but protected from rats and other vermin by wire mesh—the low humidity reduced the potatoes' water content, making a dramatic difference to their taste when cooked.

Duplicating that desert air in Chicago's alternately humid or freezing environment required developing special drying equipment, housed in the basement. More major variations from the San Bernardino model that the brothers agreed to—only over the phone.

Such continual refusals to put anything in writing meant Kroc was in violation of the agreement from the get-go—a shaky foundation for his business.

But paying the necessary price to buy out the Frejlich brothers left him with another, equally serious problem. He was not just stretched but also totally *starved* for capital.

Why Not "Kroc's" Instead of "McDonald's"?

You may be wondering why Kroc didn't simply walk away from the agreement and do what others had done: set up their own McDonald's clone without paying the brothers a dime?

He certainly considered that option. But Kroc's approach to business was that of a salesman. That was his strength—but also his weakness.

He felt that McDonald's was a marketable name while Kroc's (rhyming with *crock*) was not. He could have chosen another name, but the McDonald's *system* was a complete product, one he knew he could sell. And he would benefit from tapping the brothers' expertise and years of experience. Experience he did not have.

With a salesman's optimism, he was also confident he could renegotiate the registered-letter requirement in the agreement. That optimism was totally misplaced. When he later met with the brothers and their lawyer, they were immovable and intransigent.

Kroc's first McDonald's opened in Des Plaines on 15 April 1955 with encouraging—and profitable—first-day sales of $366.12. That may not sound like a lot today, but it works out to 2,440 sales at an average product price of 15¢. Or about a thousand customers.

Kroc hoped his demonstration store would attract potential franchisees. But it didn't. The hamburger business in the Chicago area then was mostly owner-operators running a stand, and they were only open for the seven warmest months of the year.

But one person the store did attract that same year was Harry Sonneborn.

Sonneborn had just resigned his position as vice president of Tastee-Freez after a disagreement with its founder, Harry Axene.

In 1944, Axene formed a partnership with the founder of Dairy Queen, then with just eight stores. Axene sold territorial franchises for $25,000 to $50,000 apiece, for whole cities or states. When he resigned in 1948, Dairy Queen had twenty-five hundred stores across the United States, a dramatic success that spurred dozens of restaurant-franchising copycats including Big Boy burgers, Chicken Delight, Kentucky Fried Chicken, and Taco Bell.

In 1950 Axene started Tastee-Freez, a Dairy Queen clone, with fifteen hundred stores when Sonneborn resigned.

Sonneborn visited the Des Plaines McDonald's store, and as he later told Kroc, "I can tell just by watching it from across the street that you have a winner there."[12] And he wanted to work for Kroc.

Kroc was in a financial bind. He had just one employee, his secretary and assistant, June Martino. His only income—indeed, after buying out the Frejliches, his only source of capital—was from Prince Castle and its MultiMixer sales.

As Kroc later admitted, he'd been supremely confident that profits would automatically follow sales. He also knew his finances were a mess, but the subject barely interested him. Logical (perhaps) for a salesman, but potential suicide for a businessman.

When he met with Sonneborn, Kroc knew he was just the financial man Kroc needed. But he couldn't afford to hire him—while at the same time he couldn't afford not to.

That dilemma was resolved when Sonneborn came back with an offer to work for just enough to cover his keep: $100 a week. A quarter of what he'd been earning at Tastee-Freez.

Kroc and Sonneborn were a study in opposites. Kroc was an extrovert, a "people person" who loved to sell one-on-one, focused on selling hamburgers. Sonneborn, an introvert, had no interest in hamburgers. He didn't even like them. Indeed, he couldn't care less whether a business was selling hamburgers, burritos, widgets, or whatever. What attracted him to McDonald's was not hamburgers but the fact that they were flying out the door.

Kroc knew that. But an excellent judge of character, he also knew that Sonneborn would put twenty-four hours a day into McDonald's, just as Kroc did.

Kroc's employment style was extreme delegation. Sonneborn took charge of finances and financing, and Kroc left him to it.

He soon proved his worth.

Starved for Capital

Kroc's agreement with the McDonald brothers required him to charge no more than $950 for a franchise, and a fee of 1.9 percent of sales, 0.5 percent of which went to the brothers. This was a great deal for the franchisees—and a recipe for disaster for Kroc. Every new franchise sale was cash-flow negative up front, while 1.4 percent of sales barely covered the cost of servicing franchisees.

Kroc also made a fundamental decision to spurn the industry practice of manufacturing or sourcing supplies and equipment and requiring franchisees to purchase them from the franchisor. With the one exception of MultiMixers, which did not turn out to be the cornucopia Kroc had expected. Most McDonald's franchisees needed just two, not the ten the McDonald brothers had.

In the long run this turned out to be an excellent decision. In the short to medium run it meant that Kroc's only source of revenue was the insufficient franchising fees. In the five years leading up to 1960, McDonald's sales totaled $75 million while its earnings were a minuscule $159,000.[13] Kroc didn't even draw a salary until 1961.

So where to find the capital to expand? Franchising was the obvious solution: get someone else to put up the money.

As the original home of McDonald's, with a climate where drive-in restaurants flourished twelve months of the year, California was a logical place for expansion. Nine of the eighteen franchises Kroc sold in his first year were in California.

But from two thousand miles away in Chicago it was impossible for Kroc to effectively monitor the maverick California operators. They all went their own way, diverting from the McDonald's system by charging different prices and by adding various other menu items from hot dogs to burritos and pizza. Fred Turner later termed it "fast-food anarchy."

In Illinois, Kroc turned to his friends at his golf club. They'd initially thought he was crazy to go into the 15¢ hamburger business. Some of them changed their minds when they saw the profits of the Des Plaines store.

But they were absentee investors, indifferent to Kroc's operational standards so long as they banked a profit. So Kroc had no more success enforcing his high standards on them than he'd had in California.

Then, one day Betty Agate walked into the office of Kroc's assistant, June Martino—to sell Bibles. Instead, Martino sold her and her husband on the idea of having their own McDonald's store.

Betty Agate and her husband, Sandy, were owner-operators, the opposite of Kroc's golf-club friends. They invested everything they had into their restaurant, and both worked behind the counter.

Their store opened on 26 May 1955 in Waukegan, Illinois, fifty miles north of Chicago, a working-class town like San Bernardino, and did a land-office business. In their first year, the Agates grossed $250,000 and took home $50,000 in profits. With numbers like that, it became *the* showcase for anyone interested in taking on a McDonald's franchise.

How Harry Sonneborn Turned McDonald's into a Money Machine

Stores such as the Agates' were financed by third parties. Kroc, Sonneborn, or the franchisee found a banker or a landlord willing to build the store and lease it to the franchisee.

Harry Sonneborn institutionalized this model. Instead of the franchisee leasing the premises direct, McDonald's, initially, leased the store and subleased it to the franchisee.

Later, Sonneborn refined the model, buying the land *and* building the store. A new franchisee was required to put down a *rental* deposit equal to the amount McDonald's needed for the down payment to purchase the land. McDonald's required the seller to take part of his or her payment in a note, classed as a second mortgage, so McDonald's was able to then take out a *first* mortgage from a bank with the land as security, so providing the money to buy the land *and* build the store.

McDonald's then rented the finished store to the franchisee at a minimum monthly figure that included a 20 percent to 40 percent markup over the payments McDonald's had to make to repay the bank and the seller—or a percentage of sales, usually 8.5 percent, whichever was greater.

Provided the store was profitable, it was a no-risk arrangement—which ended up with *McDonald's* owning the real estate at zero cost!

This brilliant solution provided the necessary capital for McDonald's expansion—and as an unexpected side effect, eventually made McDonald's the most profitable, by a long shot, of the three competing chains.

Furthermore, as part of the lease agreement, the franchisee was required to meet Kroc's operational standards. This gave Kroc sufficient control over franchisees' operations to ensure a far superior uniformity in the customer experience across all McDonald's stores than any of its competitors could achieve in their stores.

In 1960, Sonneborn took this model to the next level by negotiating a loan of $1.5 million from two insurance companies. As part of the agreement, McDonald's created a subsidiary, Financial Realty Inc., to house all the real estate—and give the lenders additional security.

But to close the deal, McDonald's had to part with 22.5 percent of the company's equity. Both Kroc and Sonneborn vowed they'd never repeat this incentive.

Exit the McDonald Brothers

The following year, conflicts between Kroc and the McDonald brothers came to a head. Kroc decided he had to buy them out. They were agreeable—for $2.7 million, which would give each of them $1 million after tax.

Once more, money Kroc didn't have.

McDonald's net worth was a mere $250,000. Aside from the $1.5 million it had just borrowed, McDonald's was up to its eyeballs in real estate debt, and the more stores McDonald's opened, the more leveraged it became. Its balance sheet was enough to give any banker a heart attack.

Nevertheless, Harry Sonneborn came up with yet another creative financing arrangement. One that was expensive in the short run, but turned out to be a masterstroke several years later.

McDonald's borrowed $2.7 million from a consortium of twelve trust funds, including those of Princeton University, Howard University, and Swarthmore College.

The interest rate on the loan was an about-market 6 percent—exceptionally reasonable given that McDonald's then had a close-to-zero (if not negative) credit rating.

Further, loan repayments were set at 0.5 percent of McDonald's systemwide sales. The beauty of this arrangement was that it cost McDonald's nothing—since it was committed to paying out that 0.5 percent of its 1.9 percent share of franchisees' sales anyway. The money just went to the lenders instead of the McDonald brothers.

Thanks to Sonneborn, this agreement actually improved McDonald's cash flow. While 0.5 percent of sales were due, the lenders agreed that McDonald's could hold back 0.1 percent, which would be paid at the end of the loan period.

Now free of the McDonald brothers' restraints, Kroc could increase his rate of expansion and, more important, increase franchisees' fees and charges.

But there was a kicker (in case you're wondering whether the lenders had lost their minds): when the loan was paid back in full, McDonald's had to continue the same 0.5 percent payments for the same period. So if repayment took ten years, the lenders received payments for *twenty* years.

The lenders estimated that it would take McDonald's about fifteen years to repay the loan, and their expected return would be somewhere between $7.1 million and $9 million.

In fact, the loan was repaid in five and a half years. The total cost to McDonald's: $14 million, a return to the lenders of 518 percent!

Going Public

After the buyout of the brothers and with its real estate financing strategy, McDonald's was in good financial shape. It didn't need to tap Wall Street for more money, the usual rationale for going public.

The pressure to list came from a different source.

Kroc had built an impressive management team who had come on board at below-market salaries. Although McDonald's was profitable, it still wasn't profitable enough to raise Martino's and Sonneborn's (or, for that matter, Kroc's) salaries.

Unable to increase their pay, Kroc compensated these two key associates with 10 percent and 20 percent of the equity respectively. They, along with Kroc himself, were keen to realize some cash rewards for their efforts; going public was the solution.

So when McDonald's hit Wall Street on 21 April 1965, the main sellers were Kroc, Martino, and Sonneborn—and the two insurance companies with their 22.5 percent of the equity. Not the company itself.

The 1960s: Go-Go Years on Wall Street

McDonald's timing was perfect. Its listing on Wall Street hit in the midst of "conglomerate frenzy." When McDonald's soared, from $22.50 to $30 on its first day of trading, and more than doubled in the following two weeks, restaurant chains were added to the brew.

In quick succession, Kentucky Fried Chicken, Royal Castle, and Howard Johnson went public, along with two Burger King franchisees, Self Service Restaurants (New Orleans), and Mallory Restaurants (Long Island, New York).

The "Suede Shoe Boys"

With Kentucky Fried Chicken trading at a hundred times earnings, and similar sky-high valuations for other chains, promoters—or, as James McLamore called them, "the suede shoe boys"[14]—poured into the market.

The most famous of these was Minnie Pearl Fried Chicken.

Advertising itself as the Pepsi of the fried-chicken business, the company sold large territorial franchises to gullible investors. Each franchise gave the buyer the right to a specified number of Minnie Pearl stores in a specific territory. The franchisee was required to put up a small cash deposit, further payments to be made as stores were opened.

The company then booked the entire *projected* revenue as *income*!

Minnie Pearl's stock soared in the same way and for many of the same reasons as the dot-bombs of the late nineties. Listing in 1968, it opened at $20 a share and closed the day at $40. With just $2.2 million in assets and five barely profitable stores, it reached a market cap of $81 million—before going bankrupt (though not before the promoters had pocketed a small fortune). Minnie Pearl was just one of many similar scams based on the accounting fraud of booking projected future income as if it had been received today.

Meanwhile, takeover fever infected company managements nationwide, who, like lemmings, joined the fray—and the latest hot category of fast-food restau-

Ramping up Earnings

The sixties was the decade of the conglomerate. "Synergy" was the mantra of the time. By combining a diverse collection of unrelated companies, conglomerates would supposedly benefit from reduced costs; increased buying power; slimmer, more professional management—and so, higher profits. The whole was (supposedly) greater than the parts.

For example, ITT—originally International Telephone and Telegraph—bought over three hundred companies in the "go-go years," including businesses as unconnected with each other (or telecommunications) as Sheraton Hotels, Continental Baking, Avis Rent a Car, Education Services, and Hartford Insurance Co.

Meanwhile, Ling-Temco-Vought, or LTV, added businesses from missiles to car rentals and golf equipment, while Gulf & Western scooped up hotels, real estate companies, and movie producers, to name just a few.

The theory was synergy, but the reality was mostly financial engineering. Here's how it worked.

Being in favor, conglomerates traded at high P/E ratios. Using their stock as currency, they could buy companies with low P/Es and boost their stock's value.

Hot Shot Co. Inc., with a million shares outstanding and reported* profits of a million dollars, is trading at twenty-five times earnings, giving it a per-share value of $25.

Meanwhile, Boring Bricks & Mortar Inc., with the same profits but only four hundred thousand shares, is trading at just ten times earnings—or the same $25 a share.

So Hot Shot Co. issues four hundred thousand new shares to "merge" with Boring Bricks & Mortar, with this result:

rants became an essential addition to their shopping lists. In quick succession, Servomation bought Red Barn, Ralston Purina took over Jack in the Box, PepsiCo scooped up Pizza Hut and Taco Bell, while Marriott picked up Big Boy, and Imasco merged with Hardee's.

The perfect environment, you'd think, for Burger King and Burger Chef to partake of some of that financial wizardry for themselves.

So why didn't they both join McDonald's, Kentucky Fried Chicken, and the flood of other fast-food restaurants in the rush to Wall Street?

Why, instead, did James McLamore and Frank Thomas both decide to sell out to a conglomerate—Burger King to Pillsbury and Burger Chef to General Foods?

Analyzing their decision-making underlines the difference between entrepreneurial management and what we might term the *extreme* entrepreneurial management of Ray Kroc.

Or to put it a different way:

Hot Shot Co. + Boring Co.	Profits	# shares	EPS	P/E	Share price
	$2,000,000	1,400,000	$1.43	25	$35.71

Thus a 42.85 percent boost to the share price as Boring Bricks & Mortar's earnings are "magically" rerated from ten to twenty-five times earnings.

Talk about financial fairy tales!

But Hot Shot Co. can do even better if it can borrow the necessary million bucks and simply buy Boring Co.:

Hot Shot Co. + Boring Co.	Profits	# shares	EPS	P/E	Share price
	$2,000,000	1,000,000	$2.00	25	$50.00

A double! True financial wizardry!

In reality, the wizardry was rarely this obvious. The Hot Shot conglomerates of the era usually bought companies much smaller than themselves. The result was the same over time—but in small, incremental bites rather than huge chunks.

*"Reported" profits aren't necessarily the same as true profits, especially when the stock market is hot. See my post, *Cooking the Books—and Screwing the Shareholders* (marktier.com/cooking) for a short course in how to do it.

Why James McLamore and Frank Thomas *Didn't* Go the Extra Mile

McLamore and Thomas made their decisions to sell out in 1966 and 1967 respectively. Thanks to President Lyndon Johnson's policy of guns (for Vietnam) *and* butter (to keep voters happy and his popularity rating high), inflation and interest rates were heading up. On Wall Street, stocks had crashed. Though it was not officially a recession, a significant consensus in 1966–67 was that that's where the economy was heading.

That environment ruled out an IPO.

With conglomerate offers on the table, the pressure from feeling they *had to* have a capital injection to keep up with McDonald's, and the obvious attraction of cashing in their chips, both McLamore and Thomas made decisions that, in retrospect, were disastrous for both Burger King and Burger Chef.

But those reasons were merely the *proximate* causes. Underlying those decisions were—from our point of view as entrepreneurs or investors searching for the next Starbucks—deeper flaws in both management teams.

Burger King's "Split Personality"

Seven problems plagued Burger King from the start. One—fierce competition—was external. The other six, however, were inherent in the way Burger King and its owners operated.

External

1. Fierce competition: The Florida market was dominated by Royal Castle, a White Castle clone, thanks to its sponsorship of Miami's most popular children's TV show.

In Chicago, Ray Kroc's McDonald's faced scattered competition mainly from other McDonald brothers' clones. Burger King opened in a market "owned" by a well-established competitor and its 15¢ slider. Considering that White Castle, Red Barn, and Hardee's, among many other *profitable* chains flourishing in other parts of the United States, entered the Florida market—and were all forced to withdraw—it's a wonder that Burger King survived.

Internal

2. "Schizophrenia": the division between Kramer and Burns in Jacksonville and their South Florida franchisees, Edgerton and McLamore.

Kramer and Burns sold franchises in northern Florida, but provided little support and failed to ensure consistency across different stores.

Compared to their northern-Florida franchisors, the Edgerton-McLamore operation was a class act. All the ideas for improvements came from them:

- Adding *King* to the original *Insta-Burger* name.

- Dropping *Insta* altogether.

- The Whopper, which saved Burger King—north and south—from total failure.

- And, ultimately, dumping the cranky Insta machines entirely.

Even Kramer and Burns turned to Edgerton and McLamore for advice.

This division between the entrepreneurial South Florida franchisees and the lackadaisical northern-Florida franchisors delayed the nationwide expansion of Burger King by almost a decade. Burger King grew and prospered in South Florida, but potential franchisees from other parts of the United States had to deal with Kramer and Burns. One look at the northern-Florida operation was usually enough for the potential franchisees to shake their heads and walk away (probably to McDonald's!).

3. Trademarks: Kramer and Burns registered the trademarks Burger King and the Whopper.

Edgerton and McLamore were the originators of *both* names—and Burger King's slogan, "Home of the Whopper"—but received no credit. What's more, they did not protest. The result: an asset that should have been 50 percent if not 100 percent theirs eventually cost them $2.55 million to buy back.

4. The Insta-Burger machine was unreliable: It regularly broke down, so the affected store was out of business until it could be fixed or replaced by a backup. As you can imagine, this certainly did nothing to improve the customer experience!

One day, after about two years (!) of suffering with this problem, Dave Edgerton lost his cool when the machine broke down and destroyed it with a hatchet, yelling, "I can build a better machine than this pile of junk."

"Well, you'd better get busy and build it," McLamore replied, "because right now we are out of business until we get our only spare machine in operation."[15]

Soon thereafter, Edgerton and McLamore announced they were dumping the Insta machines for their own superior replacement (manufactured, paradoxically, by the company that would soon open a McDonald's/Burger King copycat, Burger Chef!). Kramer and Burns quickly followed suit.

5. Pricing: Burger King's raison d'être, its hamburger, was priced at 18¢ compared to 15¢ most everywhere else.

Burger King's 18¢ burger patty was about twice the size (8.9 to the pound) and less than twice the cost of Royal Castle's 15¢ slider, but to customers it didn't *appear* to be a bargain price.

Burger King's higher price combined with its unreliable Insta machine and a poorly thought-out ordering system turned customers away.

The cumulative result of these problems: *all* the Burger King stores lost money until the entire operation was rescued by the Whopper.

6. *Edgerton and McLamore were slow to resolve these problems:* Taking two years to replace the unreliable Insta-Burger machine was typical of Edgerton and McLamore's slow resolution of the problems that plagued their operations.

Other examples include:

- Opening new *money-losing* stores in the hope expansion would turn the business around.

- Not willing to pay the price: starved for capital, like most start-ups, Edgerton and McLamore put off solutions to problems when they seemed too expensive.

- Staying with the 18¢ burger.

As James McLamore wrote thirty-four years later, "I believe that one of our biggest mistakes was staying with our higher-priced hamburger rather than offering one that we could design and sell for 15 cents."[16]

7. *A dysfunctional partnership:* The partnership of McLamore, Edgerton, and Harry Fruehauf became dysfunctional at the worst possible moment: when McDonald's changed the rules by going public.

Raising Capital on a Shoestring

The success of the Whopper had an unexpected side effect that helped alleviate Burger King's capital shortage: soon after its introduction, Charlie Krebs walked into their office to ask if they'd accept $20,000 for one of their stores.

Until that moment, McLamore and Edgerton had worked on the assumption that all their outlets would be company owned.

Desperate for capital, they quickly agreed. And by 1957, they had sold all their original stores and were busy building new ones—to franchise.

By 1958, McLamore had begun small-scale advertising on radio and TV. His big break came the following year when Royal Castle inexplicably decided to drop its sponsorship of Skipper Chuck's *Popeye Playhouse,* the most popular children's show in the Miami area. Immediately when he heard, McLamore agreed to sponsor the show—even though he had no idea how he would pay for it.

This was one of his few Kroc-like decisions—agree, then figure out how and where to find the money.

His decision paid off: targeting children brought more families into his stores (a strategy that McDonald's replicated many years later with its Ronald McDonald clown), adding to the bottom line. And Burger King's increased "presence of mind" in the Miami market brought in more franchisees.

Going Nationwide

At their troubled Jacksonville operation, Kramer and Burns followed Fruehauf's injection of equity with keen interest and soon decided to follow McLamore and Edgerton's example. A Jacksonville businessman, Ben Stein, took a 50 percent equity interest in Burger King of Florida and loaned the company a significant sum to finance expansion.

Kramer and Burns quickly added several new stores in the Jacksonville area—with disastrous results. The new stores were all in poor locations and poorly managed to boot. When they defaulted on the loan, Ben Stein assumed control of the company.

Stein, though an astute businessman, was unfamiliar with the restaurant business and was unable to turn the northern-Florida operation around. He turned to McLamore and Edgerton, suggesting they take over his operations, which in 1961—after two years of fruitless, on-off discussions—they did. Stein kept the trademarks in return for 15 percent of the franchise fees.

McLamore and Edgerton could now take Burger King nationwide.

Shortly afterward, McLamore asked Stein at what price would he sell the trademarks. "One hundred thousand dollars" was Stein's immediate response. An amount McLamore felt he couldn't afford.

As Burger King expanded, its payments to Stein went up—as did Stein's buy-out price: $100,000 was substantially less than the $2.55 *million* Stein received in 1967. Had McLamore "gone the extra mile" and come up with $100,000 in 1961, even at outrageous interest rates Burger King would have been substantially better off.

As McLamore later admitted, when Ray Kroc "went the extra mile" by borrowing money he couldn't afford to buy out the McDonald brothers, he "came up with the better solution."[17]

Once McLamore and Edgerton were in the saddle, they no longer had to send potential franchisees to the shabbily run Jacksonville operation. By 1965, they were adding one new Burger King almost every week; two years later that rate had doubled, matching McDonald's.

A major factor in this growth was selling franchises for whole cities or states. The franchisee agreed to open a certain number of stores on a fixed schedule, which shifted the capital cost from Burger King to the franchisee.

Keeping up with McDonald's

"We needed capital to stay in the race, and we needed to find it rather quickly"[18] was McLamore's reaction to McDonald's April 1965 public offering.

Although McLamore was concerned that by diluting his and Edgerton's share of equity they could lose control, the partners agreed that a public offering was the best option, and Fruehauf introduced McLamore to a Wall Street firm he was familiar with: Blyth and Company.

In early 1965, McLamore and Fruehauf visited New York. Burger King's numbers were certainly striking: $446,239 in earnings for the year ended 31 May 1965, with $750,000 or more projected for 1966. But Blyth seemed less than impressed.

Soon afterward, McLamore was invited back to New York only to learn that Blyth thought the partners were too young, inexperienced, and undercapitalized for an IPO.

After this discouraging rejection McLamore went straight to the airport to catch a flight back to Miami; the idea of taking Burger King public was dead.

Here's a key difference between McLamore and Kroc that made all the difference to the future courses of their two companies.

Had Ray Kroc been in McLamore's shoes—turned down by the first people on Wall Street he met—it's unlikely he'd have followed in McLamore's footsteps back to the airport. Kroc would have started knocking on all the other doors along Wall Street until he found a company that would do, or could be persuaded to do, what he wanted.

Much later, McLamore admitted that at the time he understood nothing about Wall Street and the stock market, and he should probably have brought in an experienced adviser "to guide us through the complexities." Even worse, he later discovered that he'd been talking to the wrong people: Blyth and Company's specialty was working with institutions and blue-chip companies in the bond market, not underwriting IPOs for entrepreneurial start-ups.

The partners explored other financial options, meeting with a dozen or more financial institutions, and on 14 April 1966, Mass Mutual extended Burger King a long-term loan of $1.5 million. A number of similar financings were under negotiation. Burger King could now, like McDonald's, build stores to lease to franchisees.

Just two weeks later, Pillsbury indicated a possible interest in buying Burger King.

McLamore was feeling the pinch. His salary hadn't increased since he joined with Dave Edgerton in 1954. After ten years of inflation, and with his children about to go to college, McLamore was having trouble making ends meet.

He decided the only way he could solve his cash-flow problem was to sell the company to Pillsbury.

This certainly seems like a radical way of solving a $10,000- to $20,000-a-year problem. One has to ask why he, Edgerton, and Fruehauf didn't sit down together and discuss it.

From reading between the lines of McLamore's *Burger King*, I've concluded that McLamore's relationship with Fruehauf, whom he viewed as a mentor, while friendly, was primarily professional. Edgerton was a friend to whom McLamore could pour out his troubles; Fruehauf was not.

Which is why McLamore refrained from taking the obvious course: explaining his financial dilemma to Fruehauf and requesting he agree to a salary increase.

Whatever the case, McLamore first talked about Pillsbury's offer to Edgerton, who was reluctant to agree, but was persuaded to go along with his partner's wishes.

Then the two of them talked to Fruehauf, presenting a united front, and Fruehauf, who was, like Edgerton, less than enthralled by the idea, also agreed—with a distinct lack of enthusiasm.

Ray Kroc's "Marriage" Proposal

Burger Chef and Burger King weren't alone in receiving corporate suitors. In 1968, Nate Cummings, CEO of Consolidated Foods, approached Ray Kroc to delicately suggest a "marriage" between their two companies.

Kroc's reaction demonstrated his deep-seated desire to remain independent:

"You've got a marvelous company, and that is a great compliment. The problem is that we just wouldn't consider something like that unless we were the surviving company, and I'm afraid that managing a company like yours is just more than we could handle."*

No way was Kroc going to give up his baby!

*Grinding It Out

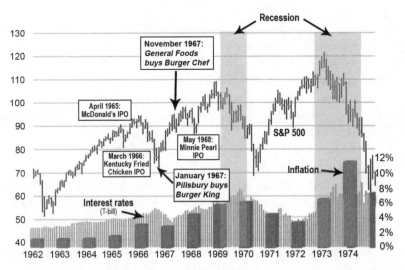

The "Go-Go" Years on Wall Street

Very expensive mistakes: By rejecting an IPO in 1965, Burger King missed the possibility of listing in early 1966—and achieving similar multiples to Kentucky Fried Chicken. Burger King and Burger Chef managements both decided to sell their companies during the 1966–67 "mini-bear market," when no other options seemed available. As a result, both missed out on the dramatic boom in franchising chains kicked off by Minnie Pearl's IPO in May 1968.

But just as the deal with Pillsbury was about to close, Fruehauf angrily complained to McLamore that *he'd* made a big mistake. An example of how a dysfunctional partnership at the top can lead to serious business blunders.

Fruehauf spoke his mind but took no action to suggest they explore other options, a topic that—like McLamore's underlying motivation—never came up in their discussions.

In fact, with the Mass Mutual loan in place, and similar loans under negotiation, Burger King didn't *need* to go public to keep up with McDonald's.

So, because the three partners didn't talk openly with each other, in June 1967 Pillsbury assumed control of Burger King—one more decision that McLamore (along with Edgerton and Fruehauf) ultimately came to regret.

Frank Thomas: A Second-Generation Entrepreneur

Burger Chef's management was also spooked by McDonald's new financial strength. So in mid-1967, when Frank Thomas and his team received two suitors, General Foods and Borden Foods, they were all ears.

Like Burger King and McDonald's, Burger Chef was profitable. But profits were reinvested in expanding the business rather than paying dividends or raising salaries. Like McLamore and Kroc, Thomas and his partners felt that selling stock was the only way they could realize some cash rewards for their efforts.

Given that Wall Street was collapsing at the time, the idea of a public offering wasn't ever seriously considered.

But Thomas and his partners' attitude toward their company was different from Kroc's and McLamore's.

Kroc and McLamore were both *first-generation entrepreneurs.* Their companies—their creations—were their *babies.* Literally. Their emotional attachment to McDonald's and Burger King respectively were identical to a mother's connection with her favorite child: her baby never (really) grows up, and she never wants to let him or her go.

As a second-generation entrepreneur, regardless of the pride he had in his creation, Thomas's attachment to his company was much looser.

In November 1967, after a mere three months of negotiations, Burger Chef accepted General Foods' takeover offer at a price variously reported as $15 million, $16 million, and $16.3 million.[19]

Four million dollars *less* than Pillsbury paid for the *smaller* Burger King the previous January.

But the appeal of General Foods' cash was irresistible. Especially given there was no other option *at that moment.*

But there were other possibilities—if Thomas had been willing to wait for the stock market to recover.

And stock markets *always* recover . . . given time.

Given that Burger Chef had a much bigger footprint than Burger King, was the fastest growing of the three chains, and could, with creative financing, have easily left McDonald's in the dust, in a few years it could have come to market with a far higher valuation than McDonald's.

Many multiples of $16 million.

On that basis, General Foods walked off with a steal.

What Went Wrong

In retrospect, the mistakes that McLamore, Thomas, and their respective partners made are clear. Even so, sufficient thought and research—which neither management undertook—could easily have shown the folly of a corporate takeover. And also the wisdom of waiting until the economic climate changed to take their companies public.

• *Markets turn around.* Always. The macro outlook for an IPO in 1966 or 1967 was certainly bleak. It was only a question of time—though an unknowable time—before the market turned up again.

• *They jumped off the deep end.* Both company managements accepted corporate offers without investigating the possible consequences. A few calls to entrepreneurs who had sold out to conglomerates would have quickly convinced them that promises of independence afterward were a chimera.

• *Burger Chef and Burger King were still growing.* Their value-proposition market was far from saturated—as all three chains proved by opening new and profitable stores, regardless of the macro economic climate. The question was not whether they could continue to grow, but whether they could keep up with McDonald's—and if they were willing to wait till the stock market turned around to cash in some of their chips.

• *Financing was still available*—as the sad irony of Burger King's $1.5 million loan demonstrated. Such financings were difficult to arrange at the best of times. Meanwhile, both chains could continue their one-store-at-a-time expansion. After all, this was the model that had grown Burger Chef faster than McDonald's.

• *You don't need control to keep control.* McLamore's fear that he'd lose control of Burger King by listing on Wall Street was misplaced. Certainly, an IPO would have diluted his—and Edgerton's and Fruehauf's—share of equity. And as a listed company Burger King could be vulnerable to a takeover. A possibility easily averted had McLamore, Edgerton, and Fruehauf agreed to vote their shares as a bloc. In reality, with just 25 percent to Fruehauf's 50 percent, McLamore didn't *have* voting control. But as the managers in residence, McLamore (with Edgerton) followed the strategy of most CEOs who own a tiny percentage of their company's equity: keep your shareholders happy.

Entrepreneurial vs. Corporate Management

Unfortunately, neither Pillsbury nor General Foods subscribed to Warren Buffett's totally hands-off management style. Despite their promises to the contrary, *corporate management* quickly replaced *entrepreneurial management* in both chains, with the result that Burger King effectively dropped out of the hamburger race, while Burger Chef disappeared from the scene, leaving McDonald's with the number one slot by default.

Meanwhile, McDonald's itself flirted with corporate management, a divisive excursion that all but halted its growth and virtually split the company in two.

But what, exactly, is "entrepreneurial" management?

Why is it the ultimate key to the success of companies such as McDonald's, Walmart, Starbucks, and Whole Foods?

In what ways does it differ from what we might call *corporate* management?

And how can corporate management be the kiss of death for a flourishing entrepreneurial company?

How General Foods' Corporate Management Killed Burger Chef . . .

In January 1968, General Foods assumed control of Burger Chef, then with 730 restaurants in thirty-nine states. Three years later, this number had increased to almost 1,200, just 100 stores shy of the McDonald's total. As Burger Chef was opening stores faster than McDonald's, to the casual observer it appeared it would shortly knock McDonald's off the number one spot.

But that growth was an illusion.

The key to any retail expansion is to only open stores that will be profitable. Burger Chef had addressed this problem successfully with its innovative strategy of hiring commissioned sales agents to find new locations and franchisees. As the agents received a percentage of the profits of each new restaurant they had a hand in developing, they worked hard "to not only find the *right* people and locations for new restaurants, but to ensure their success as well."[20]

General Foods' first action was to appoint their own man, George Perry, as the manager of what was now the Burger Chef *division*. Perry's first action was to replace Burger Chef's entire management team.

Only Frank Thomas Jr. remained—as a consultant. A consultant is someone who can be politely listened to—and then ignored. Which was Frank Thomas's fate.

The new management team quickly fired *all* the sales agents—many of whom made far more money than the incoming executives—and replaced them with real estate agents, whose only motivation was making a sale, not building a new and profitable store. In one stroke, General Foods lost the expertise that had ensured new Burger Chefs would be moneymakers.

Stores added under General Foods' management were often in poor locations run by indifferent franchisees.

While the store count rose dramatically, profits didn't follow the same trend.

Franchisees now reported to newly appointed regional managers, who were often more interested in using Burger Chef—a sideline to General Foods' main businesses—as a step up to a higher position on the company's ladder.

Coming from a command-and-control culture, General Foods' managers were used to dealing with *employees;* partnership, the essence of successful franchising, was an alien concept. Franchisees weren't happy when the new managers' attitude of dictation replaced the entrepreneurial attitude of consultation. General Foods' subsequent changes didn't make them any happier.

Burger Chef's headquarters were moved from Indianapolis to General Foods' HQ in Tarrytown, New York, while operations stayed in Indianapolis, a change guaranteed to disrupt communication and coordination within the division. Also one that ensured the managers' focus was on pleasing their Tarrytown *peers,* not satisfying Burger Chef's customers and franchisees.

The position of CEO became a revolving door: in just the two years of 1969 and 1970, Burger Chef was run by *four* different people!

By replacing entrepreneurial managers with corporate executives from the completely different business of selling packaged foods to supermarkets, General Foods simply discarded the accumulated years of knowledge and experience necessary to run a successful franchising operation. One result:

"According to Frank Thomas, the company spent 'a hell of a lot of money' trying concepts that had already been tested and discarded in years past."[21]

Eventually, General Foods threw in the towel. Relationships with franchisees had totally soured. The revolving door of the executive suite resulted in Burger Chef stores sporting *seven* different logos—just the most obvious example of the deterioration of the customer experience. By 1982, store numbers had fallen from their 1971 about-to-top-McDonald's peak to just 679—less than Burger King.

Burger Chef had changed from a profitable, entrepreneurial company into a money-losing corporate millstone. General Foods had taken enormous write-offs; in 1982 it killed Burger Chef by selling the remaining stores to Hardee's.

. . . and Pillsbury Turned Burger King into an Also-Ran

On 21 June 1967, Pillsbury assumed control of a company with 208 stores, profits of $758,000, net assets of $1.7 million*—up from the previous year's $446,239

---

*Financial year ending 31 May 1967.

and $1,056,612 respectively—and a history of producing a 50 percent to 70 percent return on equity.

All driven by an entrepreneurial, partnership culture totally alien to Pillsbury's top-down management structure.

Of the Pillsbury managers, only president and CEO Paul Gerot, who championed the acquisition, truly understood and appreciated Burger King's operational methodology.

In a harbinger of things to come, he had to fight opposition from Pillsbury directors who focused on the *assets* they were buying, not the *business*. With that thinking, $20 million was clearly far too much to pay for $1.7 million in net worth. They completely ignored that Burger King's profits were growing between 48 percent and 107 percent *per year* (and its implications for the future).

Those directors also "knew" that restaurants have a high failure rate—a failure to understand the completely different nature of Burger King's *franchising* business from the dubious prospects of a mom-and-pop, single-location restaurant start-up.

Unfortunately for McLamore and Burger King, three months after the merger Gerot retired. The first action of the new CFO, Terrance Hannold, was to impose standard debt-to-equity ratios on the new subsidiary. This immediately put an end to any possibility of following McDonald's real estate financing model. And it also broke Gerot's promise that Burger King would remain autonomous for at least its first year under Pillsbury ownership.

McLamore remained in charge of Burger King, so it avoided Burger Chef's fate. But his focus slowly changed from expanding Burger King as fast as possible to fighting a rearguard action against Pillsbury's creeping corporate culture. A fight he eventually lost on the principle that he who holds the purse strings conducts the orchestra.

Those changes came slowly, but inexorably:

- *1967:* Pillsbury sends in a management consultant who recommends McLamore abandon his entrepreneurial "hands-on" approach and become a corporate "strategist." *Result:* Franchisees have reduced contact with top management, and McLamore begins to lose his enthusiasm for the business.

- *1969:* Dave Edgerton resigns, unhappy with the creeping corporate culture. Burger King formally ceases to be autonomous.

- *1970–71:* Pillsbury management "developed an increasingly negative attitude toward franchising and real estate development,"[22] a symptom of Pillsbury's failure to understand the partnership relationship that's the backbone of a successful franchising operation.

- *1971:* A top management memo dictates that Burger King's growth can only be financed from earnings; that new stores will be company owned—although franchisees will be allowed but only as a "last resort."

● *1972:* Pillsbury management makes it clear it despises the franchisee model; and McLamore resigns as CEO. Corporate management now reigns supreme at Burger King.

The following table shows what Pillsbury's creeping corporate management "achieved":

Burger Kings added		Related events
1960	7	
1961	8	McLamore and Edgerton take Burger King nationwide.
1962	7	
1963	13	
1964	30	
1965	64	
1966	72	
1967	70	21 June: Pillsbury takes over Burger King. September: Pillsbury CEO Paul Gerot resigns.
1968	108	
1969	108	Dave Edgerton resigns. Fred Turner becomes McDonald's CEO.
1970	167	
1971	107	The results of Pillsbury's financing restrictions finally become obvious at the same time that Turner puts his foot on the accelerator at McDonald's.
1972	91	James McLamore's five-year contract ends. He resigns as CEO; remains a Pillsbury director.

In 1967, Burger King had a good chance of keeping up with and even overtaking McDonald's. Pillsbury's creeping corporate management brought an end to that possibility. Store openings to the 1970 peak of 167 were mostly in the pipeline when Pillsbury assumed control or came from territorial franchisees who had more room to maneuver than Burger King itself.

Ray Kroc, Harry Sonneborn, and the Triumph of Entrepreneurial Management

The fates of Burger Chef and Burger King illustrate the results of corporate management replacing entrepreneurial management.

The reverse distinction—the triumph of entrepreneurial management—is dramatically illustrated by the changes in the McDonald's executive suite after Kroc moved to California in May 1962 to revitalize West Coast operations.

McDonald's had expanded successfully in the Midwest and Eastern states, but Kroc was convinced that McDonald's needed to succeed on the West Coast as well to become truly viable.

A second motivation for his move to California was personal: Kroc had fallen in love. He and his wife-to-be, Joan Smith, decided to live in Los Angeles. But Joan's conscience would not let her divorce her husband, and she called the marriage off at the last minute.

Kroc moved to Los Angeles anyway and began replicating the Chicago HQ there—known as the MiniMac—confident he could leave McDonald's east of the Rockies in the hands of his trusted management team. Especially with Fred Turner as operations chief.

But things didn't work out that way.

Until 1960, McDonald's had been divided into two companies: McDonald's System Inc., the parent company, with Kroc in charge of operations; and Franchise Realty Corporation, a subsidiary, run by Harry Sonneborn, where he worked his financial magic. As a codicil to the $1.5 million loan Sonneborn negotiated that same year, the two companies were merged into one: McDonald's Corporation. Kroc remained chairman, while Sonneborn became president and CEO.

To Kroc, such titles were meaningless.

His management style was extreme delegation: hire the right person for the job and leave him alone to get on with it. Kroc's McDonald's became a highly *decentralized,* freewheeling operation, where anyone could take the initiative to solve a problem or innovate, even if it meant stepping on someone else's theoretical "turf."

This entrepreneurial attitude permeated the company.

An excellent judge of character, Kroc rarely hired round pegs for square holes. His inspirational salesmanship, together with the offer of a position with enormous responsibility—responsibility that people could only achieve elsewhere by spending years climbing a corporate ladder—attracted mavericks who were eager to work at the low salaries Kroc could afford to offer.

People such as Harry Sonneborn.

There's no question Sonneborn was the right person to bring order to McDonald's finances. Indeed, without Sonneborn's ability to raise capital for a company that had a close-to-zero credit rating—junk bond status before there were junk bonds—it's unlikely that McDonald's would still exist today.

McDonald's Business: Hamburgers or Real Estate?

While Kroc remained in Chicago, the change in titles *was* meaningless: the Kroc/Sonneborn division between operations and finance continued as before.

But with Kroc two thousand miles away in California, the dramatic differences between their two characters began to divide the company. A division that nearly tore McDonald's apart.

To Kroc, McDonald's was in the business of selling hamburgers. But his focus was not just on hamburgers but the total customer experience. His mantra to implement this aim was QSCV: Quality, Service, Cleanliness, and Value. He wanted every McDonald's store to offer a quality experience—in both product and service—at an exceptionally good value in a pristine environment.

The quality controls he established, and their continual improvement, set McDonald's apart from its competition—and transformed the production of beef, potatoes, bakery, and related products across the United States.

Organizationally, however, his primary focus was on the franchisees: he was, he often said, in the business of creating entrepreneurs.

For a franchisor, this attitude is essential to success. Franchisees are independent businesspeople. They may not be entrepreneurs in the usual sense of the word—that is, starting something from nothing—but they are entrepreneurially inclined.

Furthermore, they're the public face of the company. *They* are the ones who give every customer a good or a bad experience. Whether they're happy or not will be reflected in the customer experience they deliver. Treat them like the partners they actually are, and all will be well. Treat them as employees—as happened with Burger Chef—and you create a recipe for disaster.

Kroc went one step farther: he encouraged franchisees to innovate. The majority of the successful products McDonald's added to its basic menu, from the Big Mac to the Filet-O-Fish, the Egg McMuffin, and the Apple Pie—not to mention the Ronald McDonald character—were all created and tested first by franchisees. Often over Kroc's objections.

While *every* new product Kroc himself proposed bombed.

But to Sonneborn, McDonald's was in the real estate business. Hamburgers were just the means of building a huge real estate portfolio.

And to Boston and Wall Street financiers, McDonald's cash flow and sales growth might be impressive—but the security of McDonald's real estate portfolio was something they really understood.

When Kroc decamped to California, especially after McDonald's 1965 public offering, Sonneborn began "living up" to his title of McDonald's president and CEO.

His office was remodeled with plush sofas and dark wood paneling. He added layers of management between franchisees and the head office, chains of command, more rules, and more reports. His focus turned from raising money so Kroc could expand to protecting shareholder value from the dangers that accompanied a high debt-to-equity ratio and the like—so satisfying his Wall Street *peers.*

It was as if he viewed his earlier, highly *over*leveraged borrowings as the means to arriving at the goal of respectability on Wall Street.

Gaining and keeping that respectability meant, among other things, reducing leverage. So Sonneborn dramatically cut back McDonald's rate of expansion. His prudent strategy enabled growth to be financed from cash flow instead of debt— but it enraged Kroc.

While the culture of the Chicago headquarters took on the trappings of corporate management, in California Kroc continued his natural entrepreneurial approach, adding stores as fast as he could—ignoring all of Sonneborn's rules.

Kroc also began innovating with store designs and patio seating. Until then, all McDonald's stores—like those of most of its competitors—were pure drive-ins. Customers ate their hamburgers in their cars or took them home.

In Chicago and similar cold climates, such stores were lucky if they broke even in winter. Some drive-ins simply shut down until warmer weather returned.

Sonneborn objected to the *expense* of Kroc's changes—even though the addition of outdoor seating increased same store sales.

In the short run, Sonneborn's strategy did reduce leverage—at the long-run cost of far fewer new restaurants with lower average sales and profits.

Kroc was still in charge, though it wasn't in his nature to confront people or, having given them the authority, overrule their decisions. He and Sonneborn simply stopped talking to each other; all communication went through June Martino. And the company began to divide into Kroc and Sonneborn camps.

This division had other negative effects. The Kroc people in Chicago became increasingly frustrated and dissatisfied, and some of them accepted offers from other chains at much higher salaries—offers similar to those they had rejected before.

Fred Turner was almost one of them.

Turner was the son Ray Kroc never had. They thought the same way and Kroc saw him as his successor. As operations chief he was growing into that role. But he chafed at Sonneborn's restrictions and couldn't understand why Kroc didn't overrule him. Turner was on the verge of accepting one of many far-more-attractive offers he'd been receiving from other chains when Kroc finally took action. Sonneborn resigned, and Kroc promoted Turner to CEO. Turner's reaction: "Why did you wait so long?"

With Turner in the saddle, Sonneborn's corporate-style management was swept away, Kroc's freewheeling entrepreneurial structure was revived, and McDonald's began expanding faster than even Kroc had thought possible.

Risk vs. the Perception of Risk

On the surface, it would appear that Kroc's approach was far riskier than Sonneborn's. It's certainly true that in its early days McDonald's lived on the edge of bankruptcy.

When Turner took over from Sonneborn, he took Sonneborn's real estate financing strategy and put it into high gear. McDonald's debt load skyrocketed: by the standard financial metrics, the company was way overleveraged once again.

But the debt load was carefully calculated, *not* by the value of the real estate but by the projected sales of new stores.

These projections were based on the accumulated years of experience of selecting the right locations operated by the right franchisees. With that combination, from Turner's and Kroc's perspective, the risk of loss on opening a new store was minimal.

A perception of risk that was justified. For example, by the end of 1960, its sixth year of operation, of the 289 stores McDonald's had opened, just *one* failed—a Dallas franchisee. A stunning 99.65 percent success ratio.[23]

Filling a Void

One reason for the early success of McDonald's—and the success of its many clones and competitors—was that it filled a void in the market.

Today, you can walk into a large mall and count half a dozen or more different low-priced franchised restaurants before you've left the ground floor.

In the fifties, sixties, and seventies, the next economical eatery could be miles or even a hundred miles away.

Equally, if not more important: the prime market for McDonald's restaurants was in working-class neighborhoods where competitors with its value proposition simply did not exist.

Markets such as the McDonald brothers' San Bernardino home. And Sandy and Betty Agate's store in the working-class town of Waukegan, Illinois.

The 15¢ hamburger chains were the first "eating out" value proposition that working-class people could regularly afford. They were also family friendly—it was no coincidence that the McDonald brothers' very first customer in 1948, at their revamped store, was a nine-year-old girl, who bought a bag full of burgers to take home for dinner.

In the right neighborhood, the first McDonald's (or Kentucky Fried Chicken or Burger King) that opened had the low end of the market to itself.

This was a major confidence booster for people such as Kroc and Turner. One definition of the *right location* at the time was that it was like the Wild West in the 1800s: unowned, uncultivated land farther than the eye could see, just waiting for an enterprising homesteader to plant his hoe.

The first one to arrive could stake out the most fertile plot.

Today, most market niches are crowded, if not overcrowded. But as Starbucks and Whole Foods and *their* clones have proven, voids still exist, waiting to be filled.

Kroc and Turner could accurately judge the probable success of a new store because they were connected to their customers. Sonneborn could not have made such a judgment even if it hadn't been against his nature: he had little contact with customers or, indeed, restaurant operations.

Yes, Sonneborn could see the sales figures and see their growth, but he could never have Kroc's and Turner's confidence those sales would continue. Sonneborn understood *that* 15¢ hamburgers flew off the grills, but he didn't fully understand *why*. So when, in the late sixties, his Wall Street peers began to worry about the threat of a recession and similar macro events, so did he.

Like many of those peers, he became driven by *fear*. The reaction to fear is to retreat, not expand.

Such little customer contact he did have disappeared entirely as his management style took on more and more of the trappings of a Fortune 500 company.

Kroc and Turner were confident a new store in the right location with the right franchisee was, financially, an almost-zero-risk proposition—because *they knew what they were doing*.

Sonneborn knew what he was doing when it came to judging the value of real estate; but he had insufficient understanding of, or confidence in, projections of future sales.

The bottom line: had Sonneborn's corporate management style become the new McDonald's norm, the company could soon have been overtaken by Burger Chef and probably Burger King as well. Either way, aside from never becoming as large as it is today, it would have had lower profits, lower average store sales, a lower return on capital . . . and a significantly lower long-term return to shareholders.

And by losing its position as the number one brand in its hamburger niche, its financial fall could have been far more dramatic.

Just being the leading brand can be worth a lot. Average store sales at McDonald's and Starbucks, both the number one brands in their markets, are at least double their nearest competitors'.

The differences between Kroc's and Sonneborn's management styles can be summarized in this diagram:

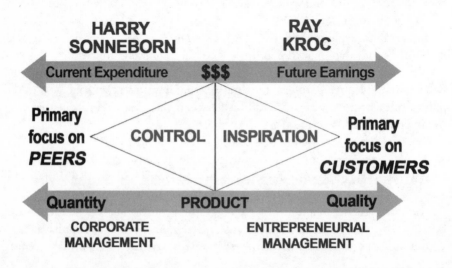

The fundamental difference is *primary focus*. Peers or people: approval from peers *versus* ensuring the satisfaction of customers, employees, and other stakeholders.

Sonneborn's chosen peers were Wall Street financiers. In most corporations, peers are a manager's immediate associates and superiors. In either case, when the primary focus diverts from the customer experience, slower growth and even stagnation can be the result.

The change in McDonald's top management and its effects were to be replicated many years later when Howard Schultz stepped back in 2000 and Starbucks lost its way. Only when Schultz returned and reinstated the customer experience as the primary focus did Starbucks revive.

In the same way, with Fred Turner in charge, entrepreneurial management returned to McDonald's, settling the question of which hamburger chain would be number one.

The relationship between corporate management and entrepreneurial management and a company's fate can be summarized graphically in this simple picture:

	Extreme ← Corporate Management (Control)			Entrepreneurial Management (Inspiration) → Superb			
1960: All three chains expand fast—under entrepreneurial management					Burger Chef	Burger King	McDonald's
1962: Ray Kroc moves to California; Sonneborn in charge in Chicago					Burger Chef	Burger King	McDonald's
1965: McDonald's goes public					Burger Chef	Burger King	Burger King / McDonald's
1967: Pillsbury buys Burger King. James McLamore remains CEO				Burger King	Burger Chef	McDonald's	
1968: General Foods buys Burger Chef. Frank Thomas remains—as a consultant			Burger Chef	Burger King		McDonald's	
1969–1974: Fred Turner, now McDonald's CEO, expands at a pace neither Burger King nor Burger Chef can match		Burger Chef		Burger King			McDonald's
1982	Burger Chef Dies		Burger King Survives				McDonald's Thrives

Underlying the entrepreneurial model is the essential relation of *partnership*, not dictation. This becomes clear when we look at—

How Ray Kroc Foreshadowed John Mackey's Stakeholder Concept

Twenty-six years before John Mackey founded Whole Foods, Ray Kroc created a system that bears a stunning resemblance to Mackey's stakeholder approach.

As we have noted, underlying Mackey's concept is the focus on relationships, the essential nature of those relationships being partnership.

Corporate management also relies on relationships, but their nature is top-down and functional, not a meeting of equals.

Mackey's approach grew from a consciously held philosophy. Kroc's evolved fortuitously, from Kroc's personality combined with the pressure of circumstances, focused primarily on just three of Mackey's stakeholders: management employees, franchisees, and suppliers.

Management employees: As we've already noted, Kroc gave management employees extreme leeway. People such as Harry Sonneborn, June Martino, and Fred Turner had enormous discretion to follow their own initiatives, becoming, in effect, entrepreneurs in their own right.

Franchisees: To Kroc, all McDonald's franchisees were his business *partners.* As independent businessmen, that's how they *should* be treated. But most franchisors, including Burger King and Burger Chef, viewed them also as *customers,* supplying equipment and ingredients and often requiring franchisees to buy exclusively from them.

Kroc totally rejected that model. He saw "a basic conflict in trying to treat a man as a partner on the one hand while selling him something at a profit on the other."[24]

When a supplier told Kroc he wanted to express his appreciation for his McDonald's business with a gift of some kind, Kroc said clearly, "I want nothing from you but a good product. Don't wine me, don't dine me, don't buy me any Christmas presents. If there are any cost breaks, pass them on to the operators of McDonald's stores."[25]

The result: the primary goals and interests of both McDonald's, the franchisor, and all McDonald's franchisees were aligned. For both parties, profits came from the same source: sales to customers.

While franchisees' operational requirements were rigid, marketing and promotion were left to the initiative of the individual franchisees, who also experimented with new products—often over the objections of McDonald's HQ.

Product innovation: For example, what eventually became the chainwide Filet-O-Fish was developed by Lou Groen, who had one store located in a primarily Catholic area of Cincinnati.

On meatless Fridays, his regular customers went to the nearby Big Boy, which offered a fish sandwich. His Friday sales dropped to around $100, down from $400 to $500 on the other six days of the week.

Groen lobbied McDonald's management for permission to introduce a fish sandwich—and met with intransigent resistance.

But Groen was persistent. He presented his case in detail to McDonald's managers, with numbers showing that without a fish product on Fridays, he probably faced bankruptcy. Part of his presentation were samples of the halibut sandwich he proposed to offer—which, more than anything else, changed management's antifish bias.

He tested the product—with stunning results. His Friday sales immediately leaped from $100 to $500, and though the fish product was only sold on Fridays, his sales for the rest of the week also went up. Two years later, his gross had risen 30 percent. "Fish," Groen later said, "was the only thing that saved me from going broke."[26]

Today the Filet-O-Fish is a McDonald's staple. The first of many products, including the Big Mac, the apple pie, the McCafé, and the entire breakfast menu, which were developed by franchisees and subsequently rolled out systemwide.

Kroc also came up with new product ideas, such as the Hulaburger (pineapple slices and cheese on a bun), a chicken potpie, and a dessert named the Triple Ripple—all of which bombed. Indeed, during Kroc's reign, only three major products, the Quarter Pounder and Chicken McNuggets—both inspired by Fred Turner—and the extra large order of french fries originated in the McDonald's HQ. The rest came from experimentation by franchisees.

Marketing and promotion: In the early days at McDonald's, all marketing had to be local. Even if Kroc had had the money, which he didn't, nationwide or even citywide advertising was impractical when hundreds of miles could separate one McDonald's store from the next.

So initially, each franchisee was responsible for its own promotion. When one franchisee developed a successful promotional concept, it was made freely available to other franchisees, who could adopt it or not, as they chose.

Eventually, when McDonald's outlets had grown to a sufficient number in a particular location, franchisees could pool their marketing resources to advertise on radio or TV. Franchisee associations in cities such as Washington, DC, Los Angeles, and New York sprang up and hired top-level advertising agencies, becoming primary sources of McDonald's advertising campaigns.

Eventually, this ad hoc arrangement was formalized into a national "parliament," dominated by franchisees' representatives. It became a forum where all issues could be raised. Though its recommendations were only advisory, management ignored its wishes at its own peril.

Suppliers: A similar partnership arrangement evolved with McDonald's suppliers.

In its early days, McDonald's was simply too small to be of any interest to major food manufacturers such as Del Monte and Consolidated Foods, whose major focus was consumer goods, not wholesale. Small firms were eager to accept McDonald's orders, and as McDonald's grew, so did they. Companies you've never heard of such as L. D. Schreiber, a Wisconsin cheese maker that won most of the McDonald's business when its previous main supplier, Kraft, refused to offer a tastier cheddar; East Balt and West Baking (muffins); and Keystone Foods (hamburgers) became multimillion-dollar operations, often with McDonald's as their only customer.

The arrangement was and remains today a handshake deal rather than a contractual one. The suppliers are selected by McDonald's HQ, but their customers are the franchisees.

Many of the innovations in McDonald's system have come from the suppliers, often on their own initiative.

For example, the success of Lou Groen's fish sandwich spurred McDonald's to roll it out nationwide. This required a product that could be delivered cut, battered, and frozen, ready to drop into the McDonald's automated production line.

Although Groen's sandwich saved his restaurant, his production method left *everything* to be desired. The preparation of the fish began on Thursday mornings and usually extended until 3:00 a.m. Friday.

McDonald's approached several suppliers, but only one responded: Bud Sweeney of Gorton Corporation. For the next twelve months, Sweeney became an unofficial—and unpaid—consultant to McDonald's, spending most of his time testing different fish sandwiches behind the McDonald's counters. Time his superiors thought would be much better spent on servicing accounts that actually produced revenue.

But after a year of testing and discarding dozens of concepts, Sweeney finally came up with a sandwich that met all of McDonald's requirements; by 1989, Gorton supplied 80 percent of McDonald's annual fish business.

Solving the Potato Problem

In the 1960s, McDonald's purchased potatoes for its french fries from 175 different local suppliers, and quality could vary widely from one delivery to the next. What's more, potatoes have a short shelf life, and the Idaho russet, which made the best fries, was out of season three months of the year.

Jack Simplot, whose Simplot Company was a major potato grower, proposed solving these two problems by offering frozen, ready-to-cook french fries of a consistent quality, which would also make the Idaho russet available twelve months of the year.

To many, if not most, customers, McDonald's fries were its best product. The resistance to any changes that might upset that applecart was enormous. Sonneborn turned Simplot down.

Simplot was advised to approach Kroc, who had, some years earlier, set up a lab near his Santa Barbara ranch to research the possibility of frozen fries. The research project was headed by Benjamin Strong, who had come up with an experimental process that overcame the many problems involved in freezing potatoes.

On a handshake, Simplot agreed to invest $3.5 million to build a production line based on Strong's process. But there were no guarantees of success—there's a big difference between producing small quantities of frozen fries in lab conditions and mass-producing them in the quantities McDonald's would require. Indeed, the risk was such that another potato supplier approached by Strong had turned McDonald's down.

But Simplot persevered, succeeded—and was rewarded with 50 percent of McDonald's business.

By 1972, Simplot had four production lines in operation, was the largest processor of potatoes in the country, and had become a multimillionaire.

As with Whole Foods, a major part of the success of McDonald's is the consequence of this partnership arrangement.

John Mackey took the partnership model further than Kroc, including *all* employees in his stakeholder concept, and adding customers, investors, governments, neighbors, and the community at large—including the environment.

Nevertheless, the result in both cases is similar: innovative entrepreneurial management extending deeply into both companies rather than being restricted to the top level.

And a loyalty between partners that is rarely seen in the corporate world. Just as most of the suppliers who stood by John Mackey during Austin's 1981 flood are still Whole Foods suppliers today, so Kroc's early suppliers still sell to McDonald's—in some cases, *only* to McDonald's.

Kroc, like Mackey, considered loyalty a prime virtue—and made it a two-way street.

McDonald's: Who's in Charge?

Ray Kroc's McDonald's evolved into an alliance of independent business owners where it was senseless to ask the question "Who's in charge?"

Kroc's legacy was a company that was not a pyramid with the CEO on top and janitors at the bottom. Rather, it was a federation of entrepreneurs regulated by checks and balances between the different partners that harnessed the energy and creativity of tens of thousands of innovative people.

Decisions made at the top had to be approved by the other partners to be effectively implemented, while innovations from the bottom could percolate through the system based purely on whether they *worked*.

So What's Gone Wrong at McDonald's?

Over the two years leading up to June 2015, McDonald's sales around the world fell dramatically:

McDonald's Comparable Sales and Customer Increases (Decreases), Year on Year				
	2014		2013	
	Sales	Customers	Sales	Customers
US	2.1%	4.1%	0.2%	1.6%
Europe	0.6%	2.2%	0.0%	1.5%
Asia Pacific, Middle East, & Africa	3.3%	4.7%	1.9%	3.8%
Other countries & corporate	6.6%	1.5%	7.0%	7.7%
Total	0.6%	0.6%	0.6%	1.9%
Source: McDonald's 2014 Annual Report				

The fall in same store sales, number of customers, gross revenues, net margins, and profits continued in the first quarter of 2015, the "highlight" being a ¥14.6 billion (US$121 million) loss in Japan, which experienced a stunning 34.4 percent drop in sales from a year earlier.[27]

Customers clearly *ain't* "loving it": a 2014 *Consumer Reports*[28] survey gives McDonald's burgers the *lowest* rating of any from the twenty-one leading American burger chains.

Nor are franchisees. In an April 2015 survey from Janney Capital Markets, McDonald's franchisees rated the chain's six-month outlook for its domestic business more negatively than at any other time in Janney's eleven-year survey history and also reported an extremely strained relationship with corporate; that metric also hit new lows.

"McDonald's system is broken," one wrote. "They talk menu reduction to help our people, simplify our menu for customers—but add products to help sales and it does not work. We will continue to fall and fail."[29]

We can pinpoint the core of McDonald's problem by comparing McDonald's today with McDonald's when Ray Kroc was in the saddle. McDonald's was then a federation of entrepreneurs—top management (Kroc, Sonneborn, and Turner, among others) and thousands of independent businessmen: franchisees and suppliers.

Today, entrepreneurs are missing from the top management level. Replaced, as the quote above implies, by corporate management with its tendency to dictate rather than consult.

This is a common corporate trajectory. The saying "from poverty to poverty in three generations" can be rephrased, for companies, as "from growth to stagnation in three generations."

Three to four generations of *management*.

The underlying cause: the founder's entrepreneurial *culture* has not been firmly entrenched throughout the company, is practiced by the second generation of management who learned it directly from the founder—and forgotten or never learned by subsequent managers who reached the top by climbing up a corporate ladder (for more detail, fast-forward to Appendix I: "From Poverty to Poverty in Three Generations"—What to Do When the Founder Departs the Scene, page 265).

Comparing Ray Kroc and John Mackey makes the source of this difference clear.

Why John Mackey's Legacy Is More Likely to Endure

We all have a philosophy of life. For most of us, that philosophy is held subconsciously; only a few of us examine our philosophy of life at the conscious level—and iron out the inevitable contradictions that arise when beliefs are inherited or absorbed from parents, teachers, and other significant people in our lives.*

Similarly, the four entrepreneurial founders we're examining here all had a firmly held *business* philosophy. Of the four, John Mackey stands out as the prime example of an entrepreneur making his business philosophy *fully conscious*.

Ray Kroc stood toward the other end of the spectrum, operating primarily from gut feel. If you read his *Grinding It Out* side by side with John Mackey's *Conscious Capitalism,* you'll immediately appreciate this clear difference in their personalities.

While it's clear from the stunning success of McDonald's under his reign that Kroc *had* a firmly held business philosophy, it was never made consciously explicit. His QSCV mantra was an *operational methodology,* not the underpinning of a business philosophy.

Indeed, when he visited a McDonald's store, he would often clean up the parking lot (what other CEO of a Fortune 500 corporation would do that!?), an indication that the C (cleanliness) part of his mantra hadn't fully sunk in.

McDonald's "federation of entrepreneurs" was the fruit of Ray Kroc's genius. Unfortunately, the fast-food pioneer appears to be losing steam today, in part because that operational methodology grew incredibly fast, and its underlying essentials, the *why* of its success, were never made explicit.

The How *and* the Why

By making his business philosophy fully conscious, John Mackey has ensured that that philosophy runs all the way through Whole Foods, from top to bottom.

At both Whole Foods and McDonald's, everyone understands the how of the system.

But at Whole Foods they understand the why as well. Indeed, personnel are selected, in part, because they share Whole Foods' underlying belief system.

The Whole Foods model entrenches the essential, underlying requirement for

---

*For an example, see my post "Warren Buffett's 'Split Personality': How His Business and Political Philosophies Just Don't Get Along with Each Other." marktier.com/split

an entrepreneurial company—the *practice* of partnership and the accompanying devolution of decision making and innovation—to an extent that few other companies do.

The result is that people promoted to new positions within the company are already steeped in the Whole Foods philosophy. So when, as will inevitably happen, the founders depart from the scene through either retirement or death, their successors, who have been implementing their legacy all along, will continue to do so. And be more likely to pass it on to *their* succeeding management generations than is typically the case.

2010: Entrepreneurial Management Returns to Burger King—the Brazilian Way

In October 2010 3G Management, a company owned by three Brazilians, Jorge Lemann, Carlos Sicupira, and Marcel Telles, bought control of Burger King for $4 billion and reinstituted entrepreneurial management after a hiatus of forty-three years.

The change in Burger King's fortunes was dramatic—and immediate.

The menu was simplified and sales and same store sales soared. By 2013, 1,493 new outlets had been added—bringing the total to 13,667. Costs were slashed as the corporate head count dropped from 38,884 to 2,425, primarily (but not solely) as all but 52 of the company-owned restaurants were sold to franchisees.

Burger King's profits and value followed suit. Relisted on Wall Street on 18 June 2012, the stock opened at $14.50 and closed 9.3 percent higher on the day at $15.85. Its market cap was $600 million more than the 2010 $4 billion purchase price. By July 2014 its value had doubled to $9 billion.

Following the 2014 purchase of Tim Hortons, Burger King—renamed Restaurant Brands International Inc.—reached a market valuation of $20 billion in 2015.

This was far from the first time that Lemann, Sicupira, and Telles had transformed a business so dramatically.

The Brazilian Model

There are many different styles of entrepreneurial management, and "the Brazilian model" is one of the more fascinating ones.

In 1971, Jorge Lemann (today, Brazil's richest man and number twenty-six on the Forbes 500 list of billionaires for 2015) founded Garantia, a brokerage company that grew into an investment bank, and instituted the model that led to one of the most intriguing rags-to-riches stories ever told.

The key to his approach was to hire PSDs: people who are Poor, Smart, and with a Deep Desire to Get Rich. People who were hungry to succeed, spurning the "rich kids" model of his competitors.

The firm was a meritocracy: promotions, and pay, were all tied to performance. Salaries were low, but bonuses were usually double the salary and could amount to ten times as much. Nepotism was banned, as were romances within the company. (They happened anyway, and if they ended up at the altar, one of the pair had to quit.)

This regime applied to everyone, from the mail-room clerks to the managing partners.

Employment was a ladder of three levels:

1. *Salaried employees:* including mail-room clerks, who could graduate to the next level of—

2. *Associates:* who worked in the trading room for a commission (plus bonuses); and,

3. *Partners:* when an associate was invited to become a partner, he had to *buy* his shares, though the purchase was financed from his future profits and dividends.

This requirement kept the new partner relatively poor, as most of his rewards had to go back to the company to pay for his partnership interest.

If a new partner's prime motivation was the money, he could only begin to enjoy his wealth when he had paid for his share in full. Until then, he was "roped in" to Lemann's future-oriented aim of building the business.

The Brazilian Model's Downside

An underlying problem with Lemann's model is the pure money motivation.

How much money is "enough"—$1 million? $10 million? $100 million?

When your primary motivation is the money, it comes with a use-by date. When you have enough, whatever that means to you, your motivation turns from making it into spending it. Which is what eventually happened to the majority of Garantia's new partners: Ferraris, luxury apartments, beach homes, even, in some cases, helicopters and private planes became more important than showing up for work.

This problem is best illustrated by one of Lemann's original partners: Luiz Cezar Fernandes.

Fernandes was one of the dozens of people Lemann's model turned into multimillionaires.

He left Garantia in 1982. The following year, with two partners, he set up a securities distributor called Pactual. From top to bottom, it was a clone of Garantia. And like Garantia, it was successful. Pactual grew at an average of 33 percent per year to 1992, and Fernandes's personal wealth soared to some US$600 million.

But in 1998 Fernandes lost control of Pactual and was forced out in 1999.

Fernandes did superbly when he stuck to the original Garantia model. But he wanted to follow in Lemann's "build-a-business" footsteps, an aim that led to his undoing.

In 1993, he bought Benetton's Brazilian operations for $1.5 million—and sold it back to the Italians two years later at a loss. Another money-losing investment was Teba, a textile company, which accumulated 43 million real (about $39 million) in losses in 1996 and 1997.[30]

And he loved to party—in a big way. In 1993, for example, to celebrate Pactual's tenth year of operations, he threw a party for five thousand guests. Including—*especially* including—Jorge Lemann.[31]

The combination of excess spending and failed investments weakened both his finances and his relationships with Pactual's other partners. So much so that when Fernandes tried to persuade his partners to turn Pactual from an investment bank into a retail one, they resisted—and within a year bought him out of the partnership.

The major difference between Lemann and Fernandes was that Lemann's primary motivation was (and still is) *not* the money, but building a great business. While Fernandes, seduced by the money, was torn between enjoying his wealth and attempting to follow in Lemann's footsteps.

Without Lemann's single-minded focus, Fernandes could not replicate Garantia's stunning success.

When Fernandes left Garantia, two other partners, Carlos Sicupira and Marcel Telles, formed a triumvirate with Lemann. The three of them controlled the company and were all on the same wavelength, motivated by the business, not the money.

Under their direction, motivation by money became a powerful management tool. *The* management tool that enabled them to reach *their* aim: building a great business. One indication of that motivation: long *after* Lemann had become one of Brazil's richest men, he made an annual "pilgrimage" to Boulder, Colorado, to attend a seminar led by Jim Collins, author of *Good to Great* and *Built to Last*.

Collins and Lemann first met when Lemann attended a seminar at Stanford in 1990. Afterward (as Collins wrote in his introduction to Cristiane Correa's *Dream Big*), Lemann "asked me if I would be interested in coming down to Brazil to share my ideas with his two partners and his company. I did not know at that time that this fortuitous moment would turn into one of the most stimulating business friendships of my life."[32]

From Garantia to 3G

In 1981, Garantia began buying shares in Lojas Americanas, a failing retailer.

Its market value was around $30 million, a fraction of the $100 million value of its real estate assets. It looked like a no-risk deal.

The following year, Garantia took control. Carlos Sicupira left Garantia to become CEO of Lojas Americanas—and began to implement the management model the partners later applied to dozens of other businesses.

Like just about everything else at Garantia, sending Sicupira to run a retailer was totally unconventional.

Sicupira's business experience was confined to the finance industry. He knew nothing about retailing. Had he applied in the normal way for such a CEO position, he would have been laughed at by "experienced" executives.

Who would also have been horrified by the new CEO's turning up in jeans with a backpack rather than a briefcase.

> [Sicupira's] first intention was to get to know the people there firsthand, select those who had talent and get rid of the others. This was a strategy that was repeated in almost all the acquisitions made by the three partners.[33]

Within months, around 40 percent of the workforce had been fired; grandiose projects such as a new executive office with a tennis court in the back were canceled; and the Garantia model of employment—low salaries with profit-related bonuses—was installed companywide.

The turnaround was rapid. Garantia had paid $24 million for 70 percent of Lojas Americanas; six months after Sicupira occupied the driver's seat, the company attracted investors interested in paying $20 million for a 20 percent share.

In just six months, Garantia's $24 million investment had turned into $70 million.

"Throw Them off the Deep End"

Time and time again, the triumvirate put similarly untrained youngsters in charge of their new acquisitions. The management equivalent of teaching your kids to swim by throwing them in the pool and seeing whether they float.

But while few of the youngsters had management experience of any kind outside the financial industry, they had all imbibed "the Brazilian entrepreneurial model."

It wasn't quite that simple.

The Garantia model was a Darwinian revolving door. Those PSDs motivated purely by money exited when they had made "enough." Those who remained were on the triumvirate's wavelength.

All competing for the next opportunity to be "tossed into the deep end."

After Lojas Americanas, the triumvirate (having sold Garantia and reconstituted their partnership as 3G) took over a series of companies, each bigger than the last, including Brazil's biggest brewer, Brahma (1989: $60 million), and Antarctica, Brazil's number two brewer (1999: $1 billion), forming AmBev, which was immediately the world's number five brewer; Interbrew of Belgium (2004, in a "reverse takeover": Interbrew bought AmBev, forming InBev; Lemann, Sicupira, and Telles increased their shareholding in InBev to a controlling stake); then InBev buys Anheuser-Busch (2008: $52 billion), creating AB InBev; Burger King (2010: $4 billion); Heinz (2013: $23 billion); and in 2014 Burger King buys the Canadian chain Tim Hortons ($11.4 billion).

"Burger King Is Run by Children"

Businessweek summed up Lemann's model with a story titled "Burger King Is Run by Children."[34]

In June 2013, a 3G "veteran," Daniel Schwartz, aged thirty-two, became CEO, while the chief financial officer, Josh Kobza, was a mere twenty-eight, and the head of investor relations was just twenty-nine.

No one raises an eyebrow when "children" such as Mark Zuckerberg, Bill Gates, or Sergey Brin and Larry Page join the *Forbes* billionaire list.

Yet they, like Daniel Schwartz, "merely" demonstrate the power of the entrepreneurial model.

The primary difference between Burger King today and the Facebook, Microsoft, and Google of yesteryear is that entrepreneurship was reintroduced to an established business.

6 Finding the Next Starbucks "by Walking Around"

How can we, with no insider information of any kind, and no access to top management (other than by turning up at a shareholders' meeting), hope to determine whether a company qualifies as a candidate for the "next Starbucks"?

It's not simple. But it's doable, and easier than you might think.

Let's reframe our five clues into an "*outsider's* guide" to finding the next Starbucks—by walking around!

Let's begin with a brief summary of what we're looking for:

- *The operational methodology* is the set of procedures—the essential links—that translate a vision into a consistent, companywide customer experience.

   Our aim is to evaluate the quality of this operational methodology. As outsiders—as you'll see—we can determine or infer much by a combination of walking around with our eyes open, talking to people—and trawling the Internet.

- *The company's vision and the customer experience.* With the company's statement of its mission and vision in hand, this is a metric that's readily available to all of us.

   The customer experience.

   Is the customer experience one you—and other customers—want to repeat? Is that customer experience consistent across different outlets of the same firm—and, more crucially, across different countries and cultures? And is the company's stated vision apparent at the customer interface?

   If the answers to questions like these are all good, you could be looking at a candidate for the next Starbucks. If not, you can quickly cross a potential turkey off your list.

- *System:* The ideal company gives excellent service—and is run by nineteen-year-olds. That is, people of any age with little or no previous work experience. This is achieved through what's called a system.

A business system consists of breaking procedures down into small, easily mastered tasks, combined with institutionalized training methods. This makes it relatively simple to replicate the business's "nuts and bolts" across multiple locations.

Such a system can be difficult to devise and apply. But it's surprisingly easy to tell, from the outside, the quality of a company's system.

● *Management's honesty, integrity, and ability:* When we're making a long-term investment, we're giving our money to people we don't know. So we must make sure they're honest, especially about their mistakes. After all, we're after the next Starbucks, not the next Enron!

1. Operational Methodology

The successful translation of a vision into a consistent, companywide experience requires an *operational methodology.* That is: a series of practices, rules, and/or routines that turn that vision into action. Otherwise, a vision is little better than a dream.

This *system* is the essential connection that translates a company's vision into a seamless customer experience. It's the behind-the-scenes nuts and bolts; while we can't see it from the outside, we can experience the effects (or lack of them), learn some of the details with a little detective work, and infer the rest.

For example, Howard Schultz's vision of replicating the Italian café experience is of no help to the newly hired barista, except, perhaps, in a motivational sense. But that barista learns how to make espressos, cappuccinos, and so forth the same way they're made in every other Starbucks store from a *manual*—an essential part of an overall business *system* that ensures consistency across locations.

A few more examples:

Southwest Airlines prefers to hire people with a sense of humor, especially for the cabin crew. Laughing customers are happy customers.

Whole Foods applies *decentralization* to achieve its mission of caring for and empowering its partners: team members within a store are responsible to their teams, and teams can make decisions within circumscribed boundaries without referring them up the management hierarchy for approval. Store and regional managers can act independently in the same way.

To ensure the consistency of the customer experience, Whole Foods hires people who already agree with its values. It's much more efficient than trying to fit square pegs into round holes and attempting to change their beliefs.

Walmart's culture of "low everyday prices" is achieved by cutting costs. So its aim is to inspire everyone in the company to look for ways to save money that can be passed on to customers as even *lower* prices.

In each case, the vision is achieved by focusing staff members' attention on specific *actions,* their sum communicating that vision to customers through the customer experience.

But if this operational methodology is "hidden behind the scenes," how can we, as outsiders, judge whether a company has one that works?

By judging what information *is* readily available, especially—

2. The Company's Vision and the Customer Experience

Why do you frequent one business in preference to another?

You'll have different answers for different businesses. Lower prices for one, better selection/higher quality for another, friendly and/or fast service for a third, convenience for a fourth, and so on.

All these reasons can be summed up in one term: *the customer experience.*

And Then There's Inertia . . .

When a company achieves a consistent customer experience, it enlists the aid of one of our most powerful drives: inertia.

We're adventurous people—but we're also creatures of habit. The problem with being adventurous is that we can be disappointed. So when we're satisfied with our experience at a particular business, when we know what we're going to get, why take the risk of being dissatisfied by trying somewhere new?

At the opposite end of the spectrum from inertia is customer loyalty. If inertia can be defined as avoiding disappointment by choosing what you know you're going to get, then loyalty is looking forward to repeating an experience without even considering other options.

Inertia is good . . . until something better comes along. And in a competitive market, someone is always trying to create a better customer experience.

When you can identify a company whose customers are so loyal they never or rarely consider alternatives, you know you've found a winner.

For example, when Howard Schultz returned as Starbucks' CEO, I was skeptical of his plans. At the time I wasn't following Starbucks, the company. But I started thinking about *why* I went into one coffee shop in preference to another. As I examined my own behavior, I realized it exhibited everything that Schultz was talking about:

- *Friendly staff* is a prime factor. Their greeting you when you walk into the store and smiling when they see you *does* make a difference, even though you know they're saying "Hi" because it's in their rulebook. But, boy, it works!

- *Smell the coffee.* Walk past a bakery, sniff the aroma of freshly baked bread wafting from the store, and your juices automatically start flow-

As "cappuccino man," when I'm traveling I'll often head to McDonald's for a coffee, especially at odd times of the day when not much else is open.

My experience is a complete lack of consistency across different countries:

Australia: better than Starbucks.

The Philippines: as good as Starbucks.

Hong Kong: drinkable.

New York: only if you're truly desperate.

Part of the difference: McCafés come in several different "flavors"—from freestanding McCafés to push-button machines behind the counter. But in some countries, Australia being a prime example, the machine-made cappuccinos can be virtually as good as the handmade ones.

ing. It's the same with coffee: there's nothing quite like the smell of freshly ground coffee.

● *Appeals to* all *the senses.* Aside from the *smell* of coffee (olfactory), does the store *look* clean and inviting (visual), are you made to *feel* welcome and do the staff *talk* to you in a friendly way (kinesthetic and auditory), and does what you buy taste good (gustatory)?

● *Efficient service.* Everything, from taking your order to delivering it, runs smoothly and quickly. Even when there's a line (unless it's *really* long), you're happy to wait as you know it will move fast.

None of this is rocket science. Individually, each one of those items I've listed is minor, almost irrelevant. But when they're put together, the sum total is an experience you're happy (if not eager) to repeat.

And finally:

● *Consistency of experience.* As a customer, do you have the same kind of experience at different stores of the same chain, especially in different countries? If not, then the company's management has failed to instill its practices across the board.

These are also some of the indicators that tell you whether the founders' *vision* for the company is communicated to *you,* via the customer experience.

When you're evaluating by walking around, keep the company's expressed vision in mind: whether you're receiving the message tells you a lot about the management's capabilities.

The Importance of Consistency

For an investor, the *consistency of customer experience* across its stores is a crucial metric. One you can easily test by simply visiting different stores in the same chain.

When achieved, it's a signal that the company's management has *successfully* installed its operating model throughout its entire business.

But when the customer experience at different outlets of the same chain is *variable*—or, even worse, is variable at the same store on repeat visits—you know you can cross this company off your list of potential investment candidates.

As you become more aware of the facets that, combined, make for a standout retail experience, you'll become highly sensitized to their lack. A few signs that will help you *remove* a candidate from your list of possible investments:

● Some staff members behind the counter are checking their cell phones, reading the paper, or doing paperwork. *All* of them obviously ignoring *you,* even when you're the only customer in line.

● Poor organization. One example: staff are lining up *behind* the counter to access the pastries, the refrigerator, or something else. Or you ordered four items but only three show up.

● Indifferent staff, who clearly couldn't care less about your presence— even, sometimes, being annoyed that you're interrupting their siesta!

● Not listening to customers, Microsoft's Windows 8—*and* 10—being prime examples: focus groups all but unanimously hated the Windows 8 interface and wanted the option to choose the familiar Windows 7 look. Customer feedback that was simply ignored.

● Disco music. Fine if you're in a disco, but a real pain when you're in a restaurant trying to have a conversation with your companions.

● And my favorite beef: waiters who've obviously attended that secret waiter school where they learn how to walk through a restaurant teeming with demanding customers—and not notice a single one of them!

> ### The Power of Music
>
> Friday and Saturday nights often got rowdy at a hot dog stand across the street from the University of California, Berkeley, campus.
>
> How to drive the inebriated students away without making them angry?
>
> The owner advised a simple strategy: "Switch the radio to the classical-music station."
>
> It worked every time: within a few minutes the rowdy students decided to create mayhem somewhere else—and left peacefully.

The Problem with Perfection

However, the closer to perfection on these metrics a business achieves, the more glaring are the exceptions.

Consider your reaction to seeing a pimply-faced teenager with an ugly mole on his or her nose. You hardly notice it.

But see that same mole on the nose of a beautiful woman with otherwise flawless skin and it turns into an eyesore.

Similarly, you walk into a store where the staff is friendly but lackadaisical, where the service is so-so and half the time you can't get anyone's attention—then you hardly notice that some of the tables haven't been cleared.

But in another store where everything is excellent, a flaw such as a single unbused table really stands out. When that table (or other imperfection) is cleared within a few minutes in *every* location, you know you've found a standout candidate for your portfolio.

Cultural Differences: The Ultimate Test

People are the same the world over—they like to be liked, treated honorably and with respect, and cared for, and they have the same basic emotional desires.

But people of different cultures can treat each other, and thus customers, in a variety of different ways.

> ### Culture Shock
>
> During the war in Vietnam, American soldiers could take a five-day R&R break halfway through their one-year term.
>
> Some soldiers' vacations were interrupted when they fell afoul of local laws.
>
> In which of these cities—Bangkok, Hong Kong, Sydney, or Manila—do you think Americans got into the most trouble?
>
> Sydney. With its culture so similar to that of the United States, Americans were simply not aware of the differences . . . until it was too late.

Airlines are a good example, especially when you, the traveler, have a problem. Some personal experiences:

Japan Airlines: Something was wrong with my coffee. When I pointed out the problem to a passing stewardess, *she was ashamed and embarrassed.*

I was flabbergasted: *she* had had nothing to do with serving the coffee, but she reacted as if she had personally insulted me.

Needless to say, the coffee was quickly and efficiently replaced—with more fulsome apologies.

Swissair: Same problem, totally different reaction. An unsmiling stewardess appeared almost immediately and with great efficiency replaced the coffee in no time at all.

Qantas: I explained the problem (related to my then one-year-old daughter) to a Qantas steward at great length. He listened attentively, indeed compassionately. There was no question that he understood everything. And then—

Nothing happened!

American Airlines: I was sitting next to a Chinese lady who was ignoring her supposedly black tea, which looked milky. I suggested she have it replaced. Shrugging, she said, "Never mind."

So I flagged a passing stewardess, whose immediate response was
"There's nothing wrong with it." A
childish "There is!" / "There isn't!" exchange ended with a grouchy stewardess taking the tea away and returning
some five minutes later with another
cup *that looked exactly the same.*

> ### How Starbucks Overcame the "Culture Gap"
>
> We chose [our] international partners very carefully, selecting only organiza-
> tions whose leaders shared our values.
> —Howard Schultz

She explained at great length that the problem lay with the machine, which,
apparently, put air bubbles into the hot water. In other words: "It's not *my* fault!"

Each of these examples is an expression of four different cultures.*

While a company operates solely within one culture—say, Starbucks within
the United States—it's relatively easy to roll out its operating model culture-wide.

The challenge for such a company is crossing cultural boundaries, and over-
coming these cultural differences to provide a multicultural consistency of customer experience.

If you've ever visited the Philippines, you know you'll always be addressed as
"sir" or "madam." In most other countries I'll be "Mr. Tier," but in the Philippines
I'm "Sir Mark"—a deference I, as an Australian, find annoying and demeaning.

Into this culture arrives Starbucks, with its policy of asking for your first name.
Being called "Mark" instead of "Sir Mark" certainly induces a greater sense of equality and friendliness. Which can be a problem for anyone raised to be deferential.

This cultural difference is not unique to the Philippines: in most countries,
you will be "Mr.," "Miss," or "Mrs." Even in the United States you'll often be
addressed as "sir" or "madam."

Australia is the opposite. At the end of a phone booking with an Australian airline,
the operator asked, "And is there anything else I can help you with today, Mark?"

An Australian friend of mine had to teach his staff to address customers as
"sir" and "madam"!

A negative example illustrates how a company's customer experience can come
afoul of cultural differences.

Many years ago, Hong Kong entrepreneur Jimmy Chan started a clothing-store
chain he named Giordano. More inspired by McDonald's than anything Italian,
the chain was a roaring success in Hong Kong.

A major reason: when you walked into the store, you were greeted by the staff
who then left you alone, but were always ready to help if asked.

This was a revolutionary achievement. Back then, Hong Kong shop assistants
made New Yorkers seem like paragons of friendliness and etiquette. You could walk
into a camera store with thousands of dollars in your pocket—and be totally ignored.

Wow! I thought. If Jimmy Chan can change Hong Kong people's habits, Giordano could be a great stock to buy. The key test: Would it travel?

---

*The American Airlines incident is an example of the effect of unions on a *company* culture at that time (in the
1980s), not the American culture as a whole. A similar example: when management and unions at United Airlines
were at loggerheads, many cabin staff wore badges saying I JUST WORK HERE.

I visited franchised Giordano stores in Malaysia and the Philippines, both countries where people are naturally friendly. In each store, the staff ignored me. So I didn't buy the stock—which turned out to be the right decision at that time.

But when you come across a company that produces a consistent customer experience *despite* such cultural differences, you know you're looking at a probable winner.

3. System, or: Can the Business Be Run by Nineteen-Year-Olds?

Walk into pretty much any franchised business and most of the people behind the counter will be nineteen-year-olds. A shorthand way of saying that they have no specific qualifications for the job other than the willingness to work.

Sometimes you'll have to revise this question. I once asked the general manager of a company if his business could be run by nineteen-year-olds. "Definitely not," he replied, and listed a series of qualifications required for every new hire.

I quickly revised the question to "Can your business be run by twenty-two-year-olds with a college degree in X?"

"No question about it," he replied.

How can you take an average person off the street and, within a few days, have him or her serving customers like a veteran?

The answer is *system*.

Leon Richardson, founder of the Hong Kong–based Magna Industrial, once explained to me how a business system should work.

One of the six product lines his company sold was a range of specialized chemicals. His salesmen had to explain the benefits of these products to customers with PhDs in the sciences.

> ### System in a Nutshell
>
> As the manager of a hotel, how can you be sure that every room will be properly cleaned?
>
> Clearly, a specific set of tasks need to be completed. Rely on the cleaner's memory, and something is bound to be forgotten. Or, perhaps, simply ignored. (Who's going to check under the bed?)
>
> One hotel came up with a simple solution. A checklist. Every task was listed and had to be ticked off for every room. A random check each day made sure that every nook and cranny was always covered.
>
> And in case anyone looked, a sign under the bed said YES, WE CLEAN HERE TOO!

Leon had two options:

1. Hire PhDs—or, at least, science graduates—who would be able to talk intelligently about the products and interact with customers as an equal. Good salesmen are a minority. Good salesmen with PhDs of any kind are few and far between. And PhDs can be expensive to hire!

2. Find another way. Which is what Leon did. He told me he could take any reasonably intelligent person off the street and in twenty-four hours he or she would know *more* about his specialized chemical products than any PhD.

Leon pulled out a heavy ring binder, as thick as a large briefcase, opened it, and propped it up on his desk (prop included: the binders were custom-made).

"In here is the answer to every possible question anyone can ask about our chemical products," he said. "All the salesman has to do is open this binder at the right page—and the customer's question is completely satisfied. *Always.*

"Learning where to find the right page in seconds is what takes twenty-four hours."

All businesses have a set of routine procedures. *Are they written down?*

In the average one-man show, the answer is no. Every new employee learns catch-as-catch-can. And if the owner forgets to mention one or two important tasks, the business will suffer.

Starbucks barista training manuals: a major component of system.

When those routine procedures are organized into teaching tools—a combination of a "textbook" (i.e., the manual, and probably videos these days as well) and staff who have been trained to teach new hires—a new employee is performing like a veteran in next to no time at all.

Judging a System by Walking Around

You can judge a variety of important system-related and other metrics just by walking around. A few examples:

Relative sales. Comparative customer traffic gives you a good idea of which chain is the leader in its niche. If you regularly see empty tables in one while you can hardly find a seat in another, you don't need to read annual reports to figure out which is the sales leader.

Speed of service. Similarly, how quickly customers are served is an index of the efficiency of a company's system.

Table turnover. Related. The number of times per hour each seat changes hands. The world record possibly goes to a Hong Kong restaurant with two thousand seats that served an average of six thousand meals every weekday lunchtime.

This metric is partly related to the price of real estate. Encouraging customers to sit all morning nursing just one cup of coffee is fine in a low-rent area. Where rents are high, pure takeout is a better proposition. Witness the new no-seat stores Starbucks is opening in New York.

The value/quality proposition. Simply looking at price lists gives you a good indication of the company's target market (rich, middle-class, poor). Add in quality by sampling the menu to gain a finer judgment of the target market and various chains' relative competitiveness.

Other sources of walking-around information include:

Trawling the Internet . . .

A lot of information can be gained just by watching the news. Or, these days, trawling the Internet.

It's quite surprising what you can dig up in next to no time at all.

For example, when I was in New York in June 2014, I came across a coffee shop called Pie Face—an Australian chain invading New York, whose coffee was better than Starbucks'.

While enjoying their coffee, I went online to find out more about it. One of the first things I came across was a story that several of the Australian franchisees were unhappy and having disputes with the company.[1]

Right away, a red flag on what I thought might have been a potential investment candidate.

Sure enough, just months later the Australian franchise went into "voluntary administration" (an Australian form of Chapter 11 bankruptcy—emerging from that status in January 2015),[2] and seven of the eight Pie Face stores in New York[3] had been shuttered. In retrospect, hardly a surprise: one of the attractions of the American Pie Face store was the lack of lines and the many empty tables (no wonder they were having problems!). Something you'll rarely find in a Starbucks wherever you go.

Going to news sites is just one of many ways you can dig up relevant information on the Internet. Most companies have Facebook pages, often a different page for every country of operation, and sometimes even for single outlets. Read the customer comments. With the help of Google Translate, you're not restricted to your native language.

That's just the beginning of what you can find. (If you have trouble finding your way around the Internet, just ask any kid to help.)

Pie Face in New York: good pies, great coffee—at the last (now also closed) Pie Face outlet left in the city.

Talking to Frontline Staff . . .

If you're a people person and make friends easily, talking with people behind the counter is a magical way of learning more about the nuts and bolts of a business.

One example: when something isn't working and it takes weeks (or in one case, months) to fix, you can guess that the company is more focused on cutting costs than maintaining, let alone enhancing the quality of the customer experience. An impression confirmed when you overhear staff members bitching that these things used to be fixed in *days*, before the company switched to a cheaper supplier.

Sometimes staff will give away confidential information. A friend of mine in Australia learned the daily gross sales of several different outlets in a local chain this way!

What if you're not a people person? Do what I did: find someone who is and ask that person to help you out.

Competitors . . .

A company's management is highly unlikely to tell you anything negative about their own operations. But they'll happily tell you everything that's wrong with their competitors.

A Few Googling Hints

If you type *Pie Face* in the Google search bar, then go to "News," you may not find anything about the company on the first page of results.

As Pie Face is an Australian company, you'll get better results by going to Google's Australian site: www.google.com.au. Which you can easily find by searching for *Google Australia*. Then, by clicking on "Search tools," you can set the country to Australia. Then, all the news stories you'll see will be from Australian sites.

Google has country-specific sites for just about every country and territory in the world. Here's a list: https://en.wikipedia.org/wiki/List_of_Google_domains.

Say you were searching the Indian chain Café Coffee Day. If you don't see many news stories about the company on Google, go to Google's Indian site: www.google.co.in.

Similarly, for any other country where Google has a site.

Getting to a company's managers is easier than you think.

Go to an annual meeting and you'll have a chance to ask questions from the floor. You may even get to talk to the company CEO.

Unlikely, I grant you, but other managers from all different levels of the company will be more accessible.

At trade shows it's dead simple to strike up conversations with officers of companies you're interested in (or their competitors): they're all eager to sell something to you—and the other attendees.

Okay, they'll start with their sales pitch, but you can always steer the conversation to the topics you're interested in. At the numerous cocktail parties and other social events you'll find at most trade shows, you will have a far more relaxed atmosphere for your "interrogations."

Plus, thanks to the Internet, you can often listen in on a company's earnings call. That's when the company's management presents its financial results, usually quarterly, and is grilled by Wall Street analysts.

And Other Customers . . .

Finding out what other customers think about a company is a valuable source of informational "nuggets" to help build your evaluation of the customer experience.

What do other customers like or dislike about the company? Why are they visiting this store rather than a competitor's? And if they're regular customers, finding out how often they shop somewhere else will give you a rough index of customer loyalty.

Or Work There Yourself!

While it's not possible for everyone, other than sitting in on top-management discussions, what better way is there to get "inside" a company than as an employee?

Once you've identified a potential investment target, apply for a job. You'll then be *taught* the company's operational methodology from the inside. What's more, questions you may be reluctant to ask as a customer will now be answered in full.

In just a few weeks or less, while you probably won't have an inside track to top management, you'll be in an excellent position to judge the quality and *efficiency* of the link between the company's vision and the customer experience.

Even more important, you'll be able to identify any behind-the-counter flaws in the company's operational methodology that negatively impact the customer experience.

And if there are hardly any imperfections? Unless the particular location is the company's showcase, you're onto a winner.

"But . . . I Don't Travel Much"

If you're not much of a traveler, how can you research the customer experience in other places and—especially!—judge whether a company's culture is consistent across different countries?

Being a stay-at-home doesn't cut you off from this information.

The first place to visit is our old friend—

1. The Internet is filled with customer reviews of restaurants, hotels, coffee shops, and all manner of other businesses. Customers will comment—and complain—on Facebook, Yelp, and similar sites about the local operations of multinational companies. And if they're not in your native tongue, thanks to Google Translate other languages are no longer a barrier.

2. If you have friends who travel or live abroad, get their take on the company you're investigating. You can even give close friends or relatives an "assignment"—though don't phrase your request that way! Indeed, if you tell them why you're asking, they'll possibly become interested in doing the research for their own account.

3. And whenever you come across a frequent flier, find out what he or she thinks.

4. Judging Management's Honesty, Integrity, and Ability

Would you give half your money to your best friend to look after?

The answer, surely, is "It depends."

It depends on whether you trust him or her to keep your money safe.

One of your friends might be the greatest person in the world, but he always seems to run out of money a few days before payday. Chances are your money would receive the same treatment if he were looking after it.

When making an investment, especially one for the long term, you're effectively asking a group of people you don't know to take care of your money on your behalf.

So you should first judge the ability, honesty, and integrity of a company's management before investing a dime.

We want a management that tells it like it is. One that openly admits its mistakes, rather than fudging its previous projections when they turn out to be wrong.

Why?

As Warren Buffett puts it, "The CEO who lies to others in public will eventually start lying to himself in private."

With that kind of management running the show, you could easily end up with the next Enron instead of the next Starbucks.

How to tell the difference?

One place to start is with the company's annual reports. Download the last five years' worth and read the chairman's letters, starting with the oldest one.

What's the tone? Straightforward or full of hype?

Does he admit his mistakes or gloss over them?

One way to tell: if his sunny forecasts of five years ago didn't pan out, did he tell you why in a subsequent letter or just continue making more optimistic projections? The last thing you want is a CEO who always wears rose-colored glasses.

Warren Buffett sets the gold standard for chairmen's letters. Read a few of his missives to shareholders* to establish a benchmark. If Buffett gets 10 out of 10, what score would you give other chairmen's letters? Less than 7 is probably a fail.

Meet Your Managers in Person . . .

The best way to evaluate people's character is to meet them in person. One venue where you can "meet" a company's top management: the annual shareholders' meeting.

Attend, and you may get a chance to meet one or more of them. But more important—if you're a good judge of character—you'll come away with valuable insights into the personalities of the people running the company.

---

*http://www.berkshirehathaway.com/letters/letters.html.

What if you're a lousy judge of character? Bring along someone who has the talent you don't.

Or on YouTube

Today, thanks again to the Internet, an even easier way to "meet" your managers is by YouTube and similar Web sites.

Videos of a person's speeches and interviews can be far more intimate and revealing than a brief encounter you might have at an annual meeting or social event. With the added advantage that you can replay what you think might be a revealing moment.

If a CEO has authored a book, read it. Similarly, look for any articles he has written, and anything written about him and his management team.

Middle Management

Between the CEO and the staff at the customer interface are several layers of middle management—people who are rarely in the public eye but are essential to a company's smooth operation.

The bigger the company, the more layers.

When the CEO is the company's founder, and your experience as a customer accords with the CEO's stated vision and mission, you can reasonably conclude, but only as a working assumption, that the company's culture, from top to bottom, is pretty much a unity.

But it would be a mistake to give a company no longer run by its founder the benefit of the doubt.

Evaluating management is not easy. Even Warren Buffett, with five *decades* of mostly successful experience in judging managements, can make expensive mistakes.

In 1998, Berkshire Hathaway bought General Re, a major publically traded (not owner-operated) company and the fourth-largest reinsurer in the world, for $22 billion. Buffett was impressed by General Re's performance and, especially, its CEO, Ron Ferguson. As he told Berkshire shareholders in his 1998 letter:

> For many decades, General Re's name has stood for quality, integrity and professionalism in reinsurance—and under Ron Ferguson's leadership, this reputation has been burnished still more. Berkshire can add absolutely nothing to the skills of General Re's and [its subsidiary] Cologne Re's managers. On the contrary, there is a lot that they can teach us.[4]

In Buffett's previous owner-created and owner-operated acquisitions, the CEO's culture ran deep into the company. General Re was different. Ron Ferguson was chairman of a public company founded in 1846.

While Ferguson clearly met Buffett's standards, middle management was another story.

When I agreed in 1998 to merge Berkshire with Gen Re, I thought that company stuck to the three rules [of underwriting and pricing insurance policies] I've enumerated. I had studied the operation for decades and had observed underwriting discipline that was consistent and reserving that was conservative. At merger time, I detected no slippage in Gen Re's standards.

I was dead wrong. Gen Re's culture and practices had substantially changed *and unbeknownst to management—and to me*—the company was grossly mispricing its current business. [Emphasis added.][5]

"I was dead wrong." How often do you think you'll hear those words from the lips of a CEO (whether of a Fortune 500 company or a one-man band)?

Buffett's mistake illustrates the importance of judging those hard-to-detect middle-management layers. And at the same time, this is a perfect example of the kind of person we, as an investor in a company, want the CEO to be: someone who candidly admits his mistakes—and learns from them.

Guesstimating a Business's Inner Workings

Clearly, as outsiders, no matter how much we "walk around," some behind-the-scenes aspects of a company's operations will remain hidden from our view. (Unless we get to know one of the top managers and he spills the beans. Don't hold your breath.)

Nevertheless, we can often infer the quality of a company's inner workings from what we *can* see.

And more important, we do not need utter precision. It's better to be vaguely right than precisely wrong. A couple of examples:

● *In the food business, the effectiveness of a restaurant's, supermarket's, or delicatessen's health and sanitary procedures. (Is it safe to eat their food?)*

Whether as consumers or investors, we want to avoid places where the handling and preparation of food is less than perfect.

At the meat counter in a deli, we can see whether the staff are always wearing gloves when filling our order. But what about the meat already wrapped in plastic?

Even when the meat looks perfectly fresh, we can never be 100 percent certain. Let alone monitor every step from the farm to the retail counter.

In practice, we depend on the retailer's reputation, the often unconscious assumption that the seller's intention is to provide us with healthy products so that we will turn into a regular customer, and that the company is abiding by all the relevant health regulations.

While occasional cases of food poisoning go with the territory, we naturally want to avoid any such business where a widespread outbreak of food poisoning is likely.

This risk is difficult to foresee. However, an analysis of past outbreaks (see "Reputational Risk: Is Chipotle Hazardous to Your Health?" on page 243) gives us some signs to look for.

● *The quality of a company's supply chain.*

While we can never know *all* the nitty-gritty details, we don't need to.

The quality of a company's supply chain is, in part, indicated by whether the shelves are always fully stocked—or whether there are, from time to time, empty shelves or shortages of particular products.

In other words, do they *always* have what you want?

A second source of information is the inventory levels reported in the company's financials. If those levels fluctuate wildly from one quarter to the next, they could indicate poor inventory management. A supply-chain problem.

Such fluctuations may indicate a brewing problem. From the outside, we cannot know for sure. But if we're comparing two companies, one that suggests perfection (i.e., full shelves everywhere we go) while the other may have problems hidden from our view, either further investigation is required or we simply go with company number one and pass on number two.

Ultimately, we can place our guesstimates of each of the metrics we're discussing here into one of three wide categories: poor, medium, or excellent. While imprecise, we can simply ignore a business we rate as mostly poor or medium. And focus on the one we rate as excellent on nearly every category.

Vaguely Right Rather Than Precisely Wrong

These metrics will help you do two things:

● Eliminate from consideration companies that clearly fail on one or more metrics.

● End up with a short list of potential investments that justify deeper investigation.

Most of the metrics are not quantitative, but qualitative. Precision, for qualitative judgments, is not possible. What's more, it's not always necessary.

For example, if you're driving along the freeway in a 100 kph zone, and your speedometer shows this—

—you don't need to know your precise speed to know that you're in danger of getting a speeding ticket.

When driving, you focus on two categories:

But the policeman manning one of those mobile radar traps is only interested in *one:* speeding.

Precision only matters when it comes to writing the speeding ticket. And only in jurisdictions where the higher the speed, the higher the fine.

In the same way, for any business we can put each of these metrics into one of two similar categories: Excellent and The Rest.

But we do need a little more precision. Five categories: Poor, Average, Good, Very Good, and Excellent:

It's unlikely we'll find companies that are Excellent on *all* those metrics. Businesses we might judge as Excellent overall will probably score Good or Very Good on a few of those metrics.

But if such a company scores Average or Poor on one or more, it's definitely a cause for concern.

When the Results Speak for Themselves

As a potential investor in a company, we need to answer another question that cannot be gauged from the customer's perspective: Is the management's focus on building long-term value for shareholders—or rewarding itself with high salaries, generous grants of stock options, perks such as first-class travel or company jets, generous expense accounts and pension plans, and similar benefits that subtract from the bottom line, thus eroding the company's profits and the shareholders' returns?

To answer questions of this kind we need to get a handle on the company's financials.

5. Judging Management—by the Numbers

A company's financial reports are a gold mine of data. Those numbers don't lie—when you understand what they mean.

Trawling those numbers helps us discover whether the management is focusing on increasing the wealth of its owners, the shareholders, by focusing on the business's long-term value. This is, if you like, a continuation of judging the management's honesty and integrity.

Past performance alone does not tell us whether that performance is likely to continue into the future.

But when we have hard evidence that a management walks the talk we want to hear, we have a higher degree of certainty that it will continue to sing the same tune tomorrow and in the years to come.

For example, a CEO might tell us his aim is to build shareholder value. It's good PR. But is that his *real* aim?

We can know a CEO is *dedicated* to that goal when financial evidence demonstrates that it is more than just hot air.

A number of key things to look for, starting with—is management aiming to *minimize taxes* or *maximize accounting profits?*

- *Minimizing taxes.* Every dollar paid in tax is one dollar less for us, as shareholders, or for reinvestment in expanding the business. Resulting in *lower* sales, profits, and dividends in the years to come.

Why Some CEOs Like to Maximize *Accounting* Profits

From a CEO's point of view, having his company pay *higher* taxes can be a *personal benefit*. Higher taxes mean higher *reported* profits, which in turn boost the company's stock price, and so the value of the CEO's options.

And having achieved a record year, a CEO may be awarded an extra cash bonus and/or more options by the board.

Fair enough, *if* those higher profits are *real* ones, the direct result of higher sales, lower costs, improved efficiency, and other improvements in the business's nuts and bolts.

But all too often the profits are the result of financial manipulation, especially when it comes to estimating the values of the intangible items that must appear on the balance sheet.

When intangible assets are overvalued, or intangible liabilities underreserved, it's evidence that management's aim is to maximize accounting profits, so boosting the company's price/earnings ratio, stock price, options value, bonuses, and—worst of all—taxes. All of which, by reducing shareholders' equity, comes straight from the shareholders' pockets.

Maximizing Profits—or Accounting Profits?

Accounting profits are what the IRS says they are.

Some numbers in a company's financial statements are fixed. For example, the money spent on purchasing goods for resale is a hard cost.

But some numbers are discretionary within a "reasonable" range. As a result, small differences in such judgments can produce quite large and misleading differences in metrics such as earnings per share, cash in the bank, a company's share price—and Wall Street's judgment about which company is a better buy.

Consider these two companies with exactly the same operating profits:

	Company A: Maximizing shareholder value	Company B: Maximizing accounting profits
Sales	$1,000,000	$1,000,000
Cost of sales	$800,000	$800,000
Operating profit	$200,000	$200,000
Adjustments		
Provision for bad debts	+$1,500	-$1,500
Pension fund	+$1,500	-$1,500
Intangible assets	+$1,500	-$1,500
Total adjustments	+$4,500	-$4,500
Reported earnings	$195,500	$204,500
Income tax	$78,995	$82,505
Net earnings	$116,505	$121,995
Earnings per share	$5.83	$6.10
P/E ratio	15.0	15.0
Share price	$87.45	$91.50

A quick comparison suggests that Company B, with higher profits and earnings, would make the better investment.

But when we look at the adjustments the two managements have made, we can see that Company A is the more conservative one. By increasing the amounts set aside for discretionary items, it reports lower profits.

Company A also pays less tax, thus leaving more money in the bank than does Company B.

These different assumptions result in a small 4.60 percent difference in the companies' share prices, at the same P/E ratio of 15.

But what if Wall Street judges these two companies differently? Perhaps penalizing Company A for "cash hoarding," while rerating Company B for having the better earnings history. If that happens, the two companies could trade at different P/E ratios with the following result:

P/E ratio	13.5	16.5
Share price	$78.71	$100.65

This small difference produces a 28 percent variance in the two companies' share prices—and market caps.

Even though their actual sales and cost of sales are exactly the same.

• *Over-reserving for losses or bad debts.* Adding one dollar to these reserves takes one dollar from the company's taxable profits.

The Long-Term Benefits of "Over" Reserving

When such reserves are maximized to the limits allowed by the tax code, aside from reducing taxable profits, in an economic downturn this company will have plenty of cash to cover the inevitable write-offs as doubtful debts become uncollectible, so avoiding the recession-induced "cash crunch."

Meanwhile, other companies that have based their loss/bad-debt reserves on historical averages, so not allowing for the possibility of the high, "outlier" interest rates typical of the last phase of a boom and the early months of the subsequent recession, are likely to be in financial difficulty.

When you see a company that minimizes taxes in this way, it's evidence that the management is focused on increasing the business's value in the long term.

Recession's "Triple Whammy"

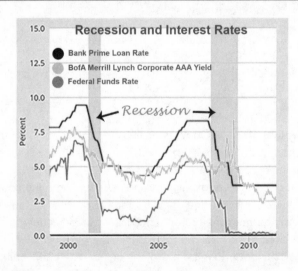

The graph, on page 114, of two recent recessions illustrates the three-stage pattern of the "cash crunch":

1. *Interest rates rise at the end of the boom.*
Highly leveraged companies can enter bankruptcy *before* the recession begins.

2. *Interest rates decline during the recession.*
But not all interest rates are equal.

Central banks usually try to alleviate the recession by pumping money into the economy. As you can see, the Federal Funds Rate—the rate at which the US Federal Reserve will lend money to banks—declines rapidly during the recession.

The Bank Prime Loan Rate—the rate at which banks lend to their best customers—follows suit. But most businesses that borrow from banks will pay much higher rates. Especially smaller ones.

And as you can see, in the 2008–9 recession, corporate bond rates spiked up toward the *end* of the recession.

Banks, too, are affected by the recession. One way they react is to tighten loan requirements, effectively restricting new lending to people who don't really need the money. They may also increase the rate of interest on variable-rate loans like overdrafts—or just cancel them entirely.

Thus, smaller or more highly leveraged businesses will have to pay higher rates of interest, while the interest bill for larger businesses that can access the bond markets will remain fixed (unless refinancing is required).

3. *Companies' sales fall while costs fall far more slowly.*
Profits and free cash flow both decline at a time when companies' interest rate bills may have risen and debt refinancing is difficult if not impossible to find.

The key to avoiding this fate is to practice conservative debt management.

- *Conservative debt management.* Debt is a two-edged sword. It can be rocket fuel: a high level of debt increases the per share amount of capital that can be invested in expanding the business. But too much debt can lead to bankruptcy when a company overreaches or when interest rates zoom up or sales and profits tank. A *recession-proof* business is, first and foremost, one with debt management aimed to survive the worst-case scenario.

Capital-intensive businesses, such as the retailers we're focusing on, can only expand rapidly by using "other people's money."

The most dramatic example of this, as we've seen, is the no-debt, no-franchising White Castle, versus McDonald's creative financing approach.

Had White Castle not spurned other people's money, it could be the number one hamburger chain today instead of McDonald's. (On the upside, White Castle *didn't* go under from having too much debt, while McDonald's in its early years teetered on the razor's edge of bankruptcy.)

All leverage, including debt, has two sides:

● the upside, where everything goes well and new facilities produce profits; and the downside, where the debt burden sinks the company— usually during a recession. To avoid the downside,

● use debt only to expand the business, and (ideally) only when you can be sure the new locations, factories, or product lines will be profitable; and

● set a maximum on the overall debt load so it can be financed through thick and thin.

Being able to meet debt repayments through thick and thin means projecting the worst-case scenario, and setting debt levels so that repayments can continue no matter what.

Debt repayments come from profits (or cash reserves). In a downturn, sales and profits usually fall, while a company's interest bill may go up. To avoid a cash crunch at a time when banks are calling in loans and aren't particularly interested in lending money even to people who don't need it (except at high interest rates with gold-clad security), a company needs to have—

● *A* manageable *ratio of profits to interest payments,* calculated to cover the worst-case scenario—so that the company *never* has to touch its cash reserve.

The worst-case scenario occurs at the depths of a recession.

The recession-proof ratio of interest to profits must be calculated using a low profit number. As a rule of thumb, say half average profits over the previous few years.

A more precise estimate can be made by comparing a company's profits in past recession years with average profits.

Figuring the annual interest payments a company must make during a recession depends upon whether the company has fixed-rate or variable-rate financing.

Companies that can access the bond market will have fixed interest rates, so their interest payments will not change.

Off-Balance-Sheet Financing

Franchising shifts the capital burden from the company to the franchisee.

A related financing model is to seek investors who will put up the money for a new retail location in return for a percentage of that store's sales or profits.

These are legitimate ways of financing that enable a company to benefit from debt while keeping it off the balance sheet.

The short-term financing often used by smaller companies (for example, bank overdrafts) will have variable rates. Worse, the bank may cancel their overdrafts at the worst possible moment.

A one-to-one ratio of estimated recession profits to interest payments is the bare minimum.

But what if the next recession is worse than the last one? Or interest rates go even higher? (Or both!?)

We need to add a margin of safety: estimated recession profits should be between 50 percent and 100 percent higher than annual interest payments.

From this perspective, the ideal company is totally debt-free and sitting on a mountain of cash.

 • *A pile of cash.* In a downturn, when money is tight, asset prices have collapsed, and doom and gloom is the prevailing mood, a cash-rich company is in a position to expand its market share at bargain prices while its highly leveraged competitors are flailing.

Without a doubt, the best example of this behavior (and its benefits) is Warren Buffett's Berkshire Hathaway.

Following the collapse of Lehman Brothers in 2008, Buffett injected $25.2 billion of Berkshire's cash "hoard" in companies such as Goldman Sachs, General Electric, and Dow Chemical, on exceedingly favorable terms.

Five years later that $25.2 billion had grown almost 40 percent, to $35.15 billion.

Wall Street analysts often penalize companies for hoarding cash (with the important exception of Berkshire Hathaway: Buffett always gets a free pass). The analysts claim it's an asset that's not working to produce profits for the company; if it's not going to be invested, it should be returned to shareholders via dividends or (preferably) share buybacks.

Apple has been criticized for hoarding. Steve Jobs simply ignored such complaints, but the post-Jobs management has given in to this pressure, increasing dividends and buying back stock.

But complaints about "excess cash" ignore the benefits of sitting on tons of money.

For example, Microsoft in its early years faced a cash crisis: one payday, it had barely enough money to pay the employees. Bill Gates vowed to avoid a future cash crunch by building a cash reserve equivalent to one year's wages.

Today, Microsoft's cash reserves are way above Gates's original target.

Cash reserves are a form of insurance. Who would argue that you should *not* have fire insurance because the chances of your house burning down are slight? And why buy life insurance when you won't be around to benefit from it?

But the major advantage of a pile of cash comes when markets collapse.

Berkshire Hathaway has been a cash-rich company for decades. In the depths of the 2008 financial crisis when stocks had tanked, Buffett repeated the comment he made in the 1973 bear market, that he felt "like an oversexed guy in a whorehouse."

On both occasions he was scooping up stocks as if there were no tomorrow.

His policy of sitting on cash gives him enormous firepower when stocks are cheap. This is a major factor in the strategy that has made him one of the world's most successful investors.

A company that focuses on increasing its market share will be forced to cut back dramatically when the economy tanks.

Meanwhile, like Buffett, the cash-rich company is now in a position to expand while all its competitors are contracting.

Thanks to the collapse in asset prices, the cash-rich retailer may be able to add two, or even more, locations for the same price its competitors added one just a year or so earlier. And/or pick up ailing competitors for a song.

Or buy back shares for less than enterprise value, thus increasing all shareholders' net worth.

In the long run, the company that follows the more conservative debt policy will, as a side effect, end up increasing its market share more profitably, and possibly even faster, than companies with market share as their expressed objective.

"Hoarding" Cash

A quick Google search produced articles with titles such as "Biggest U.S. Corporations: Still *Hoarding Cash*," "$2 Trillion *Corporate Cash Hoard*," and "Apple Isn't Only Company with *Too Much Cash*."

That gives you an idea of the conventional thinking: "hoarding" / "too much cash" is a Bad Thing.

One obvious misconception from the first article: "We thought it was time to take another look at how much money large U.S. corporations are *not* investing back into the economy."

Well, that Google is sitting on $58.717 billion in cash and liquid assets does *not* mean it is *not* being invested back into the economy. It's in a bank somewhere, and presumably that bank is lending it out to someone *else* who is "investing back into the economy."

Here's a list of the top ten "cash hoarders" from the Fortune 500 list (excluding financial companies), as of mid-2014:

Biggest US Corporations "Hoarding" Cash (Mid-2004)		
Company	Cash & cash equivalents ($ millions)	% of total assets
Google	$58,717	52.9%
Microsoft	$85,709	49.7%
Cisco Systems	$50,469	49.5%
Oracle	$38,819	43.0%
Humana	$9,158	39.6%
WellPoint	$20,114	32.3%
Intel	$7,540	26.0%
Johnson & Johnson	$31,624	23.4%
Costco Wholesale	**$7,275**	**22.2%**
Best Buy	**$3,066**	**22.0%**

Source: http://www.remappingdebate.org/map-data-tool/biggest-us-corporations-still-hoarding-cash.

Note: two retailers (in **bold**) make the top ten. Probably worth a look ☺.

● *No dividends, thank you.*

As a long-term investor, we want a management that pulls out all the stops to maximize the company's future value.

Paying no dividends is, perhaps, the ultimate confirmation of a management's long-term orientation.

First of all, a no-dividend policy is scorned by Wall Street analysts. Income-oriented investors like dividend stocks, leading to a lower demand for no-dividend stocks, and a lower price for the stock.

But overall returns to shareholders are *higher* when a profitable company with a high return on capital and equity does *not* pay dividends.

The first reason is tax.

Dividends are taxed as income. So if you receive a dividend check for $100, you'll have to pay $30 or more in tax.

Since that $100 in dividends has reduced the company's assets by the same amount, the value of your shareholding has dropped by $100, but you have pocketed $70 or less.

The alternative to receiving dividends is to sell some shares when you need the cash. If you'd sold $100 in shares, it would have been taxed at the capital gains rate, usually half the income tax rate. So you'd end up with $85 in your wallet instead of $70.

Second, having paid $100 in dividends, your company no longer has that money to reinvest in future growth.

Provided the company is achieving a positive return on capital and equity, wouldn't you prefer to have that money working to increase the value of your shares? Especially if you don't *need* that $100 right now?

When a company has excess cash it wishes to return to the shareholders, it is far more tax efficient to buy back shares than to pay out dividends.

And what if this no-dividend policy does knock a few dollars off the company's stock price?

All the better for us—if we want to increase our holdings.

Red Flags to Watch out For

To quote the sage Anonymous, "Prediction is difficult, especially when it concerns the future."

While all projections of the future are, by definition, uncertain, we can find any number of red flags in a company's financials that tell us, in no uncertain terms: *KEEP OUT!*

Some examples:

● EBITDA is short for Earnings Before Interest, Taxes, Depreciation, and Amortization.

A company's EBITDA can look fantastic—the day before it files for bankruptcy.

While depreciation and amortization may be noncash charges, interest on debt and taxes are obviously unavoidable expenses. So a company's high EBITDA may appear attractive—until you see that the interest it has to pay on the fistful of junk bonds it issued equals EBITDA, and more.

And that's before Uncle Sam comes knocking on the door.

Taken alone, EBITDA tells us nothing about the state or value of the business of the company as a whole.

A company that trumpets its EBITDA may simply be following Wall Street fashion, or it may be trying to divert our attention from some ugly numbers.

Either way, this is a sign of a company we should probably avoid. We want a management that's marching to its own tune, not Wall Street's or somebody else's. And we certainly don't want to "give" our money to people who are fudging reality.

> ● *Lavish options and bonuses* indicate a management that's more interested in looking after itself than you, the shareholder.

What's "lavish" is, unfortunately, somewhat subjective.

The key is whether such performance bonuses accord with real performance. But when you see enormous option grants or bonuses to top management, along with excessive expense accounts, beware.

A handful of companies go in the opposite direction, significantly *under*paying their CEOs. Warren Buffett's annual salary is a mere $100,000 a year. He used to be the lowest-paid CEO of a Fortune 500 company. That mantle now belongs to John Mackey, whose salary (along with that of eight other CEOs) is just $1 a year.

Other red flags include the opposites of the "virtues" we have identified above.

We definitely want to avoid companies that are overleveraged (too much debt). The last thing we want to worry about is whether our investment will go to "money heaven" in the next downturn.

Nor should we be interested in companies that pad revenues Minnie Pearl–style, underdeclare expenses, or engage in other accounting shenanigans.

Applying the Customer Experience

To see what you can discover about a company *just* "by walking around"—purely as a customer—let's apply this method to two companies we're all familiar with: Starbucks (in the Philippines) and Microsoft.

Case Study #1: Is Starbucks Philippines Going Downhill?

Starbucks Philippines is not a subsidiary of the US company but a country franchise. A *private* company, so no financial details are available.

Starbucks in the Philippines is also an unlikely story. No one considered the country to be an important market. "I don't think any of us thought this market could hold fifty stores," Howard Schultz said[6] about his thoughts when the first Manila Starbucks opened in 1998.

Today there are 283 and counting.

What's more, Starbucks Philippines sparked the same espresso revolution as Starbucks did in the USA.

Today, Starbucks Philippines is the leader in a crowded market. In addition to local chains—Figaro, Bo's, Café de Lipa, Xtremely Xpresso, Mocha Blends—plus dozens, if not hundreds, of single-store independents, a wide variety of international chains have entered the market: UCC (Japan), Seattle's Best, McCafé, and Coffee Bean & Tea Leaf (USA), Caffè Pascucci (Italy), Highlands Coffee (Vietnam), Toby's Estate and Gloria Jeans (Australia), Caffè Dolce (Taiwan), Costa Coffee (UK), and Hollys Coffee and Caffè Bene (South Korea).

For completeness, we should include noncafé chains that have added espresso to compete in the market Starbucks created. These include Krispy Kreme, Dunkin' Donuts (USA), and J.CO (a Krispy Kreme copycat from Indonesia).

To give an example of how Starbucks has expanded the market, when the world's number two café chain, Costa Coffee (UK), entered the Philippine market in 2015, it projected seventy to eighty stores. More than the fifty stores Howard Schultz thought was impossible in 1998.

Although I'm based in Hong Kong, these days I spend a lot of my time in the Philippines. So naturally I sample the cappuccinos, and Starbucks is my choice.

STARBUCKS' "GOLD STANDARD"

In my judgment, Starbucks in the Philippines is the company's worldwide gold standard for service.

A major reason: in most countries, a job at Starbucks, McDonald's, and similar chains is, for most people, temporary or part-time. For example, some 12 percent of Americans had their first job at a McDonald's.

In the Philippines, Starbucks offers a career path. What's more, a Starbucks barista's salary is higher than the average for similar jobs, so Starbucks attracts and retains excellent people. By offering an above-average salary, it can pick and choose the best—the most enthusiastic and the most compatible with the company's vision and values—and maintain a high employee retention rate to boot.

> **Where Starbucks USA Wins Out: The Benefit of Volume**
>
> One metric of the customer experience where Starbucks USA tops its Philippine associate is speed of service.
>
> The lines move faster.
>
> The reason: volume.
>
> Higher volume requires more staff behind the counter, which translates into faster service, even when the lines are long.
>
> And the higher the volume, the more profitable the store.

The company created its competition in more ways than one. The quality of its training is such that other chains actively poach Starbucks staff. An experienced Starbucks barista—someone who's just working behind the counter—can instantly be a store manager, at a higher salary, at many other restaurant chains. And can even be sent abroad to train staff in other countries where the chain operates.

Break-time reading.

As a result, Starbucks' staff turnover has gone up, and in the years I've been a regular customer, the quality of the customer experience has somewhat deteriorated.

I admit that few customers will even notice the imperfections I see. Yet, they're signs that the gold standard is slipping into silver.

Some examples:

● Tables and chairs that are impossible to level—even on a perfectly flat surface. And that aren't fixed for weeks or months.

● Bagels and cream cheese. Something I'd often order in the mornings. Until they replaced their Philadelphia cream cheese with a tasteless no-name brand. One that was quite clearly much cheaper—a fact *not* reflected in the retail price.

● Outdoor fans that don't work properly. One store has two overhead fans in the outdoor seating area. For years, the medium and high settings on one of the fans haven't worked. I visited this store the other day: same problem, except worse. The second fan didn't work at all! Unsurprisingly, plenty of seats were available at the outdoor tables, which had often been nearly full.

These are just a few of many examples I could give you that indicate that the focus of Starbucks Philippines' management has veered away from the quality of customer experience to the bottom line.

We've seen what happened when Howard Schultz stepped back from Starbucks' day-to-day management in 2000, and how McDonald's suffered when Harry Sonneborn ruled the roost.

There is always a tension between quality and the cost of providing that quality, and the quality of the customer experience always declines when the number crunchers are in the saddle.

Perhaps you're thinking that this is all minor stuff.

And, Dear Reader, you're right.

Except to the once-loyal customer who gets pissed off at one of these "minor" problems—and never comes back.

The more "minor" problems there are, the more customers you lose.

But this "minor stuff" may also represent a more fundamental issue.

Many years ago, I was on a trans-Pacific Pan Am flight.* On landing and takeoff some of the overhead-bin lids flipped open, while the movie screen in the front of the section flapped. I not-so-idly wondered whether the wings, engines, and other components that were keeping us forty thousand feet above a wet landing had been similarly neglected.

When I told the story to an airline-pilot friend, he said, "Yep. The wings and the engines get the same level of treatment."

> ### When the Focus Is Quality
>
> In the early 1960s, legendary adman David Ogilvy wrote an ad for Rolls-Royce with the headline:
>
> "At 60 miles per hour, the loudest noise in this new Rolls-Royce comes from the electric clock."
>
> The reaction of Rolls-Royce's chief engineer to the headline indicates a dedication to an exemplary customer experience: "It's time we did something about that damn clock."

What the long-term consequences for Starbucks Philippines might be are hard to say. It certainly dominates the country's café niche. Being the first mover, it has the best locations. And as the leading brand it's often invited into new shopping developments as an anchor tenant and is, generally, busier than its competitors.

Nevertheless, should a competing chain raise its quality to the level of Starbucks' or better, it could take the number one spot.

In a competitive market it's always a mistake to lose total focus on the quality of the customer experience.

Case Study #2: Microsoft's Windows Experience

In 1992, IBM was in big trouble.

It was hemorrhaging cash as the demand for its primary cash cows, especially the IBM S/390 mainframe that produced 90 percent of its profits, was plummeting.[7]

Sales had imploded from $13 billion in 1990 to a projection of under $7 billion for 1993.[8]

The twin causes: competition from Hitachi and Amdahl, which were both offering competing products at lower prices, and from the personal computer, which by distributing computing power far and wide cut into the demand for centralized computing systems.

At the same time, IBM was effectively ignoring its customers' wants. For too many managers, internal politics was more significant than satisfying customers. The company's structure, which had worked so well to propel IBM to market dominance in the 1950s, '60s, and '70s, had become a patchwork of fiefdoms that, more often than not, refused to cooperate with one another.

Past success had turned into hubris and arrogance. The IBM Way was the "right way"—regardless of customer demand or market feedback.

---

*Yes, that's how long ago it was. Pan Am went bankrupt in 1991.

IBM, in sum, was being hit by an enormous headwind, was on the edge of bankruptcy—and had its head in the sand.

MICROSOFT: THE NEXT IBM?

Today, Microsoft's once-primary cash cow, Windows, could be in a similar position to IBM in 1992.

In October 2012, the company introduced Windows 8. Followed three years later by Windows 10.

To universal acclaim?

Hardly.

Following the release of Windows 8, sales of new computers (other than Macs) tanked. The manufacturers who did best were those whose computers came with Windows 7, or *no* operating system at all.

MacBook sales went up.

What's more, Microsoft reported that *activations* of Windows 8 *licenses* were way behind sales: around half of those new computers were overwritten with Windows 7.

The primary complaint: the Windows 7 interface had effectively disappeared.

What did Microsoft do to meet these customer complaints?

Not a thing.

What's more, *before* Windows 8's release Microsoft knew from focus groups that people overwhelming wanted the option of the Windows 7 interface.

Why hold focus groups at all if you're going to completely ignore the results?

The demand for the much-loved Windows 7 look quickly led to the availability of apps for Windows 8, such as Stardock and Classic Shell, which put the Windows 7 interface back.

The proliferation and popularity of those apps resoundingly confirm the focus groups' reactions.

If *you* had introduced a product and got this kind of customer feedback, wouldn't you seriously consider putting those features back? Especially when those popular add-on programs are not *reinstalling* missing Windows 7 features, but *reactivating* them?

Then, along comes Windows 10 with some of those Windows 7 features back—and a whole host of other problems, including:

- Forced upgrades—whether you wanted Windows 10 or not.

- Updates full of bugs. Some of them even causing the "blue screen of death." Others just causing your computer to crash.

- Followed by updates to fix the bugs—that sometimes introduced new ones.

The market's response: a gadget called *GWX Control Panel*, which enables you to stop Windows 7 and 8 from upgrading to 10.

Windows 10 was *free*.

And lots of people didn't want it!

Imagine that!

What was Microsoft's reaction?

Here's this, from CEO Satya Nadella's 2015 letter to shareholders:

> We as a company stand for deeply understanding the needs of customers, translating that understanding into products that people love and ultimately into the success our customers have with our products. It's that last part that is our key motivation. The entire Microsoft team is inspired to bring their best ideas and efforts every day to build products people love, and to advance our mission to *empower every person and every organization on the planet to achieve more.* And we're seeing the impact.

Huh?

Are we talking about the same business? Is this guy on the same planet?

Talk about a customer disconnect!

This is all happening at a time when the demand for PCs is declining as people switch from laptops and desktops to smartphones and tablets.

The fall in demand for PCs has been so significant that on 18 April 2016 Intel announced "it was laying off twelve thousand people, about 11% of its workforce, as it continues to reel from a long downturn in global demand for personal computers."[9]

That, after having laid off 2.3 percent of its employees the year before.

Microsoft's overall reaction is, again, similar to IBM's way back when.

With its mainframe business imploding, IBM bought into the general belief that mainframes were passé and the future of computing was in "distributed computing."

PCs.

IBM had been a first mover in the PC market. But the company made a fundamental mistake. When it licensed MS-DOS from Microsoft, it did not insist on an *exclusive* license. The result being the PC market as we know it today: dominated by Microsoft operating systems running on PCs made by dozens of competing manufacturers.

IBM's "answer" to this "chaos" was its *own* operating system, OS/2, on its own PowerPC chips, on its own hardware.

Instead of focusing on its strength—the mainframe—IBM reentered a highly competitive market, now dominated by its former partner, Microsoft, where it had no competitive advantage.

The result: a big fail.

Microsoft's reaction to the decline in the market for its Windows cash cow has been to move into tablets and smartphones. Both markets dominated by Android, Apple, and Samsung.

Markets where Microsoft is a minor player with no competitive advantage.

Or, perhaps more accurately, where it *could* have a major competitive advantage by connecting PCs with its tablets and smartphones—if it weren't alienating a big chunk of its customer base.

Like IBM, Microsoft Windows is facing a major headwind, ignoring and, worse, alienating its customers, and the management is exhibiting arrogance and hubris based on its past lock on the computer market.

Unfortunately for us, as Windows users, there is a major difference between IBM yesterday and Microsoft today.

Microsoft is in no danger of going bankrupt.

Quite the reverse. Between 2014 and 2015 its pile of cash and cash equivalents grew from $85.709 billion to $96.526 billion.

When you're experiencing numbers like these, it's easy to ignore or be completely unaware of what you're doing wrong: $96.526 billion will finance a helluva lot of arrogance.

As you can see from this breakdown of Microsoft's revenues, sales of Windows now come in third after Office and Server products. And represent just 15.8 percent of the company's total sales.

Year ended June 30	In millions 2015	In millions 2014	In millions 2013
Microsoft Office system	$23,538	$24,323	$22,995
Server products and tools	18,612	17,055	15,408
Windows PC operating system	14,826	16,856	17,529
Xbox	9,121	8,643	7,100
Phone	7,702	3,073	615
Consulting and product support services	5,090	4,767	4,372
Advertising	4,557	4,016	3,387
Surface	3,900	1,883	853
Other	6,234	6,217	5,590
Total	**$93,580**	**$86,833**	**$77,849**

Source: Microsoft 2015 Annual Report

Of course, Microsoft is not a candidate for the next Starbucks. Or, indeed, the next Microsoft.

But it is a compelling example of how we, as mere customers, can derive significant information about a company from our personal experience, the experiences of others that we can find in the news and on the Internet, and the company's financials and management's statements.

If we were considering investing in Microsoft, we'd want to determine if the same management attitude spills over to its other product segments.

My guess is it probably does.

My only other experience of Microsoft products is Office. And in successive releases of Word, features I found useful keep disappearing.

One example: misspell a word in Word 2010 or earlier, right-click on it, and you have the option AutoCorrect (among many others).

But in Word 2013 . . . ?

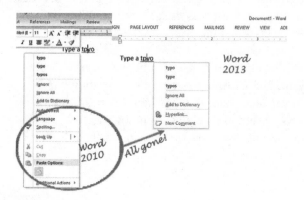

How annoying is that?

If you want to AutoCorrect a misspelled word in Word 2013, it will take you eight clicks instead of one!

Windows 8 does impress me in one major respect: I've been using it since January 2013—and it has not crashed yet. Not even once. A first for Microsoft.

Nevertheless, by 2016, while the Mac was hogging the top end in the (declining) laptop market pretty much by itself, Google's Chromebook was outselling Macs (by numbers, not by value).

Today, Windows is being squeezed at both ends of the market.

So applying the "speedometer" ratings on the two metrics we've been discussing, I would rate Windows 8 as follows:

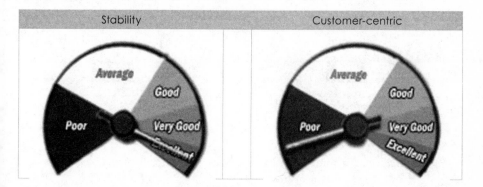

In summary, when you come across a company that—at least in your judgment—doesn't care about the customer experience, ultimately the most important of all the metrics we've covered in this chapter, that should be sufficient reason to cross this company off your list of investment candidates.

One last thing: I admit that I haven't had much experience with Windows 10.

With good reason: I've decided, from everything I've read about *other* people's experiences, to avoid Windows 10 like the plague.

Indeed, just days after Windows 10 stopped being free, it released an "Anniversary Update," which causes a wide variety of failures, rollbacks, flaky Universal Windows programs, and error codes such as 0x80070020.

What does 0x80070020 mean?

I don't want to find out! And I don't need to.

Microsoft will support Windows 7 until January 14, 2020, and Windows 8 until January 10, 2023. I figure that by then my laptops and (probably) desktops will have to be replaced, and with any luck Microsoft *may* have gotten the bugs out of Windows 10 (but probably not Windows 11).

So I see no reason to switch—at the moment.

PART 2

How to Profit from the Next Starbucks— or the Last One

The Investment and Business Opportunities

Businesses that exhibit all the "five differences that make the difference" and are relatively capital-intensive can—just like Starbucks, Whole Foods, Walmart, and McDonald's—be high-growth stocks for decades.

Yes, you can also use these five clues to spot the next Google. Problem is, you can never be sure *in advance* if such a stock will turn out to be the next Google— or the next turkey.

Or the next AOL, Myspace, or Netscape: companies that fly for a year or three before they crash and burn.

Investing only in companies whose customers *can't* be stolen with just one click by some upstart Harvard dropout or kid from Brazil, China, or India removes those risks.

It's a slower—but surer—road to wealth.

Once we've come across such a candidate, what's next?

You can profit from the next Starbucks—and the last one—in four ways. We begin with two types of *business* opportunities, followed by the different *investment* approaches:

1. *Start your own* (chapter 7).

2. *Become a franchisee* (chapter 8).

3. *Investment strategies from Buffett . . . :* take the "low-risk road to wealth" by investing in a first mover or copycat *at the right price* (chapter 9).

4. *. . . to Thiel:* invest in the next Starbucks at the IPO—or become a venture capitalist and take *profits* at the IPO instead (chapter 10).

A Business Approach to Investing

Don't skip to chapter 9, thinking, "I have no interest in *starting* a business, only investing in one." To make long-term profits from a high-growth company, we must approach it as if we are *partners* in that business.

In other words, first analyze the company as a business proposition before examining the investment opportunities.

After all, in our search for the next Starbucks, we're looking for a *business* that we confidently expect to grow at above-average rates for a long time. One we can sock away in our pension plan and pretty much (but not totally) forget about.

So, like Warren Buffett, we're looking for an investment we can hold "forever." Which we can only achieve by taking a business approach to investing.

In sum, the business approach primes us to make more intelligent investment decisions; and the investment analysis helps us make more intelligent business decisions.

Whichever our primary interest, each is enriched by the other.

CHAPTER

7 | **Dream Big: Start Your Own**

As a rule, the entrepreneurs who start a high-growth company are the ones who make the highest returns from it. Howard Schultz, John Mackey, Sam Walton, and Ray Kroc all turned their initial investment of, at most, a few hundred thousand dollars (plus many years of dedication, hard work, and, inevitably, twenty-four-hour days) into multibillion-dollar fortunes that put them on the Forbes 500 list.

The people who make almost as much money from a successful start-up are the investors who back the entrepreneurial founders at the beginning. So even if you have absolutely no interest in *ever* starting or owning a business yourself, walking through the process the successful founder follows helps you identify a strong candidate for the next Starbucks—while it's still on the ground floor.

So let's, temporarily, put ourselves in the shoes of someone whose intention *is* to start the next Starbucks (or Google), take the copycat route, or just have his or her own show. And see how applying the five clues to a start-up enables a new business to open its doors with *all* the essential ingredients to dramatically increase the chances of success.

As a reminder, here's a quick—

"Recipe" for Starting Your Own

1. Identify an *underserved market niche*.

2. Define the *vision* and *mission* that will motivate customers, employees, investors, and other stakeholders. The bigger the vision, the better: if you want to hit the moon, aim for the stars.

3. Create a *compelling customer experience*.

4. Develop a *system,* with the focus on the customer experience, to ensure that experience is *consistent* across all locations (and enable your business to be run by nineteen-year-olds).

5. Even if you have only *one* location (e.g., online), you still need to ensure that the customer experience is *consistent 24/7.*

6. The previous four components will combine into what will become the *company's culture:* the accepted way of doing things (to define *culture* simply).

> I came to see, in my time at IBM, that [a company's] culture isn't just one aspect of the game—it is the game.[1]
> —Louis V. Gerstner Jr., the CEO who turned IBM around

7. *Mental attitude and commitment.* Years of unremitting effort and twenty-four-hour days go into the creation of a new business—with no guarantee of success. Climbing Mount Everest—though far more hazardous to your health—takes just a couple of months. But it can be *years* before the entrepreneur who creates a business from nothing is fully rewarded, so only someone who is highly motivated, powerfully committed to his goal—and *hungry*—has a chance of staying the course.

8. Finally, to qualify as a candidate for the next Starbucks, the business needs to be scalable with, at least potentially, a high ratio of owner earnings to the capital investment required for expansion, and have superb entrepreneurial management.

Outside Looking In

As potential investors in a start-up, we're looking for the same qualities, but with a different emphasis.

Bill Gross, founder of the venture capital firm Idealab, which has been involved in more than a hundred start-ups, thinks the key factor is the founding team.

> The strongest correlation to success has been the founding team—much more than the idea, or the amount of money raised, or almost anything else I can think of. The best successes came when there were at least two strong people, *with opposite but complementary skills,* who had a great deal of mutual trust and respect for one another. . . . If I see a complementary team like that, I would try to find almost any way to work with them. [Emphasis added.][2]

Gross could have been describing one of the most successful start-ups of all time: Apple Computer. A company synonymous with Steve Jobs and Steve Wozniak. Jobs was the visionary and salesman; "the Woz," the developer/executioner.

This underlying theme of two (or, at most, three) founders who trust, respect, and are open and honest with each other seems to be a common factor in successful start-ups—according to a number of venture capitalists.*

Between them, the founders need to fill (or hire) the following roles:

Visionary: the driving force behind a growth company. The visionary is usually also the salesman or "hustler" who inspires and persuades employees, customers, investors, suppliers, and other stakeholders to come on *his* board. Howard Schultz, John Mackey, Sam Walton, and Ray Kroc all fall into this category.

Manager: the person with the "execution skill" who creates and delivers the product or service that fulfills the vision.

People person: to hire, retain the right people—and make sure they work as a team.

Administrator: to maintain smooth operations as the company grows.

That these are remarkably similar to the five "differences that make the difference" between a good company and a great one should hardly come as a surprise.

So when you find this combination of skills in the founders of a start-up, then you can have much greater confidence in its chances of success.

Develop Your Own Concept . . .

If you want to start your own business, where should you begin?

The first answer to this question is—anywhere.

You could start with a product idea, a manufacturing process, a sales or marketing method—or even a completely different kind of store design.

You could look for a tailwind—a business niche that appears to be about to explode; follow your passion wherever it may lead; jump on a bandwagon—or perhaps you are a highly independent person who hates the idea of having a boss so any of the above will serve (though customers can often be far more demanding "bosses" than any CEO).

Investing on the Ground Floor

One way to get in on the ground floor of a start-up is when you know (or, like Harry Fruehauf, who became 50 percent owner of Burger King, can get to know) the founder(s).

Whether you think you've found a potential stock market flier, or simply a small business that could turn into a cash cow, to have reasonable certainty of making a profit you need to be able to realistically and objectively judge the founders' abilities.

And as a partner in the business in its start-up phase, as one of the founders' "coaches," you can help keep them (and your money) on the right track.

---

*For example, see this Quora discussion: https://www.quora.com/What-is-the-perfect-startup-team.

In other words, when developing the underlying concept of a business, it doesn't matter where you begin.

But come the planning stage, building a *great* business requires a totally different perspective: begin at the end rather than the beginning.

Surprisingly, it's rather like writing a novel.

A great novel requires a great ending, one that leaves you on a high, wishing the story went on for another hundred pages. Best to figure out THE END before you start writing page one.

In business, THE END is a customer experience so compelling that people walk out the door determined to come back.

. . . or Stumble Across the Next Starbucks

Alternatively, you could strike it lucky and follow in the footsteps of Harry Axene and Ray Kroc. Neither developed the original concept for the companies associated with their names: Dairy Queen and McDonald's.

Instead, they literally stumbled over them.

Kroc had his introduction through the McDonald brothers' purchase of eight MultiMixers. Axene's discovery of Dairy Queen was a pure accident.

In 1944, while on a family visit to East Moline, Illinois, Axene, then a farm-equipment salesman for Allis-Chalmers, drove past a store and was intrigued by the long lines of customers he saw. "What are they selling, nylon stockings?" Axene asked his sister, referring to the scarcest product of the war. "No," she replied. "That's Dairy Queen."[3]

The first Dairy Queen opened on 22 June 1940, in Joliet, Illinois, and by summer's end had grossed $4,000 ($54,360 in 2016 dollars!). By 1942, there were eight Dairy Queens. But as materials were diverted into the war effort, the company's expansion ground to a halt.

Impressed by Dairy Queen's popularity and the product, Axene approached the owners and became a partner, later buying nationwide franchising rights.

In November 1946, he presented the profit potential of a Dairy Queen franchise to a group of twenty-six Chicago investors. The clincher was the investors' reaction to samples of the product: they all loved it. He then knew "he had a product that nearly sold itself."[4]

Which it did: *all twenty-six investors were ready to put money on the table* for an exclusive franchise. Some for whole states.

Axene was delighted to accommodate them, selling territories for between $25,000 and $50,000.

The bottom line: Kroc was sold on McDonald's and Axene on Dairy Queen by the customer experience. Both their own, but even more important the behavior of others.

Ultimately, everything revolves around the customer experience. So if you ever stumble across something that blows you away, it may well be worth discovering whether it offers a business or investment opportunity.

For example, while I was staying in Melbourne a few years back, I went to an Italian restaurant for dinner simply because it was right near my hotel.

My meal began with the best Greek salad I have ever had, followed by a pasta dish I had never heard of before that was equally superb. After that I simply had to try their tiramisu.

It was divine.

No question: next time I'm in Melbourne, I'll be back.

When you stumble across a customer experience of this kind, one that sticks in your mind, then you may have discovered a concept that could be the basis of a substantial business.

Creative Copycatting

As we have seen, most highly successful businesses are copycats.

Even when a business is begun with an entirely new concept, it's a lot easier to be like Sam Walton and study and copy what other people are doing than it is to reinvent the wheel.

You can apply this same process when developing your own business concept. Somewhere in the world someone has probably started a business something like the one you are thinking of.

The Internet makes it easy to find out.

You'll inevitably come across some highly unusual, if not weird, ideas that have proven successful. In half an hour I came up with these examples:

Lollypotz: expensive ($40 up to $100+: www.lollypotz.com.au) but beautifully packaged chocolate gifts delivered to your door. A combination of franchised outlets (some of them home businesses) and online ordering.

This Australian company has outlets in New Zealand—and a Web site in Ireland (www.lollypotz.ie) where you can order for delivery in Ireland and the UK.

Leather Doctor: There are actually *two* Leather Doctors: in Australia (www.myleatherdoctor.com.au), a franchised leather-cleaning and leather-restoration service; and in the United States an online store (www.leatherdoctor.com) offering a wide range of leather-cleaning products.

Metal Supermarkets: a Canadian company expanding into the United States (www.metalsupermarkets.com) that offers "Any metal. Any size." Eight thousand different types, shapes, and sizes.

So take heart: if you think your business idea is off-the-wall, there's bound to be a business somewhere in the world that makes your concept seem straitlaced by comparison.

A second way is to copy the *principle* rather than the *business.*

Consider Airbnb.

As at Expedia and Travelocity, at Airbnb you can book rooms pretty much anywhere in the world. Not hotel rooms, but spare rooms in somebody's house, or whole apartments.

This was not a new idea: you could achieve the same aim on classified-ad Web sites such as Craigslist.

But, like eBay, which made it easy to monetize secondhand goods, Airbnb founders Brian Chesky and Joe Gebbia harnessed the network effect to offer travelers more options and enable people to monetize unused space.

And, like eBay, which resulted in thousands of people starting businesses devoted to buying and selling secondhand items, thousands of people now own apartments for the sole purpose of renting them out on Airbnb.

In 2009, a year and a half after Airbnb was founded, Uber came into existence. Like Airbnb, Uber monetizes unused or partially used assets—in this case, automobiles.

Both Airbnb and Uber almost immediately inspired copycats. FlipKey, HomeAway, VacationRentals, and VRBO—of thousands of Airbnb copycats—are the main ones; while Lyft and Grab are Uber's main competitors.

More recently, this same principle has been copycatted to moving (mober.ph—"If you own a van, be a Mober") and package delivery, using travelers as delivery agents (muber.com—"Airbnb for package delivery," which at the time of writing still wasn't off the ground, even though founded in 2013.*)

Whether you develop your own concept, stumble across a winning idea, or copy an existing business, the customer experience remains the key to ultimate success.

So before investing a dime, put on your "customer's hat" and in your imagination walk through the experience you want your customers to have when they buy from you. An experience that will communicate your *vision* and *mission*.

Following this exercise you'll be able to note (and note down!) every aspect of the product and service you want to provide.

Working backward, you can then develop the *system* that will enable you to deliver that customer experience.

---

*And quite possibly will never take off. The concept—using travelers to carry packages for third parties—falls afoul of the question every airline passenger is asked nowadays: "Are you carrying anything for someone else?"

How the McDonald Brothers
Perfected Their System

In 1952, *American Restaurant Magazine* ran a cover story trumpeting the enormous success of the brothers' San Bernardino restaurant.

The result was a flood of inquiries, which led to their first licensing arrangement with a businessman from Phoenix.

The brothers decided to make this new store a model for future McDonald's stores.

On their tennis court at home, they sketched out the kitchen design for the new restaurant. That evening, after their store had closed, the night crew came over and went through the motions of making, assembling, and serving hamburgers, milk shakes, and so on. The brothers followed them, marking the best places to locate all the kitchen equipment.[5]

By 3:00 a.m., they had a design that dramatically improved the efficiency of their Speedee Service System.

When designing *your* business, follow the McDonald brothers' example.

Do more than simply imagine what it would look and feel like. *Literally* walk through it. First, as a customer. Then from the other side of the counter.

Continue working (or, should I say, "walking") through all the steps you'll need to take to turn your initial concept into a reality.

Applying similar "3-D processing" to every aspect of the business, from the underlying concept through vision and mission to the customer experience, and via system, management, and financing, back again, will dramatically improve your chances of success.

Too many new businesses falter or fail through lack of planning—like someone going on a business trip who hops on a plane, wanders around the destination looking for a hotel room, and then starts calling people he wants to meet (only to find they're out of town).

Not something you'd ever do, right?

Planning, booking, and making appointments ahead of time lead to a smooth, successful, and *time-efficient* outcome.

Inevitably, you'll make mistakes. By planning ahead in as much detail as possible, you'll make far fewer mistakes. And be in a much better position to correct the ones you do make.

An alternative travel option is to buy an "off the shelf" travel package with airfare, hotel, sightseeing, and most everything else included. The business equivalent: becoming a franchisee (addressed in the next chapter).

Why Do You Want to Start a Business?

Clarifying your underlying motivation and defining your objectives—two sides of the same coin—can make it far easier to develop your vision, business concept, and even the managerial structure.

Nearly everyone who starts a business does so from one (or both) of two fundamentally different motivations:

1. Fulfilling Your Passion

That's what just about everybody recommends. Indeed, it's hard to find anyone who advises it's better to start a business that you are *not* passionate about.*

No question. There's nothing like doing what you love to do—and getting paid for it.

And as Ray Kroc, Sam Walton, Howard Schultz, John Mackey, Steve Jobs, Warren Buffett, and hundreds of others who've created Fortune 500 companies from nothing have proven, it can be a sure avenue to success.

The disadvantage of following your passion can be that you find it difficult, if not impossible, to delegate key tasks. After all, nobody else can perform them as well as you, right?

This may not prevent you from starting a successful and profitable business, but without the ability to delegate everything, *including* those creative tasks that are so close to your heart—you know, the ones you can always do better—chances are you'll create a one-man band.

2. Follow the Money

An equally (if not more) powerful motivation is money, as the Brazilian model demonstrates (page 90).

When money is your prime objective, it can be far easier to focus on all the requirements of creating a successful business without being married to any specific aspect of it.

Whichever business model you choose, the biggest problem you will face is *you*.

For example, my own management flaw is *delegation*. My first business, an investment newsletter titled *World Money Analyst,* was a one-man show.

I had no problem delegating routine tasks, such as processing orders or updating the mailing list. But when it came to anything to do with writing, whether an issue of the newsletter or marketing materials, the buck stopped with me. I was the bottleneck. The more projects I took on, the slower everything happened.

The business was profitable, but its profitability was far outpaced by other people in the same business who were able to do what I was not: delegate successfully.

After I sold the *World Money Analyst* I teamed up with two friends and we started another newsletter business. One that was far more successful and far

---

*But see www.smallbusinessideasblog.com/passion-business.

more profitable. My delegation problem was no longer a hindrance. All three of us had considerable experience in newsletter publishing, and the division of labor resulted in each of us doing what we were best at.

In the six years I was involved in this partnership, my one-third share of the profits added up to far more money than I'd made in the seventeen years of being a "one-man band."

So if, like me, you find it hard to delegate, find partners or employees whose strengths are your weaknesses, and vice versa.

If delegation is not your weakness, something else is bound to be. Perhaps you're impetuous. Find a partner who needs a lot of convincing before he'll move. If you're focused on the big picture, you need someone who's going to handle the nitty-gritty. And so on.

In a one-man show, you can do everything yourself—except grow really big.

A business can be compared to a financially successful marriage: one person is in charge of making money; the other spouse is in charge of not spending it.

In a partnership, you are no longer in full control; with the right partner (or partners) your deficiency or deficiencies are easily overcome.

Figure out your strengths and weaknesses and find partners or employees who complement your strengths and cover your weaknesses. Otherwise, one day when you feel you're about to hit the big time, those weaknesses will suddenly bite you in the you-know-what.

The Two Kinds of Motivation

The essential character trait for success is total commitment, and that kind of commitment can only come from a powerful motivation.

Types of motivation can be divided into two broad classes:

- Away from

- Toward

For example, if you're motivated by the desire to get out of poverty, what happens when you succeed?

When you've accumulated "enough" money—whether a hundred thousand or a million dollars—then that motivation will no longer drive you.

An "away from" motivation has an expiry date.

Unless you acquired that away-from motivation as the result of a formative experience. For example, in 1944 Nazi Germany occupied Hungary. As a Jew and a teenager, George Soros spent the next twelve months hiding from the Nazis.

Surviving.

Years, and billions of dollars later, Soros admitted he had a "bit of a phobia" about being penniless again. As his son Robert recalled, "He talked all the time about survival. It was pretty confusing considering the way we were living" (overlooking Central Park).[6]

Similarly, a "toward" motivation can also have an expiry date—unless it is effectively unachievable. If you set out to change the world, that's such a large goal that it's unlikely anyone can achieve it in one lifetime.

Clarifying your motivations, dividing them into "away from" and "toward," and determining whether they are perpetual or come with a use-by date, is a powerful exercise.

While a long-term goal can be a continual source of motivation, in the meantime you have to show up at the office every day. Including those days when so much has gone wrong you may begin to doubt that you'll *ever* achieve your ultimate goal.

Getting Paid for Having Fun

Whatever your motivation, if a major source of day-to-day satisfaction comes from the *process*—from what you're *doing*, from the journey rather than the goal—and when it feels like just plain *fun*, then, like Warren Buffett, you'll "tap-dance to work."

The most powerful combination of all is getting paid for having fun, together with powerful "toward" *and* "away from" motivations.

Have the Courage of Your Convictions

You think you've got a great business idea, so you start testing it by seeing what your friends and family think.

Pretty quickly you'll find that they just don't get it. Nearly all their comments are negative. Quite likely, even people who sound supportive, even encouraging, show by their body language that they don't *really* believe it will work.

It's easy to be put off by universal criticism. But it could be a mistake.

Psychologist Nathaniel Branden told the story of meeting a penniless twenty-one-year-old "kid" who'd just arrived in New York.

"What brought you to New York?" Branden asked.

"I'm going to make a million dollars on Wall Street," said the kid.

"You'll never do that."

Obviously, the probability of someone without two dimes to rub together turning them into a million dollars in the stock market is so close to zero it's hardly worth considering.

But it's *not* zero, and before his thirtieth birthday the net worth of this "kid" was seven figures and counting, all made from buying and selling stocks on Wall Street *on his own account.*

From that experience, Branden learned to *never again* cast doubt on anyone's ambitions, no matter how seemingly unrealistic they might be.[7]

Handling Rejection

When almost universally negative, criticism can be highly discouraging. So it's crucial that you resist the possibly overwhelming pressure to give up.

Your family and friends may all be right, but only you, not they, have any real understanding of the opportunity you see. Especially when your concept is only half-formed, so your explanation may come across as half-baked.

Most people aren't business oriented. So asking them to comment on a business idea is rather like a surgeon asking a patient to evaluate a new surgical procedure.

Useless information.

But everyone over the age of three is an expert *customer.* So never ask your friends to comment on your business *idea.* Instead, ask questions *related to the customer experience.*

Here are three possible approaches to experiment with:

1. *Describe the customer experience you have created—and ask for reactions.*

    For this to work, you must first create a description of the customer experience you imagine that's compelling and emotionally involving, so your listeners can visualize and *feel* it.

    Consider the original GoPro camera, which early on was described as "a camera you can wear underwater."

    Put that way, to people who aren't surfers or divers it sounds like a crazy idea.

    As an experiment, I rephrased the slogan as "a Dick Tracy–style camera you strap on your wrist: just point and click—even underwater." When I tested this line on a few friends, most could immediately imagine and *feel* the *experience* of wearing and using it. Though it may not be perfect—"Dick Tracy" does date me somewhat ☺.

    This approach diverts the focus from the *business* to a *product,* making its potential appeal immediately understandable.

2. *Base the customer experience on an existing brand "with this" and / or "without that."*

    For example: "Would you like a café like Starbucks with a dedicated indoor smoking section?"

    Smokers (a totally underserved, even if shrinking, market these days) will love you.

Or, given that thanks to menu bloat, drive-through lines at McDonald's in the United States sometimes go around the block, how about a drive-through McDonald's clone that promises "No waiting!"

3. *Invite family and friends to brainstorm how they could make your concept (or brand X) better.*

This is, perhaps, the simplest approach of all—when properly conducted. And the easiest way is to follow a proven format:

Brainstorming—the Walt Disney Way

Let's say you're thinking of starting a Starbucks clone. To involve people in brainstorming your concept, instead of telling them what you have in mind, ask an open-ended question like "What might make Starbucks better?"

Inevitably, you'll get some weird suggestions. "Baristas in bikinis" was the first one that came up when I tried this with a few friends.

Crazy? Maybe—or maybe not.

What normally happens when someone throws up an off-the-wall idea like that is someone else immediately shoots it down.

That's a mistake: the Critic, especially the loudmouthed one, can shut down everyone else's creative thinking.

Instead, by following Walt Disney's Creative Strategy (see next page) the critic in all of us must wait his turn: *last.* Letting the creative juices flow could lead to something interesting. For example:

"Well, there's Hooters."

"Right. But for a coffee shop? Maybe in resort areas. Florida, Bahamas, Surfers Paradise . . ."

"How about the Hawaiian Café?"

Immediately, we have a different, non-Starbucks image.

"And what would the guys wear? Bikinis, too?"

"Tank tops."

"Hey, no fair! Swimming trunks."

"Maybe the girls could wear sarongs."

And so on.

Is this a marketable concept?

Possibly. But at this stage that question is decidedly *not the point.* In just a few minutes, the question "What might make Starbucks better?" produced a completely different and possibly intriguing idea.*

How many similar concepts could you come up with if you "dreamed" for just one hour?

---

*Turns out this is not an original idea after all: see bikini-baristas.com. So it goes.

The Disney Strategy is a process developed by Robert Dilts, who applied NLP "modeling" to the way Walt Disney went about developing his movies. From concept to product.

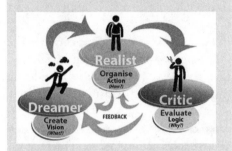

Dreamer: begin by imagining as much as you can about your concept—how it and the product might look, feel, taste, and so on.

Realist: step away from the Dreamer's position and look back at the Dreamer's construct. Your task here is to figure out how it could work.

Critic: step far away so you're looking back at what the Dreamer and the Realist have produced as if you were a third, unrelated person—and tear it apart.

At each stage, you can step back into the previous position(s) to incorporate any necessary adjustments.

Robert Dilts explains the process in more detail at www.nlpu.com/Articles/article7.htm.

Whichever approach you take, asking questions that inspire people to answer from their perspective as a customer *harnesses* their creativity and can get them excitedly involved in refining your original concept.

By comparison, the question "What do you think of this business idea?" invites a person's internal Critic to come to the fore.

Market Research

A final step is to "test" the idea without spending a whole lot of money.

If your idea is in an existing market niche, the process is relatively simple: market research.

As we've noted, the espresso revolution is far from over. So if you have the idea for an upscale coffee café—meaning a $7 instead of $4 latte—then it is easy to discover that several such companies with that same concept are prospering in many different parts of the world.

But what if your idea is something that seems completely different?

Experiment in your target market.

The GoPro camera originated when Nick Woodman, an extreme-sports enthusiast, decided he wanted to be able to show his surfing exploits to his friends.

On an extended surfing vacation, exploring Indonesian and Australian beaches, Woodman used a disposable Kodak camera to test various straps that would hold it to his wrist to make snapping pictures easier. Ideally, almost automatic.

Surrounded by surfers, he presumably received valuable feedback on his concept. On this trip he met his future partner, Brad Schmidt, who focused Woodman's attention on the need for a *durable* camera, one that would survive the pounding of the waves as well as saltwater corrosion.[8]

A "Soft Opening"

Market research and the feedback you get from floating your business idea can provide valuable input to developing and refining your concept. But one crucially important factor is missing: nobody, yet, has actually put money on the table to *buy* what *you* plan to offer.

So before rounding up enough capital to open your first location, you need a *real* market test.

For example, Howard Schultz tested his espresso café concept in a corner of the original Starbucks store. Dairy Queen's developers—John Fremont "Grandpa" McCullough, and his son Alex—tested their soft-serve ice cream in a friend's ice cream store. When they sold over sixteen hundred servings in just two hours, they knew they had a winner.

Trade shows focused on your target market can be a good venue for such a market test. Nick Woodman made the first sales of his GoPro camera at an action-sports trade show in San Diego in September 2004.[9] A market test that proved his concept in spades.

No matter if everybody raves about your business idea, you still need to find a relatively inexpensive way to discover if people are going to part with their hard-earned cash to have it—*from you*.

Financing the Idea

Taking the idea from concept to market requires money. Money that usually has to be raised from investors.

For many start-ups, family, friends, and acquaintances are a second source of debt or equity capital after the founders' own resources.

When Ray Kroc, James McLamore, and Sam Walton started their businesses, the next steps up the "capital ladder" were private bond issues of the kind Harry Sonneborn arranged, finding an "angel investor" such as Burger King's Harry Fruehauf, going public, or selling to a larger corporation.

The Zero-Capital Start-up

The ideal situation is to start a business with *no* capital whatsoever.

Is that possible?

Almost. *Some* capital is always needed, but it can be as little as a few thousand or a few hundred dollars.

That's how I started the investment newsletter that grew into the *World Money Analyst*.

I was writing a book and had completed a section on inflation when a friend of mine suggested we publish that part. Which we did: *Understanding Inflation* was a forty-page mini-book (self-published before there was self-publishing) with an initial order of five thousand copies from my partner. (And I never finished the book.)

I put an ad in the back for an investment newsletter. Twelve people sent in $100 each; suddenly I had $1,200 to start the business.

That's according to Leon Richardson, founder of Magna Industrial (introduced on page 102).

With not enough money, Richardson told me, founders are forced to economize and be creative to stretch the resources they have available. Too often, companies that have "enough" money in their early years spend $2 when $1 would be enough. As a result, when they hit a speed bump, they have neither the resources nor the nous to survive it.

Cash-Flow Financing

Such cash-flow management is a common source of extra financing. It can occur anytime a sale is made *before* the product has to be paid for.

This arrangement enabled Amazon to begin with zero investment in inventory. Ingram, one of America's two biggest book distributors, had a warehouse in Roseburg, Oregon. Amazon opened its doors in nearby Seattle. "When Amazon started, they were able to take a customer's order and money; order and receive the book from Ingram and deliver it to the customer, and then sit on the cash for a while before they had to pay Ingram for the book."[10]

Float

An even better form of cash-flow financing is float. Think of magazine and other subscriptions, Starbucks' and similar loyalty cards, American Express traveler's checks, and insurance of any kind.

What they all have in common is that customers *pay in advance* for the product or service. Until that product is delivered, the company has the use of the money. What's more, the profit from those future sales is already in the bank.

As Warren Buffett describes float in the insurance industry: "If premiums exceed the total of expenses and eventual losses, we register an underwriting profit that adds to the investment income produced from the float. *This combination allows us to enjoy the use of free money—and, better yet, get paid for holding it.*" [Emphasis added.][11]

Those avenues are still open. But over the past forty years, a sea change in the world's capital markets has made it far easier for start-ups to raise money.

Venture Capital

Forty years ago there were no "venture capitalists" sitting on large pools of risk capital searching for the next Big Thing.

Today, with billions of dollars in venture capital funds looking for new small companies that could become big, finding equity capital is much easier. And its ready availability has changed the way businesses grow.

A driving force in the expansion of venture capital was the Internet. Profiting from the "network effect" requires significant risk capital to finance the losses in growing such a business to a "critical *market* mass": the point where the network effect becomes a virtuous positive-feedback circle that will lead to profitability.

The Surge in Risk Capital

In the 1980s, the creation of a new form of risk capital, junk bonds, spurred a surge in leveraged buyouts. By 2012, $498 billion had gone into LBOs.

In the 1990s, an even larger source of risk capital was added to the pool: venture capital.

From 1995 to 2015, a massive $647.8 *billion* (an average of $31.6 billion per year, and *thirteen hundred times* the junk bond/LBO boom) had been invested in thousands of start-ups.

Although kicked off by the Internet boom, this larger pool of capital seeking profitable start-ups has also changed pre-Internet-style bricks-and-mortar

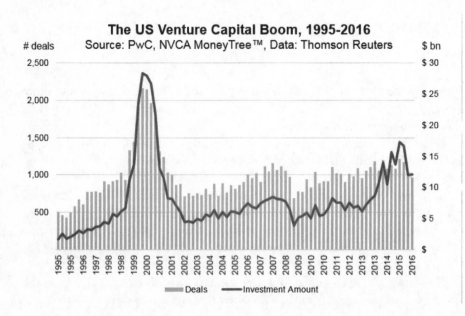

businesses, a change dramatically illustrated by the growth trajectories of Mc-Donald's and Starbucks in their respective start-up phases. Thirty-one years after being founded (Howard Schultz's Starbucks: 1985, as Il Giornale; Ray Kroc's McDonald's: 1954) Starbucks, with over twenty-one thousand stores, was three times bigger than McDonald's, with "only" seventy-five hundred outlets.

The scarcity of risk capital and the difficulty of finding it in the 1950s resulted in McDonald's focusing on the franchising model, thus attracting third parties to put up expansion capital—initially, one store at a time.

By contrast, from the beginning most Starbucks stores were company owned. Not just "at home": while Starbucks more often than not enters foreign markets in a joint venture with a local partner, it will later increase its ownership to 100 percent, as it has done in Japan and China. Or, in countries that have a local-country franchisee, purchase an equity interest—as happened in 2013 when it bought 49 percent of Starbucks Spain.

And Starbucks sources, develops, and manufactures or acquires companies that make most of the products offered and much of the equipment used in its outlets. With mostly company-owned stores, Starbucks doesn't have the conflict of interest that made Ray Kroc decide to completely avoid that practice himself.

In sum, by owning both stores and suppliers, Starbucks required far more capital than McDonald's. Nevertheless, the greater availability of capital enabled the relatively greater capital-hungry Starbucks to grow three times faster:

The greater availability of the risk capital was not the sole cause of Starbucks' faster expansion rate. For one thing, the median American household's disposable

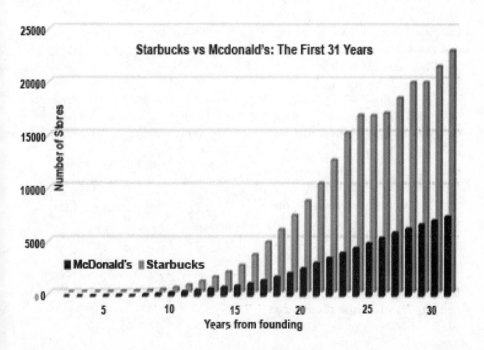

income had almost doubled between the 1950s and '90s. And Starbucks targeted the high end of the market while McDonald's focus was and is remaining low-priced.

On the other hand, when McDonald's started, it was moving into what was essentially a void in the food-service market, while Starbucks faced significantly more competition for consumers' attention.

That said, other recently formed chains such as Chipotle and Pret A Manger have been able to finance their expansion from debt and/or equity markets while spurning the franchising model in favor of wholly owned stores.

Today, the existence of thousands of venture capital funds makes it far easier to raise start-up capital for *any* business concept. But their existence can also dramatically increase the competition every new start-up faces.

Crowdfunding

The advent of crowdfunding takes cash-flow management financing to a new level.

While crowdfunding can be used to offer equity (with severe limits depending on the jurisdiction), the most common model is "rewards funding." In return for providing what is risk capital, you will receive something—when (and *if*) the project takes off.

Usually, the something is the product the company wants to finance.

Pebble Watch turned to crowdfunding when it was unable to raise any further money from venture capital investors. It offered a $150 smartwatch to anyone who

Harnessing the Network Effect

Although our primary focus has been on retailers, exactly the same principles apply to the growth and development of Internet-based ventures that depend for their success on capitalizing on the network effect.

For such a company to become profitable it must first build a critical market mass of customers and suppliers—a size where the network effect takes over to drive further growth.

But how to reach that point?

It's a bit like asking, "Which comes first, the chicken or the egg?"

There are two different formats:

•The Google/Facebook/Twitter model, which depends on building a wide customer base that can be monetized later.

•The eBay/Airbnb/Uber model, where, in order to have customers they must first have suppliers—and in order to have suppliers they must first have customers.

In both models, substantial financing is required to reach the point of profitability. With no guarantee that point will be reached. Twitter, for example, is still losing money—and losing more money—two years after its IPO. Even though its user base is still expanding.

To reach the "profit point," it's necessary to build first, build fast (to keep first mover advantage)—and monetize later.

In either approach, the founders must first build a model that's scalable. One that can be rolled out quickly when the concept reaches a "critical market mass."

put up $115—an effective 23.3 percent discount. The target of $100,000 was reached in just two hours. Six days later it reached a then-record $4.7 million for a Kickstarter campaign, closing out at $10.3 million.[12]

This money enabled the company to produce the product—while at the same time providing the perfect market test that proved the demand was there.

Similarly, M3D raised $3,401,361 from 11,855 backers to produce its Micro 3D printer,[13] while Oculus Rift raised $2.4 million for its virtual-reality head-set—and was later bought by Facebook for $2 billion.[14] Which *all* went to the founders!

A successful crowdfunding results in an injection of risk capital—without giving away a single share of equity.

The key is to reward your funders with a product that gives them value for money—whether that be the specific product under development or, in the case of a retailer, say the right to buy $700 or even $1,000 of merchandise for every $500 in funding.

The Power of Marketing

Marketing and sales are two different (and complementary) sides of the same coin.

At the turn of the twentieth century, the legendary copywriter Claude Hopkins defined advertising as "salesmanship in print." The advent of radio, TV, and the Internet have extended that definition to all forms of broadcasting, but not changed the essence of Hopkins's meaning.

Advertising is a subset of *marketing*: sales at a distance. Marketing is impersonal in the sense that only the potential buyer is present.

Sales, by comparison, is interactive: a one-on-one (or small-group) exchange between the seller and the buyer.

The success of the Whopper in turning around Burger King's fortunes is a stunning testament to the power of marketing.

McDonald's answered the Whopper with the Quarter Pounder and the Big Mac, while Burger Chef introduced the Big Shef. But none of these other names have the same marketing impact as "the Whopper," which suggests a mouthwatering treat even if you don't like hamburgers.

Such is the power of a name that Burger King's CFO, Joshua Kobza, noted that when Burger King returned to France in 2012, after an absence of fifteen years, "They still remember the Whopper. . . . We walked through the airport with Burger King logos on our shirts. The security people asked us, 'Where's the Burger King?'"[15]

Kroc was a salesman. His forte was one-on-one selling, honed from years of visiting kitchens and food-service managers around the United States. In the beginning, McDonald's grew one location at a time through personal contact from Kroc and his associates.

Eventually, as McDonald's grew, it, too, turned to marketing—as every large business must.

Word of Mouth

Ultimately, the most powerful form of marketing is word of mouth. Which results from a highly satisfactory customer experience.

But before word of mouth can become a factor, there must first be customers to spread that word. One way to get those first customers is to harness the power of *marketing*.

For example, after dinner at an exceptionally good Thai restaurant, my friend came up with what we both agreed was a great name for a Thai restaurant: Red Hot Mama's.

A little brainstorming expanded the concept:

with dishes ranging from Medium through Hot—to Nuclear.

And to juice up business on a slow night, how about:

MAMA'S RED HOT CHALLENGE
Blow Your Mind!
Every Tuesday Night
Eat the Mostest of the Hottest and It's on the House

Sound interesting?

Not if you don't like it hot.

Which is part of the idea: telegraphing what your business stands for means you only attract customers who are potential buyers for your product. No one's going to walk into Red Hot Mama's asking, "What kind of food do you serve?"

Every newly opened business is an unknown to consumers. Selecting the right name, one that *includes* your USP (marketing shorthand for "Unique Selling Proposition"), telegraphs what you're about, turns your storefront or Web site into an advertisement that works for you 24/7. At no extra charge.*

But remember: for sales and marketing to result in a long-run payoff—customers who keep coming back for more—it's crucial that the customer experience lives up to the marketing message. Otherwise word of mouth will have a *negative* effect.

It's always best to underpromise and overdeliver.

---

*For more on names and slogans for your business, see Mark Tier, "How I Saved Singapore Airlines (from Making a Big Mistake)," marktier.com/sq.

8 | The Franchise Approach

"About half of all new establishments survive five years or more and about one-third survive ten years or more," reports the American Small Business Administration (SBA).[1]

This is significantly different from the much-touted figures of the up to 95 percent failure rate for small start-ups.

What about failure rates for new franchised outlets?

A lot lower, most people think. After all, the advantage of becoming a franchisee is getting an off-the-shelf business package that includes a proven system, management and other training, employee manuals, marketing, and a product with a proven demand.

So becoming a franchisee sounds like the lowest-risk way to run that business you've dreamed of owning.

But is it?

Comparative data is hard to come by, but a table of defaults on loans from the SBA to *franchisees* is important food for thought for every potential franchisee.*

This data is skewed by the likelihood that people who turn to the SBA for loans have fewer financial resources and may thus be more likely to fail. On the plus side, the highest failure rates are for the lesser-known brands.

While this kind of data can be helpful in making a decision, ultimately it's best to consider a franchise opportu-

Not Failing ≠ Success

Not failing is not the same as succeeding.

Succeeding means your total compensation is equal to—

1. A salary equivalent to your market value, including the long hours you're putting in; *plus,*

2. A return on capital invested equal or greater than putting the same amount in an index fund, bonds, or other no-brainer interest, dividend, or profit opportunity.

Many businesses avoid failure—meaning liquidation or bankruptcy or simply closing down—while paying a below-average return to the founder(s).

---

*See https://opendata.socrata.com/Business/Franchise-Failureby-Brand2011/5qh7-7usu, and sort by failure rate.

nity as both a business *and* an investment opportunity. As such, the selection process is similar to the steps outlined in chapter 6, "Finding the Next Starbucks 'by Walking Around,'" page 95).

With one major difference: as a shareholder in a publically traded company, if something goes wrong, you can dump your shares in a few moments with a single phone call to your broker (or a few clicks).

As a franchisee, you don't have that option. So a cold assessment of the value, integrity, management ability, and market potential of a franchisor is of even greater importance.

And when you're thinking of investing in a franchis*or*, evaluating the company from the perspective of a potential franchisee offers a valuable additional metric on that company's performance.

Indeed, expressing an interest in becoming a franchisee gives you an entrée into gathering some information about the company that is not publically available from existing franchisees or the company itself.

Choosing a Franchisor

When Ray Kroc's McDonald's first began, the failure rate of its stores was exceptionally low. Two reasons:

● McDonald's and its competitors benefited from a tailwind. The automobile and the postwar boom combined to spur the move from city to suburbs, resulting in the demand for new suburban shopping centers. Gas stations, other fast-food restaurants, 7-Elevens and similar stores, plus dozens of other retailers (including Walmart) moved into the low-ranks suburban "greenfields" where being first was a major factor in success (and the rents were low).

● Kroc and his team became experts in picking new locations that would be successful.

Today's "greenfields" are no longer wide-open suburban spaces (except in poor, but fast-developing countries). Pretty much wherever you go these days you'll see one chain store (whether franchised or company owned) after another, covering pretty much every imaginable market segment, with hardly an independent operator in sight.

So today's opportunities are more likely to be found in niche markets and by following new technological trends and changing consumer tastes.

Though not always. According to *Entrepreneur* magazine, Subway, the world's largest chain by number of stores, was America's fastest-growing franchise in the years 2013 and 2014![2]

Regardless, if you want to become a *successful* franchisee, the same principles behind McDonald's early success apply today. The ideal franchisor is one benefiting from a tailwind with a high success rate (preferably 100 percent!) for newly opened outlets.

Location, Location, Location

As with a property investment, three key factors that are a major determinant of success for both franchisor and franchisee in opening a new retail establishment are *location, location,* and *location.*

Not all franchisors have franchisees' success near the top of their list of priorities (see appendix 2, "A Quick Guide to Making Money in the Franchising Business," page 275). So the ideal franchisor is one whose financial incentives are aligned with yours (as a franchisee). That way, you're both in the same financial boat.

While those factors are a good start, much more is involved. You'll find a checklist of major factors in appendix 2, and some helpful links in appendix 4, "Resources."

Your ultimate *aim* is another important factor. If you just want to be your own boss and live comfortably, purchasing or starting a single location of an existing franchise that will provide you with an above-average income can fulfill your desires.

But as a franchisee, you also have the potential of—

A Longer-Term Opportunity

Many people who become a franchisee with one McDonald's, KFC, Burger King, Subway, 7-Eleven, or other chain then add second, third, and even dozens of additional stores, becoming multimillionaires.

Some go much farther.

Dave Thomas, who founded the Wendy's hamburger chain, had his first job at twelve in a restaurant, spent three years in the US army as a mess sergeant, and cut his teeth in the franchising business with Kentucky Fried Chicken.

In 1968, he became a millionaire at age thirty-six when he sold his interest in a multistore KFC franchise for $1.5 million (1.5 million 1968 dollars is about $10.5 million today).

He opened the first Wendy's a year later. The chain grew rapidly and recently (but temporarily, from 2013 to 2015) overtook Burger King as the number two hamburger franchise in the United States.

Country Franchises

But the possibilities in this field are far greater.

For example, Starbucks is now in 72 countries. That means it's *not in 134 others.*

Even McDonald's only operates in 119 countries—so 87 countries and territories are still open for franchising.

The master franchise for one of these countries could turn out to be a gold mine.

Especially a poor but fast-developing one, such as the Philippines—even though the average Filipino's income is a mere 4.9 percent of an American's.

Starbucks' Philippines affiliate opened its first store in 1997. Today, twenty years later, there are 283 outlets, giving it an estimated value somewhere north of $150 million! It's privately held so we don't know the exact numbers, but even if my guesstimate is off $50 million either way, the potential is clear.

Similarly, when McDonald's opened up in India in 1995, Amit Jatia became a 50 percent partner for West and South India. Today, his stake now 100 percent, his franchise is valued at around $900 million.[3]

And if not Starbucks or McDonald's, there are hundreds of copycats—and other product categories—to choose from.

For example, Krispy Kreme operates in just *24* countries—meaning 182 countries are still open for expansion.

When Krispy Kreme opened its first store in Thailand, lines went around the block. Not just for the first few days: it was *six months* before the lines pretty much disappeared.

Stall owners from all over Bangkok bought dozens of boxes of Krispy Kreme doughnuts at a time—which they resold in markets and elsewhere at higher prices.

Franchising— with Venture Capital

Expansion opportunities exist even in highly competitive markets.

For example, in September 2015 Anil Patil, the UK's first Starbucks franchisee, raised £10 million (US$15.3 million) from private-equity firm Connection Capital and the Royal Bank of Scotland to finance sixteen new Starbucks sites, with a hundred planned over the next five years.

http://www.telegraph.co.uk/finance/news-bysector/retailandconsumer/11892030/Starbucks-launches-first-UK-franchise.html

A few more examples of successful international chains that may be candidates for expansion (or copycatting) in the rest of the world are:

Baskin-Robbins (www.baskinrobbins.com). 35 countries; not in 171 countries. USA. Specialty ice cream. Stores in Aruba, Australia, Bahrain, Canada, China, Colombia, Curaçao, Dominican Republic, Ecuador, Egypt, Honduras, India, Indonesia, Japan, Korea, Kuwait, Lebanon, Malaysia, Mexico, Oman, Panama, Portugal, Puerto Rico, Qatar, Russia, Saudi Arabia, Singapore, Spain, Taiwan, Thailand, UAE, UK, USA, Vietnam, and Yemen.

Café Coffee Day (www.cafecoffeeday.com). 4 countries; not in 202 countries. India. Coffee café. 1,438 stores in Austria, Czech Republic, India, and Malaysia.

Crystal Jade (www.crystaljade.com). 11 countries; not in 195 countries. Singapore. An upmarket Chinese restaurant chain. In addition to Crystal Jade (Shanghainese food) it has seven other restaurant brands. 111 stores in China, Hong Kong, India, Indonesia, Japan, Philippines, Singapore, South Korea, Thailand, USA, and Vietnam.

J.CO (www.jcodonuts.com). 4 countries; not in 202 countries. Indonesia. A Krispy Kreme coffee and doughnuts clone—but sweeter. 231 stores in Indonesia, Malaysia, the Philippines, and Singapore.

Kidzania (www.kidzania.com). 20 countries; not in 186 countries. Mexico. A working city scaled to four- to fourteen-year-olds. 20 "kid cities" in Brazil, Chile, Egypt, India, Indonesia, Kuwait, Japan, Malaysia, Mexico, Philippines, Portugal, Qatar, Russia, Saudi Arabia, Singapore, South Korea, Thailand, Turkey, UAE, and UK. Soon to open in Doha, and USA.

Krispy Kreme (www.krispykreme.com). 28 countries; not in 178 countries. USA. Coffee and doughnuts. 1,004 stores in Australia, Bahrain, Bangladesh, Cambodia, Canada, Colombia, Dominican Republic, Iceland, India, Indonesia, Japan, Korea, Kuwait, Malaysia, Mexico, Philippines, Puerto Rico, Qatar, Russia, Saudi Arabia, Singapore, South Africa, Taiwan, Thailand, Turkey, UAE, UK, and USA.

Little Kickers (www.littlekickers.co.uk). 19 countries; not in 187 countries. UK. "Learn through play": a preschool football (soccer) academy. 210 franchises in Australia, Brazil, Canada, Chile, China, Cyprus, Ecuador, England, Hong Kong, Indonesia, Ireland, Malaysia, New Zealand, Peru, Portugal, Saudi Arabia, Scotland, South Africa, and UK.

TWG Tea (www.twgtea.com). 13 countries; not in 193 countries. Singapore. Luxury tea brand. 56 stores in Cambodia, China, Indonesia, Japan, Korea, Malaysia, Philippines, Singapore, Taiwan, Thailand, UK, UAE and Vietnam; products distributed through third parties in Canada and the United States.

These are just a handful of thousands of possibilities. Find more in the links in appendix 4, "Resources," page 281.

Multiple Franchises

Another model is the *multiple franchisee:* a company that holds franchises for a variety of different brands.

The "granddaddy" of this concept is Yum! Brands, which owns Pizza Hut, Kentucky Fried Chicken, Taco Bell, and WingStreet, a chicken-wings chain the company launched in 2003. All WingStreet stores are colocated with Pizza Hut.

However, the giants of this model, at least in terms of the number of brands, are in the rest of the world, especially in countries where foreigners are prohibited from owning retail outlets. For example, consider—

Jollibee's Operating Model

Jollibee—the Philippines' answer to McDonald's—began as a Magnolia ice cream parlor in 1975. In 1978, it switched focus to hot dogs and burgers. Today it has transformed itself into an operator of multiple franchises.

By purchasing other brands and starting its own in addition to Jollibee (a McDonald's copycat, see page 24), the parent company, Jollibee Foods Inc., also owns Mang Inasal (Filipino-style chicken), Greenwich (the Philippines' answer to Shakey's and Pizza Hut), Chowking (Chinese fast food), and Red Ribbon (cakes)—plus the Philippines' franchise for Burger King.

With a total of 2,335 stores in the Philippines, just about anywhere you see a Jollibee you'll see one or more of these other franchises next door. Jollibee's bulk-buying clout gives it the power to negotiate lower prices for everything from property rental to paper cups, menu ingredients, and media buying.

Jollibee's operational model of scaling up through multiple franchises has transformed it into the Philippines' largest franchised-food operator.

The company has taken its operating model worldwide, initially by targeting overseas Filipinos in such markets as Hong Kong, Singapore, Daly City, California, and the Middle East with its domestic brands, and then by purchasing other franchises or entering joint ventures.

Today, its biggest market after the Philippines is China, where it has 422 stores, followed by the USA (86), and Vietnam (72).

From a single store in 1978, it has grown into a $4 billion company with operations in seventeen countries:

Jollibee is now extending its reach through a series of joint ventures, which give the company partial interests in Highlands Coffee (101 stores in Vietnam and the Philippines), Vietnamese restaurant chain Pho 24 (36 stores in Vietnam, Indonesia, Cambodia, Korea, and Australia), plus Hard Rock Cafe franchises in Hong Kong, Macau, and Vietnam, and 12 Hotpot (21 stores in China).

In 2015, Jollibee added Dunkin' Donuts (China) to its brands, in a 60 percent-owned joint venture with a Singapore-based investment firm. Jollibee also announced plans to expand its wholly owned operations into Canada, Indonesia, Japan, Malaysia, and Europe from 2015 to 2017.

Jollibee is far from the only international multifranchise operator. A few other examples:

Australia:
Withers Group: 7-Eleven, Starbucks
Retail Food Group: eleven food brands including Donut King, Pizza Capers, and Gloria Jean's

Canada:
QSR: Burger King, Tim Hortons

Hong Kong:
Jardine Matheson: Pizza Hut, Kentucky Fried Chicken
Maxim's (50 percent owned by Jardine Matheson): Starbucks, plus sixty-four

JOLLIBEE TODAY WHOLLY OWNED		
Country	Brand	Store numbers
Philippines	Burger King*	56
	Chowking	439
	Greenwich	231
	Jollibee	916
	Mang Inasal	460
	Red Ribbon	374
	TOTAL:	**2,476**
Brunei	Jollibee	13
	TOTAL:	**13**
China	Hong Zhuang Yuan 43	42
	San Pin Wang	59
	Yonghe King	321
	TOTAL:	**422**
Hong Kong	Jollibee	1
	TOTAL:	**1**
Kuwait	Chowking	1
	Jollibee	3
	TOTAL:	**4**
Oman	Chowking	2
	TOTAL:	**2**
Qatar	Chowking	4
	Jollibee	3
	TOTAL:	**7**
Saudi Arabia	Jollibee	9
	TOTAL:	**9**
Singapore	Jollibee	2
	TOTAL:	**2**
UAE	Chowking	20
	Jollibee	4
	TOTAL:	**24**
USA	Chowking	19
	Jinja Bar	3
	Jollibee	32
	Red Ribbon	32
	TOTAL:	**86**
Vietnam	Jollibee	72
	TOTAL:	**72**

* Burger King: Country franchise. As of December 2015. Source: Jollibee Annual Report 2016.

locally branded restaurants including twenty-four Chinese, fourteen Western, seven Japanese, and eight fast-food

Philippines:
Global Restaurant Concepts: California Pizza Kitchen, P.F. Chang's, IHOP, Morelli's Gelato, Mad for Garlic, Gyu-Kaku, Ramen Iroha

Singapore:
Osim: Osim, RichLife (China), TWG Tea (70 percent owned); GNC (franchisee for Singapore, Malaysia, Taiwan, Australia)

South Africa:
Taste Holdings: Domino's Pizza, Starbucks

Vietnam:
VTI: Highlands Coffee, Pho 24, Hard Rock Cafe, Emporio Armani Caffè, Meet and Eat, Nineteen 11, Swarovski, Aldo

Franchising: A Two-Way Flow

Most of the world's major franchising chains were "made in America." Their success led to franchising's becoming a big business all around the world. With the result, today, that franchising has become a two-way street, with many foreign-based franchisors expanding into the United States. A few examples:

Australia: *Floral Image* (floralimage.com), corporate flowers. *Cherry Blow Dry Bar* (www.cherryblowdrybar.com).

Belgium: *Le Pain Quotidien* ("daily bread," www.lepainquotidien.com), French café/restaurant.

Canada: *Smoke's Poutinerie* (www.smokespoutinerie.com). Poutine is a Quebec favorite: french fries with toppings. Smoke's is aggressively expanding in the United States, the Middle East (Bahrain, Kuwait, Oman, Qatar, Saudi Arabia, and UAE), and elsewhere.[4]

Japan: *Gyu-Kaku* (www.gyu-kaku.com), Japanese BBQ.

Philippines: *Potato Corner* (www.potatocorner.com.ph, dev.potatocornerusa .com), flavored french fries. Over 550 outlets worldwide, including in Australia, Indonesia, Panama, United Arab Emirates; aggressively expanding in the United States (31 stores, and counting).[5]

Romancing California Pizza Kitchen

Armando "Archie" Rodriguez "fell in love" with California Pizza Kitchen in the early 1990s while working for video-game company Sega in San Francisco and became determined to bring it to the Philippines.

While on vacation in Manila in 1995, he was amazed by the long lines at TGI Fridays.

"That's what drove my quest to acquire CPK," he recalls. Right away, he sent a letter to CPK officials in Los Angeles.

But—as all its US stores were then (and still are) company owned—franchising was not on the company's map at the time. So the answer was "No!"

The following year Rodriguez returned to the Philippines and started an Internet business, which he sold three years later. That was followed by a successful Mexican-themed restaurant and bar chain named Tequila Joe's.

Nevertheless, Rodriguez continued to woo CPK, sending them a business proposal every three months until, in 1998—three years after his first proposal—the American company agreed.

Rodriguez recalls CPK founder Larry Flax's jest when he came for CPK Philippines' tenth anniversary in 2008.

> "We didn't know what the Philippines was, and it was so far away. If something wrong happened, nobody would hear about it," Rodriguez quoted Flax as saying.
>
> In reality, *it was Rodriguez's dogged persistence and lucid business plan that convinced CPK to hand out its first franchise to him.* [Emphasis added.]

Today, though Tequila Joe's has folded, Rodriguez's company has flowered into a seven-brand, multimillion-dollar multifranchise operation that is now set to expand Asia-wide.

As the ancient Chinese divination text the *I Ching* puts it, "Perseverance furthers."

Note: Pret A Manger (http://www.pret.co.uk), the successful British sandwich and coffee chain that is expanding worldwide, whose stores are all company owned, may be a candidate for the Rodriguez Romancing Approach.*

"Reverse Engineering" Niche Markets

Another way to spot a business opportunity is to "reverse engineer" a profitable business in a tiny niche market in another, *smaller* country.

Normally, the flow is the other way around: from larger, richer countries to smaller, poorer ones.

For example, in my teens and twenties, I recall being impressed by ads in American magazines from *Popular Mechanics* to *Scientific American* and *Psychology Today* (okay—and *Playboy*) for hundreds of products and specialized gadgets that were simply not available in Australia.

Such a greater variety of merchandise results from a larger population and/or higher incomes, combined with lower-cost infrastructure, which create smaller and smaller niche markets.

One business to spring from this combination of factors was Sears, Roebuck. Formed in 1886 to sell watches by mail order, by 1896 it was offering a wide

---

*http://business.inqirernet/106789/in-the-restaurant-business-wisdom-is-the-dividend.

range of low-priced merchandise through its catalog to rural farms and villages that had no other convenient access to retail outlets.

What made Sears, Roebuck's success possible was the expansion of railroads plus low-cost delivery thanks to the US Post Office, which made its market nationwide.

Plus, crucially, the market's size.

In 1889, the US population was 61.6 million. Sears, Roebuck's "niche" was eventually 10 million–plus. Sears, along with its competitor Montgomery Ward, became household names.

By comparison, in that same year Australia's population was 3.08 million, spread out over an area similar in size to the US mainland. Even with the same per capita income, Australia (and other smaller countries) could not support the necessary infrastructure to offer a similar niche for a Sears clone to prosper.

Today, more than a century later, not much has changed *(relatively* speaking). Australia's population is 21.6 million compared to 318.9 million for the United States. California alone—with 38.8 million people*—is a market 79 percent bigger than the whole of Australia.

So today, as over a century ago, the United States supports a far wider *range* of niche businesses than smaller countries such as Australia. There is, in economic terms, a greater division (and specialization) of labor and production.

From Niche—to a New Industry

A more recent example, one that started an entirely new industry: the Altair 8800 microcomputer.

Featured on the cover of the January 1975 issue of *Popular Electronics,* the Altair 8800 was $395 as a kit to be put together by the purchaser. Assembled, it cost $498.

It was designed and built by Ed Roberts, president of MITS Incorporated, in a desperate gamble to save his company. MITS was a successful producer of electronic calculators— until Texas Instruments entered the market and, by mid-1974, had cut calculator prices in half, devastating MITS's until-then cash cow.

Roberts needed two hundred sales of the Altair kit to break even. Within three months, four thousand had been sold by mail order, and MITS couldn't keep up with demand.[6]

The operating system for the Altair 8800, Altair BASIC, was written by . . . Bill Gates and Paul Allen, which led to the founding of Microsoft.

*All population figures for 2014.

He was lucky: an entirely new product featured on a magazine cover jump-started sales. Even without that jump start, hobbyists and the advertising media to reach them (such as *Popular Electronics*) made the Altair 8800 a viable niche product.

In the United States, the market's size and reliable, low-cost infrastructure made nationwide delivery economical. No other market at that time could have supported a similar product.

By turning this around and scouring smaller markets for successful niche products, it is possible to find *proven* business opportunities that can be imported from the smaller to the larger country. One example:

UGG Boots

Both Australia and New Zealand claim to have invented "UGG boots." These are boots made from sheepskin, with the wool inside. They are wonderfully warm in winter.

The name was trademarked in Australia and New Zealand, but not elsewhere. The boots were imported to the United States, where they became a trendy item with surfers, mainly in Orange County. Eventually, Deckers Outdoor Corporation bought the importing business and registered the trademark in the United States in 1999, and then in many other countries.

This product came to the attention of the American company as a result of inroads into the US market made by Australian exporters.

Today, thanks to the Internet, it's much easier to find niche businesses like UGG boots that are successful in smaller markets *before* they expand internationally.

There's an important comparison to be made between the Altair 8800 and UGG boots: each resulted from that market's *specialty*.

The Altair 8800 could only have been developed in the United States as, at that time, it was the only place in the world where all the parts and relevant expertise were readily available.

Australia and New Zealand are both major exporters of wool, and UGG boots developed from that specialty. Sheep shearers wrapped sheepskins around their feet to keep them warm and dry; from that beginning, they became a commercial product in the 1930s.

When looking for business opportunities in other countries, focus on the product areas they are best known for.

Another Take on Niche Markets

The United States is not the only market that has the potential to support multiple, tiny niche businesses.

Imagine a business that appeals to just a hundred people per million and can be profitable with just five thousand or so customers.

The following table shows the potential market size for this niche product in eight different countries adjusted (in the right-hand column) for differences in per capita wealth.

	Population (million)	Potential market	
		Market potential (@ 1,000/m)	Wealth adjusted
USA	318.9	31,890	31,890
China	1,357	135,700	29,917
India	1,252	125,200	12,462
Japan	127.3	12,730	8,950
Germany	80.6	8,060	6,515
Brazil	205.1	20,510	5,628
UK	64.1	6,410	4,551
Australia	21.6	2,160	1,706

Intriguingly, only five countries' domestic markets, other than that of the United States, can support our imaginary hundred-per-million product: Germany, Japan, Brazil, China, and India. Though infrastructure costs may force Brazil and India off the list—for the moment.

So another source of business ideas is to search for successful niche products in markets of similar (or smaller) size and wealth to your own.

CHAPTER

9 | Investment Strategies from Buffett to Thiel

Warren Buffett (Berkshire Hathaway) and Peter Thiel (founder of PayPal and the Founders Fund) agree about two things:*

1. That the present value of a business is the discounted present value of the *future* cash that business can generate; and,

2. That the way to profit from that insight is to invest at a price *below* that discounted present value.

From that common insight, their investment strategies diverge into complete opposites.

Buffett is looking for a company with predictable earnings that is available at a good or bargain price (relative to its estimated future cash generation).

Thiel is looking for a company in the start-up phase that has a high probability of generating huge amounts of cash, relative to seed capital, in the future.

These two investment strategies stand at opposite ends of the spectrum of risk: from low (Buffett) to high (Thiel).

Intriguingly, however, these two investors' widely differing approaches have important commonalities.

The most significant is *judging management*. Which, as we've seen in chapter 6 (page 107), is a crucial component of a company that can qualify as "the next Starbucks."

Buffett is seeking companies whose management has a consistent record of generating profits in a business he can understand. His preferred businesses have what he calls a "moat": a unique advantage that makes it difficult for competitors to invade their market. Examples include Nebraska Furniture Mart, with costs and prices so low that competitors simply avoid the Omaha market; and Coca-Cola (Berkshire Hathaway is its largest shareholder), with its impregnable brand name. In both cases, provided management continues to do what it

---

*Whether they agree about anything else I have no idea. But quite possibly not.

has done in the past, both companies should continue to generate consistent profits.

The key to Buffett's approach is to, as he puts it, "make your profit when you buy." That is, purchase at a price lower than the discounted present value of estimated cash generation—with a margin of safety to allow for uncertainty (more about this coming soon).

Similarly, Thiel's approach also depends on judging management. He's looking for a *team* of two to three founders who get along with, complement, and inspire one another and, between them, have the necessary skill sets to develop the business they are planning—a business that makes commercial sense.

And, like Buffett, Thiel is looking for a business with a moat. Or, more accurately, a business that *will* have a moat should it succeed—by being the first mover in an otherwise unserviced market niche.

While Buffett is seeking a business with an established moat, Thiel is looking for one that will *build* a moat by doing something that hasn't been done before. Examples include PayPal itself, Facebook, Uber, and Airbnb.*

When a Great Company Is a Lousy Investment

The corollary, for both Buffett and Thiel, is that a company, no matter how great, is a lousy investment when the current price exceeds the discounted present value of estimated future cash generation.

Cash, then, is the key that unlocks a company's financials. A helpful analogy is to think of a successful business as a perpetual cash machine.†

A Perpetual Cash Machine

Unlike an automobile, which is fueled by gasoline, produces motion and exhaust gases, and eventually wears out, a successful business is fueled by cash—and *reproduces* cash. As a consequence, it can also reproduce itself.

Louis Gerstner on Cash

In 1989, Louis V. Gerstner Jr. (best known for turning around IBM) became CEO of RJR Nabisco, which had just been purchased by Kohlberg Kravis Roberts in a leveraged buyout just before the LBO boom of the 1980s collapsed.

Gerstner's four years as CEO was a race to save the company, loaded with debt,

---

*Which does not prevent Thiel from investing in copycat start-ups. For example, Thiel's Founders Fund is an investor in Lyft, an Uber copycat.
†It's only an analogy: a business is neither perpetual nor a machine.

with interest rates as high as 21 percent, from liquidation. For example, $11 billion of assets were sold in the first year.

In *Who Says Elephants Can't Dance?* Gerstner wrote, "I came away from this experience with a profound appreciation of the importance of cash in corporate performance—'*free cash flow' as the single most important measure of corporate soundness and performance.*" [Emphasis added.][1]

By following the flow of cash through a company's operations, we can zero in on the key metrics that summarize the company's financial story—and point to its financial future.

Operating Profits

Starting at the customer interface, we see the cash inflow from sales, and the cash outflow from the cost of sales.

Those costs include wages, utilities, rent, supplies, maintenance (including renovations, and the replacement of fittings and/or machinery), and the expense of goods sold.

Another operating cost is this location's share of head-office expenses and other overheads. A business with a single location must pay 100 percent of those expenses; in a multilocation business or a company with several subsidiaries, such costs are shared.

When sales revenue exceeds costs, cash is thrown off; but an operating loss means taking money out of the central cash reserve.

Operating profits are a company's "engine," and we can imagine the cash thrown off piling up like this:

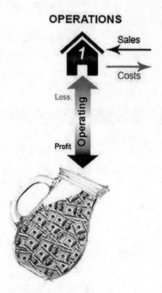

When cash reserves pile up sufficiently, something magical can happen:

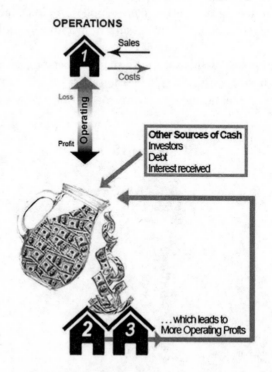

That cash turns into capital and can be invested in expanding the business. So aside from interest received, the expansion, by increasing operating profits, replenishes the cash pile.

(With any luck, we'll need a bigger jug ☺.)

Operating profits are not the only sources of cash. Other possible sources include:

1. *New investors:* selling new shares in the company raises cash—but can dilute the existing shareholders' stake in the business when sold too cheaply.

2. *Debt:* which incurs interest cost.

3. *Cash management:* if all sales are cash only (i.e., no credit) while the company has ninety days to pay its bills, it has the use of that cash in the meantime.

4. *Assets sales:* for example, when a subsidiary or other assets are sold.*

The Hole in the Bucket

To round out this picture, we must also add in the nonoperating expenses and cash outflows that while essential, occur at the head office rather than at the customer interface.

They include interest on debt, head-office expenses and other overheads, dividends and stock buybacks, taxes, and research and development, which can feed back into higher operating profits.

When management is poor, head office expenses can blow out—which is rather like having a hole in the bottom of the jug:

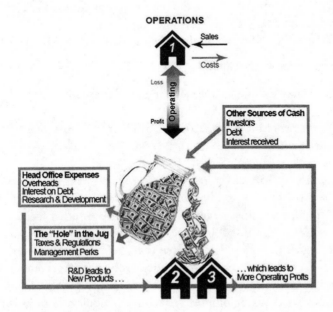

---

*Note that all of these sources of cash can be negative if the company buys back shares (1), repays debt (2), has a low credit rating so it has to buy everything for cash while giving credit to customers (3), or purchases an asset (4).

This simple (but, I would argue, not simplistic) picture of a business leads to a highly significant conclusion:

> ● The higher the operating profits (and the smaller the hole in the bucket), the faster the cash pile grows and the faster the business can expand.

The Virtuous Circle

When a business produces cash surplus to its total running costs, that money is available for other purposes, which can include:

- ● Sitting on it.
- ● Rewarding the managers with executive jets, country-club memberships, substantial bonuses, and other perks.
- ● Takeovers.
- ● Returning it to shareholders through dividends and/or share buybacks.
- ● Investing in expanding the business.

Here, we're primarily interested in the last option.

Assuming we've found a company we're convinced has the capacity to grow substantially—if not forever, at least for the foreseeable future—we need to determine *how fast* and *how profitably* it is likely to expand.

Financially speaking, the potential rate of expansion depends on—

1. How fast the cash piles up.

2. How profitably that cash can be invested in expansion.

The first factor is a result of the second: the higher the return on cash invested, the faster the cash pile will grow.

A virtuous circle.

To illustrate the difference the rate of return makes, consider a business that requires an investment of $1 million to open a new location—whether a retail store, factory, production line, server farm, warehouse, or other facility.

If a new location adds $100,000 (10 percent of investment) per year to the cash pile, without outside financing it will be ten years before a second location can be added. At the other extreme, if the annual rate of return is 50 percent ($500,000), the next location can be opened in just two years.

This chart shows the compounding effect of different rates of growth over a twelve-year period, assuming the return on cash is constant and is all invested in opening new locations:

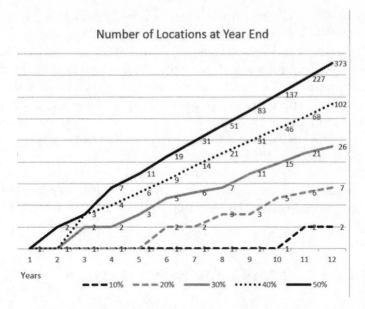

Number of Locations at Year End

As you can see, the differences are stunning, varying between 2 (for the 10 percent return) and 373 (for the 50 percent return) locations at the end of twelve years.

Even more stunning is the valuation of the business at the end of that period:

Rate of return	Number of locations at end of year 12	Annual earnings ($ million)	Value ($m) @ 18 x earnings	Present value ($m), discounted @ 5%
10%	2	$0.20	$3.6	$0.03
20%	7	$1.40	$25.2	$0.19
30%	26	$7.80	$140.4	$1.08
40%	102	$40.80	$734.4	$5.66
50%	373	$186.50	$3,357.0	$25.87

(Before you get too excited, note that these numbers are before tax—a *big* hole in the bucket—which demonstrates the importance of minimizing taxes payable to maximize future growth.)

Buffett vs. Thiel

Clearly, it is far easier for Warren Buffett to estimate future cash generation than it is for Peter Thiel.

The basis for Buffett's projections is "If this goes on . . ." Buffett is measuring the likelihood of past performance continuing into the indefinite future.

The basis for Thiel's projection is a much riskier "If this business succeeds . . ."

Following the Buffett approach, it's possible to put all your eggs in one or two baskets. Thiel's approach requires putting your eggs in many baskets on the assumption that (perhaps) just one or two out of ten of your eggs will hatch.

In between those two extremes is investing in a company with some financial history, such as Starbucks or McDonald's in their first few years, that have the promise of continuing future expansion.

We'll consider in the next chapter how we, as effective novices in the venture capital field, can apply Thiel's approach.

As the financial data for a start-up or a relatively new business can be skimpy, to get a handle on all the necessary financial components we'll first outline the approach to analyzing an investment candidate with a complete financial history.

Measuring Surplus Cash

What I've been calling surplus cash is equivalent to the measure Warren Buffett terms "owner earnings." Both have the same definition: cash-generated surplus to *current* operating requirements—which the owners can do with what they wish.

To figure out owner earnings, we begin with the company's reported earnings.

Then, we add back in the noncash charges in the Profit & Loss statement (P&L) that have been deducted from revenues to arrive at GAAP*-compliant reported earnings.

These noncash items, says Buffett, include "depreciation, depletion, amortization, and certain other noncash charges."

Some of these, being noncash and sometimes pure accounting charges, don't change the "cash pile" that's surplus to current operating costs.

But a running cost that may be included in the depreciation charge is *maintenance*.

Maintenance is the cost of keeping existing facilities in working order—equivalent to the servicing and other expenses (such as replacing worn-out parts) of keeping our car on the road.

In a business, every year something will need replacing or refurbishing. But that "something" will differ from one year to the next.

Just as one year our washing machine goes kaput and we have to buy a new one, while the year before all we had to do was replace a few broken dishes, so annual expenditures on maintenance are "lumpy."

We need to iron out those lumps to arrive at an annual average for such expenditures.

For example, if a company buys a widget maker for $100,000, it must depreciate it in its accounts.

---

*GAAP is short for "generally accepted accounting principles."

If it has a useful life of ten years, the company could use straight-line depreciation and put aside $10,000 every year so that when it must be replaced, the company has that $100,000 in the bank.

In the meantime, that money can be used for something else. Such as expansion.

However, during that ten-year life, the widget maker will from time to time need repairs. And just like your car, the older it gets, the more maintenance will be needed.

Since such expenditures can vary wildly from one year to the next, from the company's accounts we should estimate actual maintenance expenditures for a five- or even ten-year period to determine the annual average.

Say a widget maker will need a total of $10,000 in maintenance, an average of $1,000 a year. Although most of that expense will come toward the end of its life, for simplicity's sake we can assume that $9,000 of that depreciation allowance is available for other purposes—until such a time as the widget maker needs to be replaced.

As an example, from its financials let's calculate—

> ### Warren Buffett on Owner Earnings
>
> Warren Buffett defines *owner earnings* as:
>
> (a) reported earnings,
>
> **plus**
>
> (b) depreciation, depletion, amortization, and certain other noncash charges,
>
> **less**
>
> (c) the average annual amount of capitalized expenditures for plant and equipment, etc., that the business requires to fully maintain its long-term competitive position and its unit volume,
>
> **plus or minus**
>
> (d) changes in working capital.
>
> Our owner-earnings equation does not yield the deceptively precise figures provided by GAAP since (c) must be a guess—and one sometimes very difficult to make. Despite this problem, we consider the owner-earnings figure, not the GAAP figure, to be the relevant item for valuation purposes—both for investors in buying stocks and for managers in buying entire businesses. We agree with Keynes's observation: "I would rather be vaguely right than precisely wrong."
>
> Berkshire Hathaway 1986 "Letter to Shareholders," berkshirehathaway.com/letters/1986.html.

Starbucks' Owner Earnings

Combing through Starbucks' 2014 annual report illustrates the problem of identifying maintenance expenditures from the reported numbers.

In the Consolidated Statement of Earnings (page 24) we find that "Depreciation and Amortization" for the year ending September 2014 totaled $709.6 million.

As this line was not broken down, we have to estimate from other information the portion of that $709.6 million that is amortization, and how much of the remainder is actual maintenance expenditure.

On page 68 is the reported amortization for "Definite-Lived Intangible Assets" for the years 2014, 2013, and 2012. Plus a projection of estimated future amortization expenses. From this information we can estimate an annual amortization charge of approximately $8.5 million.

Presumably, though it's not clear, this section reports all the assets subject to amortization. But as $8.5 million is a mere 1.2 percent of the total, any unreported numbers are effectively immaterial.

That leaves a depreciation total of $701.1 million. How much of this is for current maintenance?

On page 54 we find:

> The portion of depreciation expense related to production and distribution facilities is included in cost of sales including occupancy costs in the consolidated statements of earnings. The costs of repairs and maintenance are expensed when incurred, while expenditures for refurbishments and improvements that significantly add to the productive capacity or extend the useful life of an asset are capitalized.

This implies that most, if not all, maintenance expenditures are expensed as they occur.

Confirmation of this can be found in the Profit & Loss statement, which includes the line "Capital expenditures (*additions* to property, plant and equipment)."

So we can conclude that the entire depreciation expense of $701.1 million is a noncash charge and should be added back in to determine owner earnings. Being conservative, let's deduct 10 percent and use the figure of $630 million, with the same calculation for the previous two years.

($ million)	2014	2013*	2012
Operating earnings (after tax)	$2,068.10	$1,801.10	$1,383.80
Noncash charges added back	$630.00	$558.90	$495.27
Owner earnings	$2,698.10	$2,360.00	$1,879.07
Earnings per share	$2.71	$2.36	$1.79
Owner earnings per share	$3.54	$3.10	$2.43

*Starbucks' actual profit after tax for 2013 was $8.3 million, as it lost a case with Kraft and had to pay a settlement of $2,784.1 million. I have added this back in, adjusted for estimated tax payable, as our focus is the earning power of the business. Provided such a payment does not sink the business, as a onetime event it can be *temporarily* ignored to calculate the business's potential.

When we compare the price-to-owner-earnings ratio with the standard P/E ratio, we can see the considerable difference in actual returns to the owners:

THE DIFFERENCE OWNER EARNINGS MAKE

($ million)	2014	2013	2012
Share price (end September)*	$37.95	$38.70	$24.37
P/E ratio	14.0	16.4	13.6
Price/owner-earnings ratio	10.7	12.5	10.9

*The end of September is the close of Starbucks' fiscal year.

And that Starbucks' owner earnings comfortably exceed its capital expenditure on expansion.

($ million)	2014	2013	2012
Owner earnings	$2,698.10	$2,360.00	$1,879.07
Capital expenditure (expansion)	$856.20	$1,151.20	$1,160.90
Capex as % of owner earnings	31.73%	48.78%	61.78%

Proxies for Owner Earnings

Four easily found metrics—*earnings per share* (EPS), *return on equity* (ROE), *return on capital* (ROC), and *free cash flow*—can also indicate how effectively management is using its capital to produce returns for its owners.

Poor numbers on these metrics will correlate with poor owner earnings.

Good numbers will merit further investigation.

Of these four, the closest to the concept of owner earnings is—

Free cash flow. Unlike owner earnings, free cash flow is a regularly reported financial metric. As you can see from this comparison, free cash flow is a much simpler number to determine:

	Owner earnings		Free cash flow
	Reported earnings		EBIT x (1 – tax rate)
Plus	Depreciation, depletion, amortization, and certain other noncash charges	**Plus**	Depreciation & amortization
Minus	The average annual amount of capitalized expenditures for plant and equipment, etc., that the business requires to fully maintain its long-term competitive position and its unit volume	**Minus**	Capital expenditure
+/-	Changes in working capital	**+/-**	Change in net working capital

There are obvious similarities between the two concepts. But important differences.

Owner earnings is the amount of cash available after paying all the expenses of running the business as is, including all maintenance and other capex.

Thus, owner earnings is cash the owners can take out of the business without disrupting it in any way.

Free cash flow is the amount of money generated by the business that is not required for *operating* expenses *in the current period*. But given that EBIT (earnings *before* interest and taxes) is the starting point, not *all* that cash is really "free."

So when comparing businesses, free cash flow numbers can be used as a quick proxy for owner earnings to screen out poorly performing companies.

Another way to understand the difference is to imagine you receive a bonus or windfall of, say, $10,000.

But your car is reaching its use-by date. So it will have to be replaced in the next six months or so.

If you already have the necessary money in the bank, you can use that $10,000 for anything you like.

That's owner earnings.

But if you were stretched for cash, some or all of that windfall will cover the purchase. In the meantime, you can use that money in any way you like—provided the necessary cash is available when your car runs out of gas.

That's free cash flow.

• Conservative Debt Management

As we've seen (in chapter 6), long-term survival depends on a judicious, conservative debt strategy.

Two numbers give us a fast take on a company's debt strategy.

The first is the *quick ratio,* which is the measure of a company's ability to pay off all current liabilities solely from cash and liquid assets.

Starbucks' quick ratio is 1.01, which means it can pay off all its short-term liabilities and still have a little bit of cash left over.

A second measure that, like the quick ratio, can easily be found on Yahoo! and Google Finance and similar sites is called the *current ratio,* which is current assets divided by current liabilities.

Current assets include cash and cash equivalents, accounts receivable, inventory, and other assets that can be turned into cash in the next twelve months.

Current liabilities—bills, debts, and other obligations that must be paid in the coming twelve months—is the same number as in the quick ratio.

Like the quick ratio, the current ratio is a measure of solvency. Starbucks' current ratio is a healthy 1.37.

To be on the safe side, when making a long-term investment you should prefer a company where both these measures are greater than 1.

That, however, is just a first screen. We also want to know whether a company can comfortably survive the next major recession.

The key to answering that question is to determine a company's ratio of interest to profits.

Here's how Starbucks rates:

	2014
Net earnings	2,068.10
Interest	417.7
Interest cover	4.95

Starbucks' 2014 earnings are a comfortable 4.95 times its annual interest bill. As most of its debt is at a *fixed* rate, its net operating earnings can drop nearly 80 percent without affecting its ability to meet its annual interest bill. A *very* manageable profits-to-interest ratio.

And when we compare the total amount of money it owes to the amount paid in interest, once again the effective interest rate is a manageable 7.62 percent:

	2014
Interest	417.7
Total liabilities	5,479.20
	7.62%

And its long-term debt is carried at a very reasonable average interest rate of 3.6 percent:

$ millions		Rate
2016 notes	$400	0.875%
2017 notes	$550	6.25%
2018 notes	$350	2.00%
2023 note	$750	3.85%
Total	**$2,050**	**3.60%**

In sum, Starbucks' *2014* numbers demonstrate it has been able to generate stunningly high returns on equity and capital with a conservative debt strategy.

But one year's numbers are not enough. We need to look back in time to see whether these ratios show a consistently conservative debt strategy, year after year.

And if we find a company with high earnings per share and return on equity, but low returns on capital, it's a company that's too highly leveraged.

• Sales and Same Store Sales

We can consider many different financial metrics in judging whether we have discovered a growth company. We'll go into more nitty-gritty detail in appendix 3. Here, let's just consider two: *same store sales* and *pricing power*.

Components of sales growth can come from four broadly different categories:

1. Higher unit sales per customer

2. Higher prices

3. New products

4. New outlets

Same store sales for outlets open for more than a year is a closely watched number for retail companies that summarizes the first three of those categories. But this metric by itself is not necessarily predictive of future trends. We need to make a judgment about the second metric:

• Pricing Power

With inflation driving up prices pretty much every year, higher prices for a company's products are not necessarily a good index of its sales growth.

But when same store sales increase with or faster than price hikes, it's an indication that demand for the company's products is relatively price resistant. Otherwise termed pricing power.

When same store sales decrease, or increase less than price rises, it's an indication of a company that may have reached its sales peak.

Here are the numbers from Starbucks' 2014 annual report, which show consistent growth in these metrics, with overall sales growth exceeding price changes:

Fiscal year ended	28 Sept. 2014 (52 weeks)	29 Sept. 2013 (52 weeks)	30 Sept. 2012 (52 weeks)	2 Oct. 2011 (52 weeks)	3 Oct. 2010 (52 weeks)
Percentage change in comparable store sales					
Americas					
Sales growth	6%	7%	8%	8%	7%
Change in transactions	2%	5%	6%	5%	3%
Change in ticket	3%	2%	2%	2%	3%
EMEA					
Sales growth	5%	-%	-%	3%	5%
Change in transactions	3%	2%	-%	3%	6%
Change in ticket	2%	-2%	-%	-%	-1%

China/Asia Pacific					
Sales growth	7%	9%	15%	22%	11%
Change in transactions	6%	7%	11%	20%	9%
Change in ticket	-%	2%	3%	2%	2%
Consolidated					
Sales growth	6%	7%	7%	8%	7%
Change in transactions	3%	5%	6%	6%	4%
Change in ticket	3%	2%	1%	2%	3%

Includes only Starbucks' company-operated stores open thirteen months or longer. For fiscal 2010, comparable store sales percentages were calculated excluding the fifty-third week. Comparable store sales exclude the effect of fluctuations in foreign-currency exchange rates. Source: Starbucks Annual Report, 2014.

Assuming "change in ticket" represents an increase in prices, we can see that overall after-inflation sales growth has been consistently positive:

Sales increase after price rises	3%	5%	6%	6%	4%

These are not precise figures, as we don't know the exact percent of price increases. "Change in ticket" could also include an increase in a number of items purchased per customer. If that is so, the actual after-inflation increase is higher.

Either way, we can reasonably expect positive growth to continue for the immediate future.

The $64,000 Question: What Price to Pay?

As we've noted, a great company can be a lousy investment when you pay too much. The $64,000 question is, how much should you pay to be highly confident of making a profit in the long run?

The answer to that question is a series of estimates that will inevitably differ from one investor to another.

The *idea* is deceptively simple: to buy at a price below a company's "intrinsic value": the discounted present value of a company's future cash generation.

Intrinsic Value

The concept *intrinsic value* was first introduced by Benjamin Graham in his book *Security Analysis* and later refined by Warren Buffett.

A company's intrinsic value, said Graham, is "determined by its earning power."[2] As such, the valuation is not a concrete number such as book value, but an estimate (or even a guesstimate).

But, as Graham puts it:

> The essential point is that security analysis does not seek to determine exactly what is the intrinsic value of a given security. It needs only to establish either that the value is adequate . . . or else that the value is *considerably higher or considerably lower* than the market price. For such purposes an indefinite and approximate measure of the intrinsic value may be sufficient. [Emphasis added.][3]

In *The Intelligent Investor* Graham introduced a formula that has come to be known (mistakenly) as his intrinsic value formula:

IV = EPS x (8.5 + 2g)

where—

IV = intrinsic value

EPS = trailing twelve months' earnings per share (in dollars)

8.5 = the P/E ratio of a stock with 0% growth

g = the projected growth rate for the next seven to ten years (% x 100)

What Graham *actually* said was quite different: "Our study of the various methods [of appraising a growth stock's value] has led us to suggest a foreshortened and quite simple formula . . . which is intended to produce figures fairly close to those resulting from the more refined mathematical methods."[4]

Furthermore, he adds, "Let the reader not be misled into thinking that such projections have any high degree of reliability."[5]

To see how this formula works, let's apply it to Starbucks:

GRAHAM'S PROJECTED *BUSINESS* VALUE FOR STARBUCKS

EPS (December 2015)	$1.89	$1.89	$1.89
g	10%	15%	20%
Intrinsic value (per share in 7–10 years)	$53.87	$72.77	$91.67

These estimates of value compare to Starbucks' stock price of $62.19 at the time of writing.

In the 1960s, Graham revised this formula as follows:

IV = [EPS x (8.5 + 2g) x 4.4] / Y

where—

4.4 = Graham's minimum required rate of return

Y = the chosen discount rate of interest to calculate the present value

This variation produces the *present value* of the intrinsic value estimate.

GRAHAM'S PROJECTED VALUE FOR STARBUCKS (FORMULA 2)

EPS (December 2015)	$1.89	$1.89	$1.89
g	10%	15%	20%
Intrinsic value (per share in 7–10 years)	$55.50	$74.98	$94.46

These projections, using the AAA corporate bond rate of 4.27 percent, are not markedly different from the previous ones.

But if the discount rate were 8 percent, the projected values would be far lower.

GRAHAM'S PROJECTED VALUE FOR STARBUCKS (FORMULA 2)

EPS (December 2015)	$1.89	$1.89	$1.89
g	10%	15%	20%
Intrinsic Value (per share in 7–10 years)	$29.63	$40.02	$50.42

Buffett's Refinement

Warren Buffett's definition of intrinsic value is similarly based on a company's earning power—with a very different focus. Intrinsic value, he writes,

> is an all-important concept that offers the only logical approach to evaluating the relative attractiveness of investments and businesses. Intrinsic value can be defined simply:
>
> *It is the discounted value of the cash that can be taken out of a business during its remaining life.*
>
> The calculation of intrinsic value, though, is not so simple. [Emphasis added.][6]

Quite so. When you consider the variables:

1. The business's remaining life (who knows?).

2. The amount of cash that can be taken out over that unknown time (ditto).

3. The chosen discount rate to calculate the present value of that unknown amount of cash (take your pick).

The concept of intrinsic value *is* useful—indeed, it can be crucial. But it's not set in stone.

A formula or a spreadsheet *always* produces a hard-and-fast number.

Don't be misled by it: it is only as good as the assumptions.

Garbage in, garbage out.

And since those assumptions *have yet to be realized,* that "hard-and-fast number" will inevitably be wide of the eventual mark.

Troll Yahoo! or Google Finance and you may well find listed companies with an intrinsic value significantly less than their market price. But that difference is only worth a damn if you have good reasons to expect that the company's existing management is both capable of and likely to actually *achieve* their growth assumptions in the future.

Without that information—without the "five clues"—the concept of intrinsic value by itself is about as useful as asking how to get from New York to San Francisco and being told, "Thataway" (just hope the guy is pointing west!).

To stretch the analogy: intrinsic value points you in the right direction—when you have a driver who knows how to get where you want to go.

How to Use Intrinsic Value

Whatever method we use to calculate a company's intrinsic value, we should follow Warren Buffett and only do so at the *end* of the analysis.

Having identified a company we would love to own (in all or in part), only then should we consider what price to pay.

This is where intrinsic value comes in.

To make it clear how subjective this estimate can be, let's compare three different computations: Graham's formula (version 2), a more conservative variation of that formula,* and Buffett's present-value calculation of projected future cash generation.

To calculate intrinsic value Buffett's way, we must first project future owner earnings—and then discount them to arrive at their present value.

The owner earnings figure used should be *after* capex, as that expenditure is what is generating the growth.

Assuming owner earnings grow at 20 percent per year, I projected a gross of $88.4 billion of cash that could "fall into" Starbucks' owners' pockets over the next ten years. Discounted at 5 percent per year and rounded down (this is a guesstimate, after all), it's the equivalent of $59.45 per share (in today's dollars).

Here, we have three different calculations of Starbucks' intrinsic value per share, ten years from now, based on three different sets of assumptions, compared to the current market price of $61.75:

Graham's formula	$94.46
Old School Value formula	$46.98
Buffett's projected cash generation	$59.45

---

*The formula used by oldschoolvalue.com (see appendix 4, "Resources," page 281): IV = EPS x (7 + g) x 4.4 / Y.

Which one should we use?

The answer is—none of them is *right*. Indeed, they should all be treated with suspicion.

But, to repeat Graham's point: we only need to establish that a company's intrinsic value is "adequate" or "*considerably higher* or *considerably lower* than the market price. For such purposes an indefinite and approximate measure of the intrinsic value may be sufficient."[7]

Here are two more variable and subjective terms: *adequate* and *considerably*.

The simplest way to allow for the "considerable" number of subjective and variable terms in these projections, any one of which (if not all of them) could turn out to be wrong, is to determine a buy price by first deducting from our chosen estimate of intrinsic value a—

Margin of Safety

In *Security Analysis,* Graham introduced a second concept, *margin of safety,* which he urged every investor (and speculators, too) to include in their calculation of how much to pay for an investment.

Inevitably, every projection about the future will be wrong in some respect (and too often, in all respects).

We are all extremely pleased to be wrong on the upside—except when we sell too early.

Being wrong on the downside is always painful—and not just in the wallet.

To guard against being wrong on the downside, we should subtract an amount—a margin of safety—from our calculation of value.

How much?

That depends on how confident we can be on the accuracy of our estimates.

The fundamental consideration is not the numbers themselves, but the quality of our judgment about whether the current managers are capable of generating such numbers in the future.

The size of our margin of safety should be related to our ability to make such judgments of management. The better our judgment, the lower our margin of safety can be.

For example, imagine that you, I, and Warren Buffett are all looking at the same company. Along with Buffett, we ask the same questions. The primary one being, do I want to buy this company with existing management in place?

Buffett has the great advantage of far more experience than either you or I (indeed, probably more than both of us put together).

My suggestion: be as conservative as possible.

Furthermore, make an extra allowance for hubris. We all tend to overestimate our abilities. Especially when we're a beginner in a particular field. So if you think you're a 7 or 8 on a scale of 10 on judging the quality of management (or any of the other criteria we've been analyzing), reduce your score by at least 1 to 2 or even 3 if you're a raw beginner.

The following chart illustrates the most conservative of the intrinsic value figures, with a 25 percent margin of safety deducted:

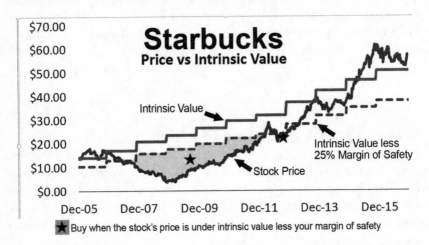

Source: www.oldschoolvalue.com (see appendix 4, "Resources," page 281).

As you can see, Starbucks' stock price was well below *this* calculation of intrinsic value (less margin of safety) for most of the period 2007–2012.

This picture also illustrates my personal preference when it comes to investing: *timing*.

Though generally associated with speculation, I prefer to buy almost solely when prices are depressed. During a recession.

Sure, I miss out on some opportunities. But it certainly makes the calculation of what to pay compared to intrinsic value dead simple.

And sleeping at night is *really* easy.

Invest in the First Mover—or a Copycat?

When a niche is being "blown" by a tailwind, you have a wide variety of ways to profit from the trend: investing in the first mover, a copycat, a franchisee, or a supplier to or a partner of a chain that brings other resources (such as locations and local knowledge) to the party.

Once the first mover has paved the way, copycats spring up left, right, and center. Often—especially when the first mover's stock has run ahead of its value, investing in these copycats can be far more profitable, at a much lower risk.

Consider two coffee companies: Starbucks and Hong Kong's Pacific Coffee. Both are expanding into China.

Say both of them can establish a thousand stores in China, so raising both companies' profits and shareholder value. Which one would make the better investment?

A thousand stores on top of Starbucks' existing 20,366 is an increase of 4.9 percent. For Pacific Coffee, with 150 outlets, another thousand multiplies their total 6.7 times.

Assuming those multiples flow through to the bottom line, you could expect a small rise in Starbucks' stock compared to an eye-popping profit from Pacific Coffee's.

And that follows even if Starbucks' profit per outlet is higher than Pacific Coffee's.

Indeed, if Pacific Coffee opened just 150 new locations, the result could be a double.

Unfortunately for us, a Hong Kong company, Chevalier, made a similar calculation and bought Pacific Coffee in 2005. Five years later, Chinese state-owned China Resources came to the same conclusion and purchased an 80 percent interest from Chevalier. As an operator of forty-four hundred retail stores in China, including hypermarts, China Resources solves one of the problems all retailers have—prime locations—which could give Pacific Coffee a powerful advantage over Starbucks in the Chinese market.

Perhaps that's why another Starbucks competitor, Coffee Bean & Tea Leaf, recently signed a joint-venture agreement with a South Korean conglomerate, E-Land, to roll out seven hundred–plus Coffee Bean stores across China.

With over seven thousand retail outlets in China alone, E-Land, like China Resources, has both the capital and the knowledge to select and establish profitable locations.

Such arrangements are not unusual. Indeed, in France, Starbucks itself recently came to agreements with Casino Restauration (127 hypermarts and 444 supermarkets) and Monoprix (over 300 department stores) to expand its presence in the country.

In sum, opportunities abound, and it can be a mistake to consider just the market leader in a niche.

Speculating vs. Investing

Though our primary focus is finding a long-term investment, this is not the only way we can profit in the markets. We can also take a more speculative approach.

To make the distinction clear, let's define these terms:

Investment: the purchase of an asset we anticipate will produce a stream of consistent or (preferably!) rising revenues, profits, and dividends, which will be reflected in a higher capital value over time.

Speculation: the purchase of an asset we anticipate will rise in value for reasons unrelated to its underlying cash flow, profits, and/or dividends. A few examples:

• *The trend is up.* The Fed is pumping out money, interest rates are falling, business confidence is rising, reflected in rising capital expenditure and consumer spending, and the stock market is skyrocketing as a result. If we expect this to go on for some time, we can profit from the trend—provided we take our profits before the bubble bursts.

• *Hot stocks.* When a market sector is hot—meaning investors are excited about it, or the niche is benefiting from a tailwind—you can ride the momentum.

• *Go short.* As a speculator we can also profit from a falling market by taking a short position. And making leveraged trades with futures or options. Such positions, however, are definitely *not* buy-and-forget investments.

Speculation and investing intersect during a market crash. When stock prices have been hammered, you can buy into great businesses for peanuts or follow the "dart-throwing" investment strategy with your eyes closed: buy pretty much anything with the expectation of selling out at a dramatic profit in the next boom.

Benjamin Graham put the difference far more succinctly: "In the short term, the market is a *voting machine* (speculation); in the long term the market is a *weighing machine* (investment)."

Another way of looking at the distinction is in terms of the preferred exit strategy:

Investment. The time to sell is when the business no longer meets the criteria that led us to buy. For example, if incompetent managers have taken over, competitors are successfully invading the market niche taking away customers, or the company has taken on excess debt or changed in some other way so that this company no longer qualifies as the long-term investment we were looking for.

Speculation. The time to sell is when a predetermined price objective is reached, or the trend we have identified as the power behind this stock's appreciation comes to an end.

A related difference, given that speculation is more uncertain than investing, is that a stop-loss is often advisable in the speculative approach, but rarely when investing.*

Stock prices, % change 2008 to 2015

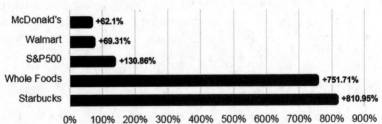

McDonald's	+62.1%
Walmart	+69.31%
S&P500	+130.86%
Whole Foods	+751.71%
Starbucks	+810.95%

0%   100% 200% 300% 400% 500% 600% 700% 800% 900%

The year 2009 was a time to buy pretty much anything that moved. Pictured above: percentage increases from 1 January 2009 to mid-September 2015 for Starbucks, Whole Foods, McDonald's, and Walmart, compared to the S&P 500 Index. Source: Yahoo! Finance.

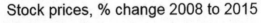

*For more on exit strategies, see chapter 14 of my book *The Winning Investment Habits of Warren Buffett & George Soros.*

Building Your Own Investment Strategy

Achieving above-average profits in the markets requires an investment of your time and money. Time—to develop an investment strategy that works for you, and then to do the necessary research to apply it. And money—to test it.

1. Establish a Benchmark

Here, we'll consider just the first and the last steps of creating your personal investment strategy.*

Step one. Before making an investment of any kind consider the *lowest-risk alternatives*. For example, you could leave your money in the bank, invest in "risk-free" (before inflation) government bonds, high-yielding dividend stocks or corporate bonds, or a low-cost stock market index fund such as those of Vanguard, which will harness the annual average long-term stock market growth of 9 to 11 percent per annum.

None of those options is particularly exciting.

But if it's excitement you want, go skydiving. *Far* less hazardous to your wealth.

Or, with current interest rates, not very rewarding. The upside: you won't *lose* money.

And more important, all of them require little or no investment of *your* time and energy.

Two No-Brainer Investment Strategies That Will Preserve Your Wealth

"Investment Rule #1," says Buffett, "is Never Lose Money.

"Investment Rule #2: Remember Rule #1."

Preservation of capital is always the first priority of every successful investor. Here are two simple strategies that will increase the purchasing power of your wealth over time—slowly, but surely.

The Permanent Portfolio

Developed by Harry Browne, the permanent portfolio is divided into four equal parts: cash (at interest), long-term government bonds, gold, and high-beta stocks.

Once a year, adjust the portfolio back to 25-25-25-25.

The Millionaire Teacher

Could you become a millionaire on a teacher's salary?

Impossible?

Andrew Hallam did—and explains how in his book *Millionaire Teacher*.

In a nutshell: Divide your savings into two parts. One part in an index fund. The other in bonds. The ratio is age dependent: if you're twenty, 20 percent in bonds; if you're sixty, 60 percent in bonds. Adjusted once per year.

For this investment of time and money you should be suitably rewarded by achieving superior returns to what we could call "no-brainer" investment strategies. Ones that require little or no investment of your time in order to receive some, even if minimal, return.*

---

*Are you an Investor, Trader, or Actuary? Discover your Investment Personality at www.marktier.com/ipp.

---

*These steps, their crucial importance, and how they fit into an investor's overall approach, are covered in detail in *The Winning Investment Habits of Warren Buffett & George Soros*. Since building a successful investment strategy is a book-length topic, I refer you to the one I have already written rather than repeat myself here.

As making above-average investment returns requires an investment of time and energy, as well as money, the ultimate question is, can you get higher returns by investing that time and energy in your existing occupation or business—or in the markets?

2. Establish Your Exit Strategy

When George W. Bush invaded Iraq, his father—former president George H. W. Bush—reportedly said, "I hope he has an exit strategy."

As we know, George Jr. didn't, and more than a decade, trillions of dollars, and hundreds of thousands of casualties later, the United States is still buried in a mess even worse than the one when Saddam ruled the country.

In the markets, failure to have an exit strategy is a major reason why investors lose money, even when they have correctly identified a profit opportunity.

An *exit strategy* can be simply defined as the *opposite* of the reason(s) you bought a stock, commodity, or other investment in the first place. So if you bought a stock for its high-dividend yield and one day the company announces it's cutting the dividend, it's time to say good-bye.

10 Buy the "Next Starbucks" at the IPO— or Before

For most of us, our first opportunity to invest in a company has been when it lists on the stock market. At the IPO.

Is this a good time to invest?

The answer is—maybe. It depends on a number of factors, not all of which are predictable.

The number of companies launching themselves onto the stock market varies with the market itself. The higher the market, the more companies IPO.

This makes perfect sense: the company and/or its shareholders are *sellers* of stock, so their aim is to get the best possible price. On this basis—from the *company's* point of view—the ideal IPO is one where the price goes *down* immediately after it lists.

For an investor coming in, that would be the worst possible time to buy.

But (and it's a *big* but), while early investors who want to cash out might be happy, other investors, and the management itself, may have contrary interests.

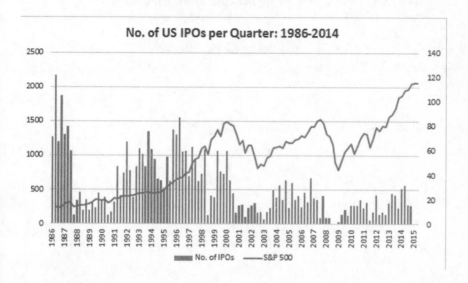

No. of US IPOs per Quarter: 1986-2014

They might prefer an IPO where the price "pops" on the day of issue because:

1. That increases the value of the executives' remaining stockholdings.

2. It can make it easier for the company to raise equity on the next financing round—often on better terms.

Another important constituency prefers a lower-than-optimum issue price:

The underwriters. Who don't want to be stuck with unsold underwater stock after a company lists.

The Mood of the Market

A second major factor is external: market sentiment at the time a company floats.

As the saying goes, a rising tide lifts all boats. So a raging market can be rocket fuel for all stocks, especially those in the hottest space.

But assessing the mood of the market is not always easy.

Consider Facebook and Twitter.

Facebook IPO'd on 18 May 2012 at $38, closed on the day at $38.23—and dropped to $19.69 five months later. On 2 August 2013, more than a whole year later, it recovered to its IPO price—and hasn't looked back since.

Twitter, on the other hand, which IPO'd on 7 November 2014 at $26, opened trading at $45.10, closed the day at $44.90, soared to $73.31 on December 26—and fell ever after.

If you'd just looked at the financials of the two companies, you'd expect the result to be the opposite. Facebook was making money, Twitter was not.

Sooner rather than later, those fundamentals asserted themselves. Today, Facebook's profits and stock price are higher than at the time of the IPO.

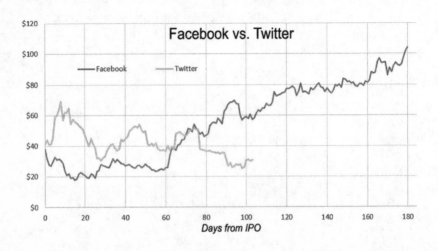

Twitter's losses since the IPO have multiplied *five times*, from $73.1 million to $555.15 million today. Its stock price has followed.

If you'd been able to buy into Facebook at the IPO *at its offering price*, you would have lost money in the days following the IPO. With Twitter, you would have been in the black—for a couple of weeks.

On an intrinsic-value calculation, *neither* company was, at its IPO, priced low enough to be considered a long-term buy-and-forget investment.

Wall Street's Verdict: Facebook's IPO "a Disaster"

When Facebook's stock did *not* zoom a zillion percent on its first day of trading, Wall Street's reaction was neatly summed up by a *CNN Money* article: "Facebook IPO: What the %$#! Happened?"

The IPO was so bad, apparently, that *two years later,* after Facebook's stock had soared, *Fortune* ran an article titled "How Facebook Overcame Its Disastrous IPO."

Disastrous? Really?

When the IPO was first announced, the aim was to offer stock between $28 and $35 a share. The target price was raised from $34 to $38 four days before the IPO. Two days later Facebook announced it was increasing the shares on offer by 25 percent "due to high demand."

On May 18, $16 billion poured into Facebook's (and its investors') coffers, making it the third-biggest IPO in American history (it dropped to fourth place following Alibaba's record-breaking IPO of $25 billion two years later).[1]

Definitely a disaster—especially if you were sitting in Mark Zuckerberg's (suddenly $19 billion) shoes or were one of the investors who took some profits, right?

On the contrary, that Facebook closed its first day of trading a mere 23¢ above its $38 offering price demonstrates that for once, an IPO was perfectly pitched.

Supply equaled demand.

It seems a little strange to me that underwriters should be castigated for doing, with such rare perfection, what they're being paid to do.

Twitter's IPO, according to the same judges of these things, was a standout success. "#WOW! Twitter Soars 73% in IPO," *CNN Money* reported, describing it as a "clean debut."

Never mind that Twitter (unlike Facebook) *needed* that extra money. The additional billion-odd dollars the company would have raised had the offer been perfectly pitched would have covered its losses for the next several years.

Sarcasm aside, Facebook's IPO was "disastrous" for an important Wall Street constituency: the underwriters—who *want* an IPO to be underpriced.

Why?

Normally, the underwriters are committed to taking a certain number of shares on their own account. If they can't sell them to the general public *before* the IPO, they want to be able to sell them afterward.

When a newly issued stock pops on the first day, the underwriters can off-load their excess shares at a profit.

When it doesn't pop, they take a loss. Which is why Facebook's IPO has been termed "disastrous."

A fate underwriters prefer to avoid.

Given that the company's best interests may be in conflict with those of management, early investors who want more than the IPO price, *and* the underwriters, it should come as no surprise that the average first-day return on IPOs is somewhere between 7 percent and 15 percent (with the exception of the dot-com boom, when the average jumped to 65 percent!)[2]—and "the average IPO leaves $9.1 million on the table."[3]

This would suggest that buying in at an IPO can be a profitable strategy. With two "if"s:

1. *If* you can buy in at the *issue* price, *before* the stock lists.

2. And *if* treated as a *speculation* (except when the offering price is below intrinsic value).

While the *average* first-day return may be between 7 percent and 15 percent, that means that some IPOs go up more, while some drop. With any speculative strategy, profits are realized from purchasing a *variety* of offerings, applying an approach that results in *overall* profits exceeding overall losses.

Naturally enough, the mood of the market can be a major determinant of whether a stock soars on day one—and by how much.

An IPO's Story

The path from start-up to IPO follows a typical pattern.

Stage One: The founders put up the initial capital, perhaps with the help of family and friends, and issue the majority of the stock to themselves. That initial funding can be small when the business's concept requires a greater investment of time than money.

Employees with key skills, knowledge, and talents will receive stock or stock options as a means of attracting and keeping them. (This may continue through the various stages.)

Stage Two: When the founders have proven the concept or have a good story to tell, they can approach investors to fund the next stage. If the company was valued at, say, 10¢ a share in Stage One, it will now be valued at 25¢ or 50¢ or more for this financing round.

Stage Three: The product is proven and in development. A further injection of capital is now needed to make the transition from development to production. The valuation is now a dollar or so. Or way more depending on the story, the business's prospects—and the mood of the market for that particular niche.

Stage Four: The product is selling and the early investors are pestering the founders to go public so they can cash in all or part of their profits.

The valuation at the IPO will be significantly higher than the value at Stage Three, enabling *all* investors and option holders to profit, regardless of when they bought in.

Becoming a Venture Capitalist

A major attraction of becoming a venture capitalist oneself is best described by a friend of mine, Larry Abrams, who—when I first met him—was a one-man venture capital fund, specializing in biotech.

When it came to researching this chapter, talking to Larry was at the top of my to-do list.

Today, some fifteen years after we met, we're both a touch longer in the tooth, and Larry told me he's changed his primary focus from biotech to IT and wound down many of his VC activities. Though he remains in the field primarily as a limited partner in a number of VC funds.

"At our age," he explained, "security becomes more important." Another risk, he pointed out, which doesn't apply to a youngster, is that come a certain age you may not live long enough to bank any profits from a business start-up.

How he began is an intriguing story.

While reading prospectuses of a wide variety of IPOs, he saw that some investors had come in at pennies per share while the company was now floating at dollars.

"The idea of coming in at pennies rather than dollars certainly attracted me!"

Second, he noticed that several names cropped up again and again in these prospectuses. Some of those names were of venture capital funds. So he approached them and began investing through them.

Later, he was involved in a number of start-ups, where he funded someone with an idea.

Most of those businesses failed. But, as is typically the case for a successful venture capitalist, profits from the successes far outweighed losses on the failures.

Larry's Criteria for Turning Pennies into Dollars

The key to becoming a successful venture capitalist, he stressed more than once, is to make sure "the odds are in your favor."

Top of his list:

1. *Only buy in at a reasonable valuation.*

   But determining a reasonable valuation, he says, "is art, not science."

   As with Peter Thiel and others, a crucial part of his investigation is judging the management.

2. *You want smart people managing the business*

3. *Who are mentally agile.*

4. *They should be hungry* (desperate to succeed—i.e., PSDs)

5. *And preferably young*—"which, as you may recall, means you have more energy." (Tell me about it.)

6. *They should have the necessary knowledge of and expertise in the business space that is your focus,* plus

7. *Specialized knowledge and expertise* (where applicable).

   For example, if you're looking at a company that intends to unravel the human genome, one or more PhDs in biology are essential.

   But biology has many subdisciplines, so the PhD(s) must be in the right area.

   Unless you, too, are a PhD in the same field, how can you judge whether someone has that specialized knowledge and expertise?

   "I look for experts," says Larry, "and ask their advice." Plus, "researching online is easy these days—as well as often being *monumentally* helpful."

8. *Research the competitive landscape.*

   When you're looking at a start-up, it's imperative to check out the potential competition.

   This can be difficult—except for the IT space, where it is *very* difficult, if not impossible.

   In a capital-intensive area such as retail, it doesn't matter so much if you're looking at a start-up in Los Angeles and come across a similar one in New York or Miami. It will be some years before they become direct competitors—assuming they all succeed.

   IT is very different.

   Say you were evaluating a microcomputer venture back in 1976. Would you have any idea that a couple of kids named Steve Jobs and Steve Wozniak were about to beat you to the market?

   You might have had a chance, as at that time the computer-hobbyist field that spawned Steve Jobs, Steve Wozniak, Bill Gates, Paul Allen, Bill Joy (Sun Microsystems), and others was a small community.

   Today, forget it. You could be looking at the greatest thing since Airbnb or Uber—and have no idea, and no way of finding out, that a couple of "Steves" in a garage somewhere in the United States (or Brazil or India) are a step or two ahead of you.

   That possibility must be allowed for in your entry price.

9. *Your psychological makeup is crucial.*

If you can't stand the thought of losing money eight or nine times out of ten, the venture capital space is simply not for you.

But venture capital investing, says Larry, is *not* gambling.

When you gamble, the odds are against you—the house always wins.

When you understand what you're doing, *and when you ensure the odds are in your favor,* you're not gambling but investing (or, as I would put it, speculating intelligently).

To make sure the odds are in

your favor, you must only buy in at a price that reflects your understanding of the venture. The less you understand, the lower your entry price must be. So you must always be willing to walk away from what otherwise seems a sure thing—if, *in your judgment,* the entry price is too high.

On one point Larry seemingly disagreed with Thiel. "Investing in a one-person start-up is okay—if that person can build the team."

I tested Larry on this point, saying, "What if I came to you with a fantastic business idea—but told you that my major weakness is that I'm hopeless at delegating?"

"If you told me that, I wouldn't invest a dime."

Fair enough, too!

What's more, of the four companies we've been focusing on, only one, Whole Foods, began as a partnership in the traditional sense of the word.

Starbucks, Walmart, and McDonald's were all started by one person. But they all—as we saw in depth with Ray Kroc—built a partnership-style management team.

Other Characteristics of Successful Start-ups

The story that a successful start-up is two dropouts in a garage is a myth.

True, Bill Gates, Steve Jobs, and Mark Zuckerberg (not necessarily with the garage) are all exceptions.

But they're *outliers.*

The characteristics of the *average* founder of a successful start-up are starkly different. Indeed, the average founder is so normal he could be the guy next door:

1. Age: thirty-eight, with sixteen years of work experience (38 percent are over forty!).

2. Education: master's degree (college dropouts are "statistically negligible").

3. He has previously failed and/or worked for a venture capital–backed company. A successful founder who has only ever had one job is rare.[4]

Finally, to quote experienced angel investor Tucker Max: "Both women do better and experienced people do better at starting companies than young men."[5]

Choosing a Venture Capital Fund

Larry points out that the advantage of investing via a venture capital fund is that someone else does all the "heavy lifting" in evaluating a business start-up.

The question then becomes, how competent are the general partners of a fund at evaluating the potential success of a start-up?

To make that evaluation, Larry first evaluates a fund's past successes and failures. "They might have had a fantastic success," he says. "But if that success is just one out of, say, twenty-five, I'll pass."

When a fund makes his first cut, he then researches the general partners' abilities by talking to people he knows in the business; finally meeting them in person before making a final decision on whether to invest with them.

Coming Soon to Your Neighborhood: How Anyone Can Be a Venture Capitalist

Thus far, the possibilities we've been discussing in the venture capital field mainly come with two qualifications that only a minority of investors can meet.

First, you need to have a substantial sum of money in order to invest widely enough to have a chance of profiting one or two times out of ten.

Second, depending on the jurisdiction, you also need to be an "accredited" (US) or a "sophisticated" (UK) investor, which also restricts opportunities to high-net-worth individuals.

That's all changing.

Just as Amazon disrupted the book business, and Uber effectively deregulated the taxi industry (over the objections of both regulators and holders of taxi licenses), so Kickstarter-style crowdfunding sites are beginning to open up opportunities in the equity field so *anyone* can invest in a new business—even before it goes public.

Regulations vary from Singapore, where crowdfunding of any kind is illegal, to the United States—the original home of the crowdfunding concept—where until recently *only* accredited investors could buy into a public offering that is not SEC registered, to Ireland, where there are no specific regulations, so crowdfunding platforms end up being regulated by different authorities—if at all.

Typically, equity crowdfunding falls into the jurisdiction of a country's investment regulators.

At the time of writing, Australian regulators were talking about legalizing equity crowdfunding; China had licensed six such crowdfunding platforms; in Belgium, Israel, Italy, Malaysia, New Zealand, Portugal, Sweden, Switzerland, the United Arab Emirates, the United Kingdom, and the United States, equity crowdfunding is publically available (sometimes with limits); while in Canada the provinces of Ontario and Saskatchewan legalized equity crowdfunding in 2009 and 2013 respectively. Other provinces are expected to follow suit soon.

The general model places limits on the amount of equity a company can raise via crowdfunding, and a limit on the amount a nonaccredited investor may invest. Requirements on the information a company must provide vary from none to a regular prospectus, with audited accounts.

New Zealand offers the freest model. As of 2013, any New Zealand company may raise up to $2 million each year via crowdfunding platforms without having to go through regular prospectus-registering hoops. And the amount an individual can invest is unlimited.

In the United States, the SEC's "Regulation A+," promulgated in 2015, allows companies (which must file a prospectus) to raise up to $50 million from nonaccredited investors, who are limited to investing a maximum of 10 percent of their income or net worth via crowdfunding sites.

Meanwhile, an example from the UK shows us what the future of venture capital will most likely look like.

Chilango's "Burrito Bond"

The loosening of restrictions in the UK enabled Chilango, a small but growing British "fast casual" Mexican restaurant chain, akin to America's Chipotle, to finance its expansion via equity crowdfunding.

They'd been considering debt issues, but the minimum bond requirement of £100,000 was too much of an ask.

Then, in 2014, the regulations changed and the crowdfunding site Crowdcube came up with a new "minibond" product. Chilango was first out of the gate, offering an imaginative, four-year "Burrito Bond," which carried an 8 percent interest rate.

Crowdcube's minimum investment: just £10!

Investors also received two free burritos, while anyone who invested over £10,000 also received a Chilango Black Card, entitling them to a free burrito every week for the duration of the bond.

Launched on June 9, 2014, with a target of £1 million, when the offering closed on August 26, Chilango had raised over £2 million.

> "The beauty of it was that we were able to combine the twenty thousand people a week coming through our restaurants with the seventy-five thousand registered users Crowdcube had at the time," says [cofounder Eric] Partaker. . . .
>
> "The Burrito Bond was as much an exercise in brand-building as it was in fund-raising," says Partaker. "Not only did we have the cash that we needed to grow, but we also had over seven hundred new brand ambassadors promoting Chilango after the campaign ended. I always thought from day one that it would be great if Chilango's growth and success was funded by its guests and fans."[6]

In 2015, Chilango went back to the market with a second Crowdcube offering of £1 million. This time, thanks to a further relaxation of regulations, with an offer of *equity*.

This round also exceeded its target of £1 million for 3 percent of the company, raising £3.4 million from fifteen hundred investors who received 10 percent of the company's equity.

Naturally, such crowdfunding sites open doors for both entrepreneurs and investors.

But whatever the size of an offering, or the portal through which you invest, the fundamental rule remains:

Buyer Beware

The smaller your investment and the farther away you are from a company's management, the more difficult it will probably be for you to judge the quality of the company's—or the intermediary's—management.

And judging the intermediaries is always crucial. *Especially* as there are several other dangers in the crowdfunding/VC space.

Internet Bucket Shops

Old-style bucket shops still exist, often set up offshore with teams of people on the phone (or Skype) smiling and dialing, pumping and dumping some (sometimes nonexistent) stock that's about to go to the moon to people who don't know any better—assuming they know anything at all.

These terms from the pre-Internet days have been updated.

A lot easier to set up a fake crowdfunding site.

No phone bills; no "smilers and dialers" to pay. No stocks to deliver. Just bank all the money.

Whether any such fake sites currently exist I don't know. But you can be sure they soon will.

But you can also be scammed on a reputable crowdfunding site.

In June 2015, the American Federal Trade Commission took its first legal action in a crowdfunding case against Erik Chevalier, who sought money from consumers to produce a board game called the Doom That Came to Atlantic City via a Kickstarter campaign.

Chevalier raised more than $122,000 from 1,246 backers but, according to the FTC's complaint, used most of the funds on unrelated personal expenses such as rent, moving himself to Oregon, personal equipment, and licenses for a different project.

The result: no board game, none of the promised rewards, and no money left for refunds.[7]

You Can Be Screwed

As a minority shareholder, you're not in control.

You can be "recapped."

A start-up's product is promising. But development has taken longer than expected. Thanks to the cost of various tests, retests, and refinements, the company is running short of money.

The management is desperate. So their bargaining power is limited, if not emasculated.

Along comes a venture capital fund willing to bail them out. It's the only one interested. But, they say, "You're close to bankruptcy. The only way we'll come in is if you recap the original investors."

Which basically means that company's equity is recapitalized so the venture capital fund can buy in at a lower price than the original investors paid.

The result: your share of the company is dramatically diluted, possibly to next to nothing.[8]

According to Tucker Max, the majority of venture capital funds *lose money*.[9]

Why?

Imagine you're a partner in a venture capital fund. You've got millions of dollars ready to invest in the Next Whatever.

What if you can't find it? Will you tell your investors, "Well, sorry, this year we just didn't come across any start-ups that met our criteria"?

Maybe one out of a hundred (or a thousand) will have the guts to admit he's "failed."

I say "failed" rather than failed because in reality he hasn't. By walking away he *hasn't lost any money.*

But, like the average mutual fund manager (who also underperforms the market), the VC fund manager is paid for *activity*. No activity means all the fund's money goes away as investors withdraw.

A fund may lose money, but the managers still get their fees. Admittedly, the managers don't get their share of profits. But the way most funds are structured, the *managers do not share in the losses*.

And while there's activity, there are stories to tell that will keep investors' dreams alive. And maybe even attract new ones.

Rule Zero

As Larry points out, you must be psychologically prepared to lose money most of the time in the venture capital space.

But I believe one psychological aspect is even more important, possibly more important than Larry's rule number one: buying in at a reasonable price.

Always be prepared to walk away.

Problem is, your emotions can get in the way.

Great money-raising successes (from the *seller's* point of view) come with a great *story*.

We all love a great story. Which appeals to our emotions, not our intellect. We get sucked in. We do the numbers, and they don't look too hot. But our emotions are in control.

We don't want to miss out. So instead of buying the steak, we fall for the sizzle.

It's really tough to walk away from a great story.

But you can. What's more, you can learn how.

A friend of mine was in New York with his son late one Sunday afternoon. Walking along Forty-seventh Street, he pointed to a camera in a shop window and said to his son: "I'm going to buy *that* camera half-price."

"You'll never do that, Dad."

"Wait and see. And learn."

My friend grew up in Egypt, where bargaining is a way of life.

After an hour of wandering along Forty-seventh Street, stopping in just about every camera store, he got what he wanted at the price he was willing to pay.

He explained to his son, "Even at half price, the store still makes a profit. A small profit, but a profit nonetheless. Tomorrow, they can restock. Still have that camera on display for someone who'll pay full price.

"What's more, most of the owners are Jews, like us. Most Americans don't understand bargaining. They do.

"There are dozens of camera stores on this street. They all know that if they don't sell to me, someone else will bank that profit. Most of them said no. But did you notice that nearly all of them offered me a discount?

"They're all ready to bargain.

"But I'd already fixed my buy price. I wasn't willing to pay a cent more. And it's near closing time. If they don't sell to me, that camera will still be sitting on their shelf tomorrow morning.

"It was just a question of going back and forth. Telling the owner, 'The guy next door offered me thirty percent off.' So he cuts his price to thirty-five percent off. Until one of them comes down to fifty percent."

Another friend of mine did essentially the same thing.

He wanted to buy a house. He decided which part of the city he wanted to live in. Drove around noting every house for sale that looked reasonable and offered the real estate agent 20 percent *less* than the asking price.

Eventually, one seller accepted. One was all my friend needed.

He was from India, another culture where bargaining is a way of life. And the house he bought was in London, where fixed prices are the general rule.

Learning to Walk Away

You can do the same.

Provided your emotions aren't in control.

So if you *really* want that camera with all those bells and whistles (and you aren't from Egypt or India), you won't get a true bargain.

The secret to learning how to walk away is—*choose something you don't want.*

If nobody meets your price, why would you give a damn?

Practice makes permanent.

Repeat a few times with different items until you're ready to apply walking away to something you do want.

Even when you have a lot of bargaining power (i.e., money), you can still be screwed if you can't walk away.

One Last Thing

Remember this:

Whether it's venture capital or anything else, the person who gets the best deal is the one with the most bargaining power.

In the VC space, bargaining power = money.

A lot of big fish are out there, not to mention sharks, with oodles of money to burn.

If you're not one of them, then, as with having sex without a condom, you can all too easily get (investment) AIDS.

11 | Catch—or Create—a Tailwind

The year 1908 was a bad time to be in the buggy-whip business.

That was the year Henry Ford introduced the first Model T.

At the time the United States had at least thirty-eight different makers of what were then called horseless carriages. Not a single one of those brands, with names such as Webb Jay, Chief, Bugmobile, Dixie, and Middleby, exists today.[1]

By the 1950s, the industry had consolidated into the three major manufacturers that still survive—General Motors, Ford, and Chrysler—together with a handful of others, such as Nash, Studebaker, and American Motors, which were either taken over by one of the big three or were liquidated.

This is a common pattern in every new industry. Dozens, if not hundreds, of small players eventually consolidate, as the industry matures, into a handful of major producers.

Businesses that were once big become small or disappear entirely. You can still buy a buggy whip today, but it's now a specialty product.

With twenty-twenty hindsight, we can see that the automobile business benefited from an enormous tailwind, as what was initially an expensive and unreliable toy for the rich became an everyday item that almost everyone can afford. Becoming a necessity.

By implication, a tailwind in one industry becomes a headwind in others.

Like a rising tide that lifts all boats, a tailwind is a combination of factors external to an industry that promote its growth.

Those factors can include rising incomes, population growth, and economic booms. These general economic factors are a precondition for a tailwind; alone, they can only produce a gentle breeze. For example, if disposable incomes are rising at 2 percent a year, *all* industries benefit. Just as in a recession, all industries suffer.

A tailwind can arise in a market niche that is growing as a result of changing consumer tastes, falling prices, and/or technological innovation that results in new products and even totally new industries.

A tailwind can also be created by an entrepreneur who introduces a new product no one realized they needed until he created it. Recent examples include Steve Jobs and the iPod, iPhone, and iPad. And Howard Schultz and Starbucks.

> A lot of times, people don't know what they want until you show it to them.
>
> —Steve Jobs

Especially Starbucks.

Walkmans, phones such as the BlackBerry, and the now-defunct "personal digital assistant," the PalmPilot, all preceded iPods and iPhones.

Even so, Steve Jobs was taking a risk when he introduced the iPod, as there was no external indication that such a product would take off.

When Howard Schultz opened his first Il Giornale, all he had behind him was his intuition, based on his visit to Milan, and his first market test in the corner of a Starbucks store (then just a retailer of coffee beans).

There was certainly no indication in 1987 that espresso would take the United States, let alone the world, by storm. In this sense, Schultz (like Jobs) can be credited with creating a tailwind by awakening a latent consumer demand.

It's often impossible to figure out the precise cause(s) of a tailwind. For example, did Henry Ford create the dramatic increase in demand for automobiles by lowering prices? Was it primarily the result of the 1920s boom? Or a combination of both?

Whatever the causes, Ford can certainly take the credit for turning the automobile into a consumer product. The dramatic growth of automobile production in the 1910s and 1920s was a hallmark of every tailwind: a rate of growth dramatically higher than that of the economy as a whole.

The tailwind that drove the growth of McDonald's and Walmart was a combination of the post–World War II boom, the automobile, and the population shift from city to low-rent suburban greenfields.

The growth of Whole Foods and its clones was driven by changing consumer tastes toward healthier diets—harnessed by John Mackey's attractive marketing of what had formerly been a niche product.

Identifying a company or a market segment that stands to benefit from a tailwind dramatically reduces the investment risk.

But how to spot one before it's obvious to everyone else?

Causes of a Tailwind

Six primary factors, singly or in combination, can cause a tailwind:

Awakening latent consumer demand. Difficult to spot until an entrepreneur has made it happen. But when you see it happen, it's time to consider diving in as quickly as you can.

Changing consumer tastes. A continual source of new business trends.

New technology often creates entirely new industries, along with dozens, if not hundreds, of new business opportunities. As we've noted, the automobile was a major factor behind the growth of McDonald's and Walmart. But the automobile also led to paved roads, suburbs, freeways, the dramatic expansion of oil and steel production, and all the industries associated with those activities.

The Internet continues to produce similar transformations in our lives.

A new form of business. Franchising in the 1950s; monetizing partially used assets as do Airbnb (your spare room) and Uber (your car) and their clones today.

Falling prices. The dramatic fall in the cost of computer memory is the driving force behind the computer and later the smartphone revolutions. This principle can also be harnessed by the *low-cost producer* in an industry. Examples include Walmart, Nebraska Furniture Mart, and no-frills airlines such as JetBlue and Southwest.

Relaxed government regulation led to the dramatic expansion of Southwest Airlines in the United States, and similar growth for newly created budget airlines such as Ryanair and EasyJet across Europe. And as I write these words, this last factor is the cause of—

A Massive Tailwind: The Marijuana Business

The spreading legalization of marijuana is creating entirely new business and investment opportunities.

Given that the black market supply of marijuana is substantial, the question of latent demand hardly arises. The demand is there; everybody knows it; the willingness of people to engage in criminal activity to supply it—and their subsequent wealth—proves it.

Legalization is resulting in an "instant industry" and entirely new business and investment opportunities.

In Colorado, where both medical and recreational use have been legalized, and Canada, where medical use is legal nationwide, hundreds of new enterprises have arisen, as if from nowhere. Just as happened in the early automobile industry. With the difference that thanks to the *proven* market, growth of the marijuana industry is way faster. As *Entrepreneur* magazine reported in its July 2015 issue:

> In the past year, legal cannabis has become the fastest-growing industry in the country. Sales in 2014 totaled $2.7 billion, up a whopping 74 percent from the previous year, according to The ArcView Group, an Oakland, Calif.–based investor network focused on the substance. Their analysts have boldly predicted fourfold growth to nearly $11 billion in sales in the next five years, as the U.S. sees more states easing up on weed laws.[2]

In time, the industry will consolidate into a handful of major manufacturers and, perhaps, a dozen or so McDonald's-style retail chains competing with thousands of independents.

It might seem logical that the major drug companies would be primary candidates for investment in this area. But while medical marijuana remains illegal or, as in the United States, in a gray area, legalized by some states while still banned federally, established companies cannot take the risk.

It is rare for established businesses to be in the forefront of a new industry.

For example, the computer revolution was driven by Microsoft, Apple, Sun, Dell, and other newcomers, while IBM, Digital Equipment, and other existing mainframe manufacturers mostly sat on their thumbs until it was too late.

Only when medical marijuana is fully legalized will major drug companies become involved. But by then the field will be dominated by outsiders, so the most likely way for an established drug company to enter the industry will be through a takeover.

The following table illustrates the growth trajectory of marijuana legalization, as a percentage of the world's population, for the two separate categories of medical and recreational.

Where Marijuana Is Legal					
Medical marijuana			Recreational and medical use		
Year	Country/state	Population (millions)	Year	Country/state	Population (millions)
2016*	Australia	23.30	2012	Spain	46.80
	Bangladesh	156.60	2013	Uruguay	3.40
2001	Canada	35.20		**USA**	
2015	Chile	17.60	2015	Alaska	0.70
2015	Colombia	48.30	2016*	California	38.80
2015	Croatia*	4.25	2012	Colorado	5.40
2013	Finland*	5.44	2016*	Maine	1.30
2015	France*	66.00	2016*	Massachusetts	6.70
	Germany*	80.60	2016*	Nevada	2.80
	Israel*	8.41	1998	Oregon	4.00
2010	Venezuela	30.40	2012	Washington	2.10
	USA				
1998	Alaska	0.70			
2010	Arizona	6.70			
2016#	Arkansas	2.96			
2000	Colorado	5.40			
2012	Connecticut	3.60			
2011	Delaware	0.90			
2016#	Florida	19.60			
2015	Georgia	4.50			
2014	Guam	0.17			
2000	Hawaii	1.40			
2013	Illinois	12.90			

2014	Maryland	6.00			
2008	Michigan	9.90			
2014	Minnesota	5.50			
2004	Montana	1.00			
2013	New Hampshire	1.30			
2010	New Jersey	8.90			
1978	New Mexico	2.10			
2014	New York	8.40			
2016#	North Dakota	0.74			
2010	Northern Mariana Islands	0.05			
2015	Puerto Rico	3.50			
2006	Rhode Island	1.10			
2015	Texas	27.00			
2007	Vermont	0.60			
2011	Washington	7.10			
2010	Washington, DC	0.70			
	TOTAL	618.82		TOTAL	112.00
Percent of world population		8.42%	Percent of world population		1.52%

* Only limited cannabinoid medicines legalized.
\# In November 2016, voters said "yes" to an initiative to legalize medical marijuana.
* In November 2016, voters said "yes" to an initiative to legalize marijuana.

	Coming			Decriminalized	
	Czech Republic**	10.50		Australia	
				Australian Capital Territory	0.39
				Northern Territory	1.70
				South Australia	1.67
			2009	Argentina	41.45
			2001	Portugal	10.46
			2007	Chile	17.60
			2008	Ecuador	15.74
			2003	Belgium	11.20
				Bolivia	10.67
				Cambodia	15.14
			2005	Chile	17.62
			1994	Colombia	48.32
				Costa Rica	4.87

				2013	Czech Republic	10.50
					Estonia	1.33
					Germany	80.60
				2011	Greece	11.03
				1985	India	1,000.20
				Proposed	Ireland	6.47
				2015	Jamaica	2.70
				2015	Jordan	6.45
				2009	Mexico	122.30
				1976	Netherlands	16.80
				2014	Peru	30.38
				2003	Russia	143.50
				2015	Spain	46.77
				2003	Ukraine	45.49
TOTAL	10.5				TOTAL	1,721.35
Percent of world population	0.14%			Percent of world population		23.42%
** Legalized in 2013, but not yet implemented						
				Legalization proposed		
					Canada	35.2
					TOTAL	35.20
				Percent of world population		0.48%
GRAND TOTAL	629.32			GRAND TOTAL		1,868.55
Percent of world population	8.56%			Percent of world population		25.42%

The table includes only countries, states, or territories where medical or recreational (which includes medical) use is *legal*. And where the marijuana *business* is also legal. Marijuana use in North Korea is reportedly legal—but doing business (of any kind) is not, so this country is not included.

Many countries have *decriminalized* marijuana use, The Netherlands and Portugal being the most notable examples. Decriminalization usually means no one is prosecuted for owning a small amount of marijuana for personal use, but it remains a crime to grow, trade, and/or sell it. If these countries eventually move to full legalization, the potential growth of the market for recreational marijuana use would grow to one-quarter of the world's population.

It would seem only a matter of time before these countries make the logical move from decriminalization to legalization. But logic, especially in politics, doesn't always apply.

The irony is that the country that's *leading* marijuana legalization is the same country that's the "general" leading the worldwide War on Drugs.

The United States.

While the federal government staunchly opposes legalization, state governments are moving in the opposite direction.

The most likely scenario is a rerun of what happened when alcohol prohibition was repealed in 1933. A patchwork of "wet" and "dry" states (and even towns and counties within states).

Eventually, pushed by the states, the federal government will end the War on Drugs. Well, at least the War on Marijuana. The first step has already been taken: in December 2015, Congress passed a bill that aims to prevent the Department of Justice from applying federal law to marijuana producers and retailers in states where medical or recreational use is legal, by denying funding for any such actions.

Once Washington folds, legalization worldwide is likely to follow rapidly.

Established companies ready to scale up rapidly when that occurs will provide enormous returns to investors.

Other market segments currently benefiting from tailwinds include:

Upmarket and luxury brands. Increasing wealth and purchasing power lead to higher demand for luxury products—and more conspicuous consumption.

Consolidation and branding. A mature market with hundreds of competitors offers the opportunity of *consolidation* and *branding*.

One example is Berkshire Hathaway Home Services, a real estate brokerage that has expanded into twenty-five US states to date, by purchasing dozens of smaller companies.

Services. Ironically, as wealth and wages rise, time becomes more precious.

A hundred years ago, maids and other servants were regular features of the wealthier American household.

Today, only the very rich can afford such modern luxuries.

The services such servants performed have been replaced by automation (washing machines, dishwashers, and the like) and by companies offering services such as housecleaning, gardening, repairs, and so forth.

Online businesses are going to generate tailwinds for many years to come.

Demographics. Worldwide, birthrates are falling and life expectancy is increasing. The consequence of this demographic shift to an aging population is an increasing demand for health care and health products, while in countries such as Japan, where this trend is most marked, primary schools and other products and services for children are in decline.

Biotech. Related, but not limited to the over-sixty-fives, will be the growing demand for life-extension products, more highly targeted drugs, and new techniques to counter the growing number of antibiotic-resistant diseases including, quite possibly, "antivirus" viruses and other similar possibilities developing from genetic research only found, to date, in science fiction stories.

Outsourcing. Initially used by corporations as lower-cost ways of answering the phone and handling back-office processing, outsourcing now—thanks to the Internet—reaches down to the tiniest of businesses.

One example of thousands: an Australian accountant I know hired a qualified accountant in Indonesia to do all his bookkeeping work.

Until wage rates equalize around the world, outsourcing will continue to be a growing industry—while, simultaneously, producing a double-barreled wealth effect:

● In poorer countries, rates paid to call-center and outsourced back-office employees raise wage rates, resulting in increased spending power.

● In richer countries, the lower costs paid for the same work contribute to falling consumer prices and/or more spending on other products and services.

Globalization—shorthand for the combination of falling trade barriers, increased capital flows, and the leveling effect of outsourcing—will continue to generate faster rates of growth in the world's poorer countries, so increasing demand for products and services from McDonald's and Starbucks to iPhones, power generators, and pretty much everything else most Westerners take for granted.

Subsidized sectors. From growing sugar, making weapons, growing corn for ethanol, to wind and solar power, a wide variety of businesses are government subsidized through regulation, tariff walls, tax breaks, production quotas, or direct payment.

But any business that requires subsidies, tax breaks, or tariff walls to prosper can be an iffy *long-term* proposition. Its continued prosperity depends on the industry's having an influential voting bloc combined with a powerful lobby in Washington. In the United States, farmers in general and the sugar industry in particular are heavily subsidized. Current growth industries such as ethanol production and wind- and solar-power generation would barely exist without massive tax breaks and other government-sourced benefits.

Any change in such government policies would inevitably result in a collapse of businesses in these sectors.

In sum, potentially thousands of possible investment and business tailwinds are waiting to be created—or unearthed.

12 | Finding the Next Tailwind to Ride

The ideal long-term buy-and-pretty-much-forget investment is a company practicing all the five clues that is also being pushed by a tailwind.

Finding that combination is not easy.

But it can be done, even if you are not able to travel around the world to investigate all (or even some) of the various opportunities and possibilities in person.

Remember, in the markets what everybody knows is of little or no value. Big profits are rarely made by following the crowd. Investors who do their own research and discover what nobody else knows are the ones who clean up.

So when you come across an opportunity that nobody else knows about, follow in the footsteps of the world's most successful investors: keep your mouth shut and buy.

Now, let's investigate the possibilities in three niches that (with the exception of the first) I, personally, have little or no experience of. I trust these examples will inspire you to undertake your own investigations.

Those three areas are:

● *Education.* The world's most heavily regulated industry. A space ripe not just for disruption, which is beginning (at the edges), but for a total revolution. Is it possible to come up with a profitable business idea that could spark the deregulation of education—around the world?

● *Tea.* Second only to water in popularity. A space that has (at the moment) no equivalent of Starbucks or McDonald's.

● *"Fast casual."* A recent almost-fast-food trend, originating in the United States. And within that category, specifically Mexican fast casual, led by the fast-growing American chain Chipotle.

Education vs. Learning

Major tailwinds can arise through the disruption of heavily regulated industries. As proven by Uber, which upended the taxi business; Skype, which decimated the world's phone monopolies' high-priced international and long-distance call revenues; and e-mail, which has all but destroyed post offices' first-class and junk-mail business.*

None of these competitors were licensed to compete against the government-regulated or government-owned monopolies.

By the time the regulators woke up to what was happening, it was too late.

In *every* country, education is the most heavily regulated industry of all.

Is there a similar opportunity in the education space?

To find out, let's unpack education, as it is today, into its various subcomponents. Then we'll be able to see if we can discover a disruptive opportunity. One that can also generate a profitable, Uber-style business model.

Why We Went to School

As children, we didn't really have much say in the matter.

But after an initial period of disorientation—the anxiety that can come from being separated from our mother and father for the first time—most of us looked forward to going to school every day.

If not school itself, seeing our friends.

We also became proud of our accomplishments†—but discouraged when we received low marks or failed a subject.

Nevertheless, school and college have become modern coming-of-age rituals, final graduation being proof of the completed transition from childhood to adulthood.

Whatever our experience while at school, we were there for reasons that were not only out of our control, but mostly out of our parents' control as well:

> ● *It's compulsory* in almost every country. So our parents didn't have much say in the matter, either.

> ● *To learn.* Our parents probably chose the best school they could afford on the expectation that we would learn more and learn it better.

> ● *Certification.* The progression from primary school to high school to university or college results in a series of certificates that most people believe enable us to be more financially successful adults.

---

*And when was the last time you sent a fax—or a telegram!?

†For example, I can still feel the pride I felt when, in primary school, I was taken from first grade directly into third grade.

● *Child minding.* For some parents, having their children looked after for most of the day is a great boon. Enabling both parents to have an income.

● *Indoctrination.* It's natural to want to pass our beliefs on to our children. So many of us select a school for our children that reflects our religious or secular beliefs. In some countries, the government curriculum mandates various courses aimed to foster certain beliefs and traits such as national pride, good citizenship, and/or other values the politicians or the education bureaucracy deem to be essential. Or beneficial (usually to them rather than the kids).

● *Because everybody else does.* Few parents try to create a different learning environment for their children to that offered by schools. Or even consider the possibility. Even in the United States, which has the loosest regulatory environment of any country, only 4 percent of children are homeschooled.

Most people equate education with learning. But as you can see from this list so far, learning may not be the primary goal of education.

To see why this could be the case, let's consider two periods of everybody's life: before school, and after school or university.

Every Child Is a "Learning Machine"

What do you think are the two most powerful and enduring learning experiences of your life?

These are two skills you learned entirely on your own.

They are two activities you engage in every day.

Let me put the question another way: Who taught you to walk and to talk?

Sure, you may have had a little bit of help. But basically—unless you had a genuine learning disability such as being crippled or mute—your only teacher was yourself.

Every child is born insatiably curious.

Aside from wanting to walk and talk like everybody else, children also want to know *why* about *everything.*

They ask "Why?" so often it eventually drives most adults crazy.

Then they go to school. Where, unless a particular subject interests them, or they're lucky enough to have an inspiring teacher, they zone out.

Meanwhile, *out* of school they continue to learn all sorts of interesting (to them) other noncertificate stuff. From shooting hoops to programming Dad's computer.

Education, Learning, and the Real World

When we "graduate" into the real world, we revert to our preschool method of learning. Learning something because we want to or need to.

A friend of mine—let's call him George—graduated from university with a degree in economics. He landed a job at BHP, the big Australian mining company. As part of his job, George had to learn about metallurgy. Hardly surprising given the nature of his employer.

Eighteen months later, his boss commented that George knew more about metallurgy than anyone he knew with a degree in that subject.

On-the-job training. Nothing surprising about that. Except that George had acquired *more* metallurgical knowledge than a university graduate in that subject, in half the time—all while doing his job, as well.

And his economics degree?

Never used it.

Your experience may not be as extreme. But, like George (and me), you spent twelve to sixteen or even eighteen years of your life at school and university "learning" stuff.

● How much of what you were taught do you use today?

● How much of what you were taught did you have to *unlearn* when you entered the real world?

I have yet to ask someone those questions and receive "everything" and "nothing" in reply.

This is true even for graduates with professional degrees in such fields as medicine, law, finance, and teaching, where you'd expect the program to be highly targeted.

A teacher told me she had to unlearn everything she'd been taught about how to handle students in the classroom after she'd graduated into the real world. While a finance graduate, who today is a successful investor, said the only things he brought from college into the real world were the accounting basics needed to analyze company balance sheets and profit-and-loss statements.

All I retain today from my eleven years in primary and high school are reading, writing, and arithmetic. Plus some higher math that I use occasionally.

I passed French—but I can't speak it, though I can read it (if it's simple enough). Even on my occasional visits to France, this poorly mastered skill has been of little use to me.

Years of wasted time.

I have a university degree in economics—but when I got into the real world, I had to unlearn almost everything I had been taught.

Looking back, I realize the only truly useful skill I acquired at university was the ability to do effective research in the library and elsewhere.

I also became pretty good at billiards.

Far more significant than anything else: as editor of the student paper I was introduced to the publishing business, where I've been ever since.

This *extracurricular* learning experience was my greatest takeaway from all the years I spent at university.

But I've yet to receive a piece of paper "qualifying" me in this field! (Unless you count all that green stuff.)

Use It or Lose It

The ultimate test of whether you've had a real learning experience is whether you use it.

Because if you don't use it, you lose it.

Once upon a time, I could solve complicated mathematical problems in my head. Quickly.

Today I can't.

I've been using calculators and spreadsheets for so long, that ability has disappeared from lack of use.

Sure, we didn't spend all those years sitting in class and learn nothing.

Obviously we absorbed enough to pass our final exams and get that all-important graduation certificate.

But how much did we *retain*?

One of my high school classmates defined "education" succinctly:

"All year you cram your head full of stuff—and then spew it out over the exam paper. And it's gone."

Studying for exams isn't called cramming without good reason.

So most of what we "learned" in school and college we used to pass the certification exam—and we then promptly began to forget it.

When judged by what is useful in the real world, education is clearly a highly inefficient industry. Perhaps the most inefficient industry on earth.

An industry ripe for disruption.

The Regulatory Environment

Education as we know it is a product of the regulatory environment.

This environment is based on two misconceptions:

1. To learn something, you need to go to school.

2. To be certified, you need to go to school.

Here we have the springboard for the disruptive business opportunity we're looking for.

Decoupling Certification from Education

The key first step to an "education revolution" is, I believe, to decouple certification from education.

To do that successfully (and profitably) it's best to focus on the certificate that is most universally desired, and the most portable worldwide: the high school diploma.

Can you get a high school graduation certificate without going to school?

In the United States, the answer is yes.

In most other countries, the answer is no.

Graduation certificates come in two "flavors":

- Passing an exam (or series of exams).

- Passing exams, plus a variety of other requirements depending on the jurisdiction.

In certain states of the United States, passing an exam plus having someone (whether a parent, a teacher, or a school) certify that you have spent a certain number of hours studying the subject are all that is necessary to gain a high school graduation certificate.

A certificate that will be recognized as a college-entry ticket in almost every other country of the world.

By contrast, many other countries have a host of additional requirements. From the general (certain subjects must be taught to a specified standard) to the rigid (it's 10:00 a.m. on a Thursday and you're nine years old so it's math).

The fundamental similarity is that in addition to passing the exit exam, you must have proof that you sat in a classroom for the previous twelve-odd years.

The SAT Model

In most countries, the ticket to university is a high school graduation certificate.

But not in the United States. The only exam you need to pass is the SAT.

Anyone can take this exam, from anywhere in the world. The *only* qualification required: the ability to pay the necessary fee.

That's it.

If we apply the SAT model to *high school,* we can decouple certification from education.

Here's how:

1. *Go jurisdiction shopping.* Set up shop in the country, state, province, or city that has the fewest government edicts specifying what you *can't* do.

In the education space, the freest jurisdiction is probably an American state in the New England region.

2. *Duplicate the SAT model* by creating a series of exams that qualify for the high school graduation certificate in that jurisdiction. Or even simpler: team up with an existing high school.

3. *Offer those exams worldwide.* Online would be ideal, but cheating is an inevitable problem.

And it's crucial that everything be kosher. To avoid gaining a reputation as a "degree mill," it would be essential to offer *physical* exams all over the world.

This may sound like a logistical nightmare—but that's exactly how the SAT works. The logistical trail has already been blazed.

There are two simple ways to duplicate the SAT model:

1. Hire the **Educational Testing Service** to hold the exams. The ETS is in the business of creating and holding exams around the world for, among others, the **College Board**, the creator of the SAT.

2. A little more difficult but not impossible: find out where the ETS holds its exams and make an arrangement with the local suppliers.

Where's the Market Potential?

It's fourfold.

1. *In the United States:*

Students, such as homeschoolers, who would like to have an official graduation certificate. And students in the more highly regulated states who wish to accelerate their graduation from high school.

While not necessary to attend college in the United States, a certificate may be an advantage for a student who intends to study abroad.

In other words, the *primary* market is not the United States. It's the rest of the world.

2. *Foreign students who want to study in the United States (or other Western countries):*

The American credential is recognized everywhere. The same cannot be said of high school graduation certificates offered in many third-world countries.

3. *Foreign (and American) students who want to circumvent local schooling requirements:*

Any third-, fourth-, or fifth-grade student who is able to pass the American exam may be able to accelerate his or her graduation from school to college by a year or more.

For example, most Philippine colleges have three entry requirements: an admission exam, an aptitude test related to the specific course being applied for, and an interview.

The foreign credential gives what's called "a backdoor entry": you can skip the admission exam entirely.

On the same basis, there'll be a demand within the United States from high school students who wish to get out of school early.

4. *Foreign private schools:*

Initially, the largest and the most accessible market will probably be private schools outside the United States that would like to enhance their local market potential.

Any school that can offer an internationally recognized diploma in addition to the local one, at a modest additional cost, will have a great marketing advantage over its competitors.

International schools that teach the American, British, or other curriculums can now be found in just about every major city. Initially started to cater to the children of expatriates, today they are filled with local students whose parents pay *up to five times the price* of the best local private schools.

The demand for such internationally recognized certificates is there.

So if just one school in a country decides to offer the American credential, the result should be a snowball effect, as its competitors realize they have to follow suit—or lose their customers.

To maximize the impact—and revenues—one additional feature must be added: practice exams, and online courses so students can bone up on subjects they may not have covered in their local school.

Such practice exams are a part of the SAT model that should be duplicated.

Offering instruction is not as difficult as it might seem. Hundreds of sites catering to American homeschoolers are equally available to anyone with an Internet connection. A directory of such sites—combined with resources from TED Talks, the Khan Academy, and dozens of similar sources can, between them, provide a student with most everything he or she needs to fully prepare for a high school exam on just about any subject.

And if not, online tutoring, via the model of freelancer.com, 99designs .com, and dozens of similar sites that put suppliers and customers together, could be an additional source of revenue.

Testing the Market

My sense when I came up with this idea was that a *big* market exists for this product.

Market testing bore out this assumption.

We asked a series of parents with children in private schools, "How much extra would you be willing to pay for your sons and daughters to gain an American high school graduation *in addition to* the local certification?"

The answers ranged from "a thousand dollars" to "up to two thousand dollars."

> ### And College . . . ?
>
> One of the first questions that came up during our market testing was, could I get an American college degree the same way—by just taking the exams?
>
> Why not!
>
> This is a more complicated option since, comparatively, the requirements for high school diplomas are fairly standardized. While college courses and the subsequent degrees come in hundreds of flavors.
>
> Before we've even started, we already have a possible brand extension!

We also asked parents if they'd be willing to pay a price similar to the cost of taking the SAT to have their kid sit for the exam. Working parents (middle- to lower-middle-class, earning around $400 per month) universally answered, "Yes!"

We even had local *college* graduates who overheard the question butting in to ask if *they* could do it, too. (Why? An American high school certificate can have greater credence abroad than a local college degree!)

The principals of the private high schools we talked to all thought it was a great idea "depending on price." The main attraction: "It would add to our school's reputation if we could offer such an internationally recognized credential."

As it happens, this model already exists.

The General Educational Development Test (GED)

The GED was developed during World War II by the American Council on Education to enable military personnel who hadn't graduated from high school to pursue tertiary education after the end of the war.

From this beginning, the GED—a high school equivalency diploma—became available across the United States and Canada as an option for people who had not finished high school.

As a result, it gained the reputation of being "for dropouts." Actually totally unfair, given the wide variability in the quality of American high schools. And thus their graduation diplomas.

Regardless, the GED is recognized by virtually all employers, colleges, and universities not just in the United States and Canada, but worldwide.

In 2011, GED's parent, the American Council on Education, and the British company Pearson, teamed up to "redevelop and administer the General Education Development test [as] a for-profit business."[1]

As of 2016, the GED had local affiliates in Bangladesh, Mexico, Myanmar, South Africa, South Korea, Sri Lanka, Ukraine, and the United Arab Emirates.

For example, the GED program requirements offered in South Africa via the Boston City Campus & Business College are "minimum of a Grade 10 Certificate and 16 years of age to enroll in the programme and take the GED test."

Meaning a South African high school student can skip the last two years of school and "on successful completion the Learner will be issued a USA High School Equivalency Credential issued by the Department of Education for Washington, DC."[2]

What's more, a South African GED holder who has only finished grade ten (of twelve) can enter a South African university if he or she has been accepted by an American one.

In other words, what began as a "think piece" has been confirmed in all respects. Does this nix the idea?

Absolutely not.

Quite the opposite. It proves that the concept works and that the demand exists.

The GED is offered by a *nonprofit organization*. Which means until the joint venture with Pearson, it was not effectively *marketed* (and, in my opinion, still isn't).

With the result that to this day it's relatively unknown.

Refining the Concept

In starting businesses and creating products I've found that coming up with the name and the USP (Unique Selling Proposition) and writing an ad are the best ways to bring everything into focus.

So I did.

A name: Graduate High School Today. Subject to improvement, but it contains the USP, is workable, and—unlike GED—does not need to be explained.

And here's an ad:

Get into College *Today*— Without Finishing School

Once upon a time, only geniuses could get into college early
Not anymore
You can too!

With an <u>American</u> high school diploma
recognized *worldwide*

You no longer need to wait a year or two or more to graduate from high school.

Thanks to GraduateHighSchoolToday.com, you can get an internationally recognized high school diploma right now—wherever you are in the world.

Why an *American* High School Graduation Diploma?

Recognized worldwide, it's your entry ticket to a higher-paying job, or the college or university of your choice—wherever you'd like to go. Any country in the world—except North Korea. (Can't have everything ☺.)

You Don't Need to Finish School!

You can take the exams anytime you like. Any age. Any grade. No school records, endorsements, or similar requirements needed.

Instead of sitting in a classroom for the next two or three years, you could be in college or university instead.

Until now, only geniuses could skip grades and get into college early. Today, anyone can do it.

Including you.

It's Easier Than You Think

You probably already know much of what's needed. English and math, for example.

You'll probably need to brush up on a few other subjects such as American history.

We'll help you. You'll find virtually everything you need online. Mostly free, too!

Courses. Practice exams. Tutorials. Readings. And the other instructional materials you'll need.

What's more, you can learn from the world's greatest minds and greatest teachers, who make the subjects come *alive,* make them easier to grasp—and get you ready to take the exam way faster.

And you *don't* have to take all the exams at once. (Unless you want to.)

Do one at a time. When *you* are ready.

You Could Graduate Right Now!

On GraduateHighSchoolToday.com, you'll find our *Tryout.*

It's like a practice exam. Except when you're done, you get a precise assessment and suggested study guide to cover everything you need to pass the actual exam.

And if you get a passing grade the first time around, you're ready to do the real thing.

Try it out right now.

No charge.

No obligation.

This draft ad contains all the fundamental concepts of the business model we're exploring.

Compare this to ged.com and "the power of marketing" (introduced on page 149) becomes crystal clear.

This ad also conveys a *single-minded focus* in the same vein as companies such as Uber and Airbnb.

Pearson is a large company with a wide range of products, the GED being just one of dozens.

Scale is certainly an advantage. But, arguably, the single-minded focus of a one-product business is a much greater advantage.

A Beginning . . .

We've identified and outlined a business concept that could be as disruptive in the education space as Uber and Airbnb have been in the taxi and accommodation industries.

Clearly, an enormous amount still needs to be done. For example, we don't have a supplier. A school or state we can team up with to offer the product in the same way GED has done with the Washington, DC, Department of Education, just to begin with. And if you're wondering where "the world's greatest minds and greatest teachers" promised in the ad are coming from, the answer is—an online directory selected from the Khan Academy, the many homeschooling sites in the United States, and many elsewhere.

So in terms of this concept, while we're nowhere near the beginning of the end, we're close to the end of the beginning.

And just as important, we've identified a process for coming up with a new business idea from scratch. A process you can apply in whatever field you choose.

Meanwhile, if your kids or grandchildren are in high school and you'd like to accelerate them into college, you don't have to wait for this concept to work. Just go to ged.com.

Tea: The Next Retail Revolution?

Worldwide, only one drink is more popular than tea. Water.

Yet, in the "tea space," there is no Starbucks or McDonald's equivalent.

As the table shows, there is certainly a tailwind (or, depending on the segment, a steady breeze) in the tea business. Unlike the "espresso revolution," which was driven by Starbucks, this steady increase in tea consumption is primarily a result of changing consumer tastes.

Businesses are reacting to the trend rather than driving it.

Tens of thousands of them. Mostly small. Especially at the *retail* end of the "tea chain" in—to use the British idiom—*tearooms*.

> **We will do for tea what we did for coffee.**
> —Howard Schultz

Is there a next-Starbucks opportunity in the tea market?

Howard Schultz certainly thinks so.

Which is what he said when Starbucks bought the 284-store Teavana tea chain for $620 million in December 2012.

That's a big promise.

Will he keep it?

Before we can address that and related questions, let's take a quick "walk" around the tea industry.

While we do, we should keep in mind that Starbucks created and rode the espresso revolution by persuading drip and instant coffee drinkers to switch.

The potential opportunities in the tea space appear to be somewhat different.

Tea's Growth in the USA

Wholesale tea sales ($ value), annual rate of growth: 1990–2014

Supermarkets/retail	7.86%
Ready to drink	26.25%
Food service	6.45%
Speciality teas	14.95%
Total	**13.51%**

Source: Tea Association of the USA Inc., http://www.teausa.com/14654/state-of-the-industry.

World Tea Production and Consumption

Annual rate of growth (weight): 2009–2013

Production	5.81%
Exports	3.44%
Consumption	5.45%

Source: Food & Agricultural Organization, http://www.fao.org/3/a-i4480e.pdf.

Howard Schultz Is Not Alone

Howard Schultz is not the only CEO who has expressed an interest in this space.

Louis Vuitton: In 2009, a team of executives from LVMH (which includes Louis Vuitton and Christian Dior), including Chairman Bernard Arnault, seriously studied the possibility of adding Singapore's upmarket tea chain, TWG, to the company's portfolio of luxury brands.

Unilever: In 2014, Unilever—the world's largest tea wholesaler—purchased the Australian packaged-tea chain, T2. Within a year, the brand had been extended into London and New York, with more places to come.[3]

The Tea Chain: From Producer to Consumer

Like coffee, tea begins as an agricultural product, which is then processed and packaged by manufacturers around the world into a variety of retail products.

The basic mass-market product is black tea (plus, in Asia, green tea), Lipton, Tetley, and Twinings being the major global brands.

222 How to Spot the Next Starbucks . . .

You'll find them in supermarkets pretty much everywhere, along with regional and local brands.

Over the past several decades, the tea market has fragmented in three directions:

1. From basic black and green teas to a wide and increasing diversity of specialty teas, including flavored teas and "nontea" teas such as chamomile and other herbal infusions.

2. Price, as the number of premium, luxury, and midmarket brands and blends have proliferated.

3. The addition of new categories, especially bubble tea, which originated in Taiwan.

These differences have always existed, but they are now becoming mass-market phenomena, thanks to a number of factors, including rising disposable incomes and the reputed health benefits of tea compared to other drinks.

One gauge of this trend is the widespread availability of bottled teas (and nontea teas) in supermarkets, 7-Elevens, and elsewhere.

And tea is available in just about every café, restaurant, and hotel dining room wherever you go. Even in coffee shops: Starbucks grew the Tazo Tea brand, which it purchased for $8.1 million in 1999, into the billion-dollar brand it is today.

But when we turn to retailers specializing in tea we find—

A Crowded and Highly Fragmented Market

Tea-themed retailers can be divided into two broad categories: retailers of luxury and/or specialty teas, and the café/restaurant where tea may appear to be the primary theme, but often is not.

Consider how this second space comes in a multiplicity of smaller market segments. From the posh and expensive British tearoom, whose specialty is afternoon (or, sometimes, "high") tea, also found in those five-star British hotels such as Claridge's; to the traditional Chinese teahouse, China's equivalent of Starbucks' "third place." But way cheaper.

And in between are a variety of other niches such as Teavana's "tea bar," Japanese and Korean versions of the tea service, Russian tearooms, and what seems to be the fastest-growing segment: bubble tea.

But nowhere do we find a handful of chains that dominate the tea space, as is the case in the coffee café market.

What's more, I'm willing to bet that 99 percent of people cannot name the leading tea café brand. (It's *not* Teavana!)*

The following table is an admittedly incomplete list of the major tea-retailing brands from around the world:

---

*The world's number one tea chain turns out to be Chatime, a Taiwanese bubble tea "teahouse." It's called a teahouse even though it has no resemblance whatsoever to a traditional Chinese teahouse. The other Taiwanese chains listed above are also bubble tea outlets. Sources: company Websites, yelp.com, and elsewhere.

The World's Major Retail Tea Chains

	TOTAL	Chatime* Taiwan	Teavana USA	Gong Cha Taiwan	Coco Fresh Tea & Juice Taiwan	Davids Tea Canada	Ten Ren Tea Taiwan	Kusmi Tea France	T2 Australia	Tea At Sea Canada	Argo Tea USA	TWG Singapore	Moon Leaf Philippines	Mariage Freres France	Serenitea Philippines	Palais Des Thes France	Boston Tea Party UK	Dammann Freres Franc	Infinitea Philippines	Yauatcha Abu Dhabi	Bettys UK
TOTAL		1002	411	405	383	187	81	71	66	51	46	45	42	42	39	33	17	15	10	7	6
USA	445	14	327	8	16	32	23	1	2	9	36					2				2	
UK	32	5		2				5				1		1			17			2	6
Australia	89	62		27			1		59												
Austria	2							2													
Belgium	4															4					
Cambodia	25	20		4								1									
Canada	279	15	61	2	3	155	6		1	42											
China	198	8		186								4									
Czech Rep.	2							2													
France	100	1						49						22		22		6			
Germany	2							8						2							
Hong Kong	39	4		30	3		1					1									
India	5	5																		3	
Indonesia	22	11		3	4				2			2									
Ireland	1															1					
Israel	1															1					
Italy	3							1										2			
Japan	27	2		1			3					4		17		1		2			
Korea	16	11		4														1			
Lebanon	2							2													
Macau	1	1																			
Malaysia	154	143		5	1		1					5									
Myanmar	5	5																			
Mexico	16		16																		
Middle East	31	7	7								10	3						4			
New Zealand	2								2												
Norway	5							3								2					
Philippines	153	34		20	5							5	40		39				10		
Singapore	82	5		66	2		1					9									
South Africa	5				5																
Sweden	1							1													
Taiwan	395	15		50	326		46					4									
Thailand	28	7		1	14							6									
Vietnam	10	10																			

*Note: The numbers for Chatime are not complete. The country store numbers of 430 come from yelp.com. But the *Taipei Times* reported Chatime had 1,002 stores in 2013 while Chatime's Web site claims "over 1,000." Chatime, Gong Cha, Coco Fresh Tea & Juice, Ten Ren Tea, Moon Leaf, Serenitea, and Infinitea are not the only bubble tea chains of reasonable size. Others, for which no accurate store numbers are available, include Hung Fook Tong (Hong Kong), Zagu (Philippines), and two chains that could be bigger than Chatime—Happy Lemon (Taiwan), and Easy Way (Taiwan)—though accurate store numbers are impossible to find.

The companies in this list range from the luxury end of the market (such as TWG and Bettys, and Yauatcha, a modernized version of the traditional Chinese dim sum teahouse) to retailers such as Chatime and Infinitea that specialize in bubble tea. Also known as pearl milk tea and boba milk tea, it's essentially a tea-based version of Starbucks' iced Frappuccino.

With the exception of TWG—which has nine outlets in its home market of Singapore—not one of these companies is dominant in its primary market. Not even Chatime in Taiwan.

This is *one* of the opportunities in the tea café market: *branding* and *consolidation*.

My Journey into Tea

What aroused my interest in the tea business was not Howard Schultz's comment. I came across that long after I had stumbled over an unusual chain named TWG Tea, which led to the discovery of a surprising number of great businesses in this market niche.

I should add that coffee, not tea, is my favorite drink. I can certainly tell the difference between tea from a Lipton tea bag and from a high-quality loose-leaf tea. But, to me, that minor (in my opinion) taste difference just isn't worth the major (more often, *major*) difference in price.

That didn't prevent me (and shouldn't prevent you) from finding and judging a great business when you see one.

TWG Tea

TWG (short for The Wellness Group) was founded by Taha Bouqdib, Maranda Barnes, and Rith Aum-Stievenard in Singapore in 2008. An upmarket retailer of high-quality teas, today it has forty-five stores in twelve countries. Including one in the United Kingdom—located inside the iconic British department store (and supplier to royals) Harrods. And is available through another twenty third-party outlets in Canada, the USA, Portugal, Germany, Australia, and elsewhere.

Their teas are not cheap. At New York's Dean & Deluca, US$34 gets you a 3.5-ounce packet of TWG loose-leaf tea. That's $9.71 per ounce.

TWG in Harrods.

Compare that to Lipton from Walmart: $4.50 for 8 ounces, or 56.3¢ per ounce.

TWG's tea is even more expensive than one of the world's rarest coffees. You can find Jamaica's Blue Mountain coffee at Starbucks Reserve for $29.50. That 8.8-ounce packet weighs in at just $3.35 per ounce. A "bargain" at one-third the price of TWG's offerings.

If you order tea at one of TWG's stores, you will drink it from a Limoges porcelain cup. Be careful not to drop it: the cup and saucer set cost $48.

And while you're there, you might like to pick up a teapot like the one above, finished in twenty-two-karat gold. Just $575 (plus tax, where applicable).

TWG is definitely *not* a mass-market retailer. If executives at Lipton's and Twinings don't sleep soundly at night, it's definitely *not* because TWG is invading their market.

Upmarket Tea: The Potential in This Niche

 TWG's forty-five locations *do* prove that there is a market for a truly upscale tea shop. In its Singapore home, population 5.4 million, it has six locations (not counting three at Changi Airport), or around one store per million.

Based on the penetration of TWG and four French chains—Mariage Frères (ironically, the inspiration for TWG), Palais Des Thés, Dammann, and Kusmi Tea*— we can confidently project somewhere between 2,000 and 3,000 outlets in this space, worldwide.

This is clearly a market segment with enormous potential growth.

TWG, as a subsidiary of another Singapore-based retailer, OSIM, does not

---

*Between them, these four chains have eighty-four locations in France. At one per 1.25 million people, their penetration is similar to TWG's presence in its home market.

offer an investment opportunity in this space. While OSIM does not break out TWG's sales or profits in its financials, TWG's 52 outlets are a mere 6.8 percent of OSIM's total of 762 retail locations.[4]

But it's not the only one at the luxury end of the market. For example, consider what could be—

The World's Leading Tearoom?

Bettys. No apostrophe. Based in Harrogate and York, in the UK. A two-and-a-half-hour train ride north of London.

Bettys was established in 1919 by Swiss confectioner Frederick Belmont.

"Belmont spent his teens in apprenticeships for all manner of bakers and confectioners across Europe. By the time he arrived in England, his head was filled with knowledge of their craft."[5]

In 1962, Bettys acquired Taylors of Harrogate, a specialist in teas and coffees, founded in 1886.

Today, Bettys has six outlets—the original café in Harrogate, and five in York, just twenty-one miles away. Via their Web site they deliver anywhere in the UK and (for selected products) "as far as Tokyo."

By all accounts, Bettys is renowned for its mouthwatering cakes. But what *really* sparked my interest was the number of comments mentioning *long lines* of customers waiting for a table. Sometimes, thirty or forty-five minutes.

Long lines of *waiting* customers—what every retailer loves to have.

I'm definitely interested in *any* business that has customers backed up around the corner.

Bettys is certainly doing something right. But what?

A quick Internet search brings up hundreds of customer comments, nearly all four and five stars. A few examples (from tripadvisor.com)[6] give the "flavor":

> This is the most amazing and delightful place for morning or afternoon tea—it's like stepping into the past. The service is superb and the atmosphere terrific. . . . I enjoyed the best coffee I have tasted since leaving Australia and the lightest and tastiest raspberry tart ever. This is a must for anyone visiting York—breakfast, lunch and morning and afternoon teas. Clean toilets. —Lonescot, England

The original Bettys in Harrogate: 3:00 p.m. on a cold December day.

Lovely, charming place and traditional in all respects. Never disappoints. Tea or coffee choice to please all. Cakes or snacks to please all. Staff there to please all. What more do you want? —kwc973, Melton Mowbray, UK

It was like stepping back in time. Old fashioned tea room service, with someone playing the piano, it's no wonder it's the most popular place in York! Loved the Tea Trolley! Lovely atmosphere with great friendly service. Can't wait to come back again! —dieterjonentz, Forres, UK

First impressions suggested Bettys' primary appeal was its cakes, and these are the product most often singled out for the highest praise. A tribute, indeed, to Bettys' founder, and his successors.

But clearly, Bettys' overall appeal is its total ambience. The total customer experience.

The answer to the question "Bettys is certainly doing something right. But what?" appears to be *everything*.

My next step was to ask people I know in the UK about Bettys. One friend, Henry Newrick,* ran a credit check for me:

As for Bettys. It sure ain't your ordinary tearoom.

I did a "credit" search. I have done thousands over the years on companies (in fact 300 this weekend). It is the *only* time I have ever seen a company with a 100% credit score. Even the strongest blue chip businesses almost always end up in the 80s or low 90s.

Bettys has 6 shops and just look at its balance sheet [screen shot below]. £7.7 million in the bank and a net worth of £45 million!

Its parent company does even better with a net worth of £96 million and almost £14 million cash:

Yet for some strange reason the parent only has a 98% credit rating!

Clearly what they are doing right is "service" targeted at the British and foreigners' love of British tradition. I'd be surprised if a lot of their customers are not Chinese and Japanese visitors.

---

*If you want to run a credit check on a UK company, Henry will be happy to help you out. See appendix 4, "Resources," page 281.

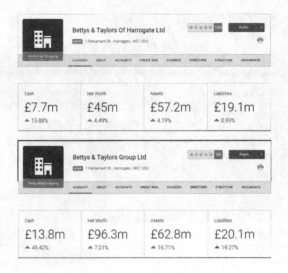

Without ever going near the place I'd say exemplary service and premium pricing.

Wow!

A 100 percent (or AAA) credit rating and two great big piles of cash!

To put this in perspective, compare Bettys' AAA credit rating with that of some of Britain's biggest companies:

Company	Credit rating	US equivalent
British Petroleum	86	A+
Tesco	86	A+
Vodaphone	49	BBB+
Lloyds Bank	86	A+
Barclays Bank	100	AAA

Source: CompanyCheck

Bettys is up there with the only British bank with a 100 percent credit rating: Barclays. Fortuitously, my daughter, Natasha, was traveling around Europe at the time. So I asked if she'd like to have afternoon tea in York. One look at the cakes on Bettys' Web site was enough to convince her:

> I went to Bettys in York, which is just like a normal café. And in the afternoon to the original Bettys in Harrogate.
>
> I arrived at Bettys in York at 10 o'clock in the morning and it was already busy. Packed. I didn't have to wait for a table, which was lucky, as a line was starting to form outside.

Inside, there was a long line for the bakery. People taking cakes home for their morning tea:

I thought both the York and Harrogate Bettys were lovely. Here's the view from my table in York:

I asked a few people why they came to Bettys. Some said they were there just because they'd never been there before. [Such, it would appear, is the power of Bettys' reputation.]

The general consensus of people who live in the area and keep coming back is that Bettys' [customer experience] is always consistent. They said the service is always good, the food is always high quality, which is why they're happy to come back again and again.

I talked to a lady from Harrogate who said she hadn't been to Bettys for ten years. She was there to treat a visiting friend, as though going to Bettys is a *must* if you're ever in the area.

My own experience confirmed everything I'd heard. The service was impeccable. Fantastic! Everything was beautifully presented. And the food was amazing (right):

Even though it was morning, I had the afternoon tea.

I tried the sandwiches obviously. They were great. Unlike sandwiches you normally get in England, Bettys' don't skimp on the filling, which impressed me.

The scones and cakes are great as well. I had a layered coffee cake, a fruit tart, and a macaroon. I have to say that I was very unimpressed with the macaroon but the other cakes were amazing.

In the afternoon I had a second afternoon tea at the original Bettys in Harrogate.

It's enormous (below):

If you have the "Lady Bettys" afternoon tea there, everything is much more posh. You're greeted by the staff when you arrive, have your coat taken, and are seated in a private dining room with live piano music (next page):

The regular afternoon tea costs £18, which seems about right to me. The "Lady Bettys" was £32, or £39 with champagne:

I think that was a bit much. But it was a beautiful, beautiful setting. The food was really great too.

Not to mention the view.

As you can see (top right), the "Lady Bettys" is a lot fancier.

The tea's good, you can have as many sandwiches as you like, the raisin and lavender scones are wonderful, and come with proper clotted cream:

And the cakes are to die for. Like this chocolate cake with raspberries on top:

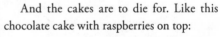

I couldn't eat everything.

I had a half-eaten sandwich and I asked the waiter to pack it for me. He said: "Don't worry about it. I'll give you a new one."

When you get the bill, they give you a 30-gram tin of special blended Bettys tea to take with you that you can't buy anywhere else.

I was so full I couldn't eat anything for a whole day!

I don't know about you, but just from the pictures I'm lusting after those cakes!

I've devoted, perhaps, more space than necessary to Bettys. Especially since Bettys won't franchise and has no intention of opening outlets "too far from their bakery." Which effectively means not outside the York/Harrogate area.

So where's the business or investment opportunity?

First, Bettys clearly offers a retail gold (if not platinum) standard of service. So seeing and experiencing what this company does could lead to an upgrade in the customer experience of just about any business.

Second, Bettys will actually teach you some of their "secrets." Four or five days a week Bettys' Cookery School is open for business.[7] If you're in a similar market niche, spend a couple of weeks in York and you'll be able to walk away with several of Bettys' most popular recipes.

You'll also be able to nose around a bit and learn some of the company's backroom "operational methodology."

But what if you have neither the intention of traveling halfway around the world just for afternoon tea nor the money to do so?

You don't need to.

Use "3-D processing," combined with the Disney Strategy (page 143) instead.

Create a mental image of Bettys' customer experience from the description above, plus the abundant comments, articles, and even videos to be found.

In just half an hour or so you'll have a detailed appreciation of the customer experience "as if" you had actually been there.

If Bettys is not in the business space that interests you, simply choose an exemplary company that is.

This exercise enables you to create your own gold standard for the customer experience. You can then apply that to create or improve the level of service in your business and to critically judge the customer experience at businesses you frequent regularly.

Put on your copycatting hat and check it out.

A Third Model: Teavana

TWG and Bettys represent two different segments in the upmarket tea café space.

TWG's prime focus is the tea. It operates restaurants where you can sample their teas, but TWG's food has nowhere near the attraction of Bettys'.

TWG also appeals to what I call the conspicuous consumption market. I know of a number of people who serve TWG teas at home not because they're tea connoisseurs but to impress their friends. (When their friends aren't around, they drink Lipton or Twinings.)

Bettys is quite different. Though called a tearoom, the real attraction is the food, especially the cakes.

Yes, they're also known for their high-quality teas. Indeed, their Yorkshire Tea brand is Britain's third most popular packaged tea.

But Bettys' prime focus is afternoon tea.

From a commercial point of view, one benefit of the tearoom concept is that the restaurant area can be busy in the mornings and the afternoons, times when many restaurants are empty or even close their doors.

The light meals offered also appeal to the lunch and breakfast trade. So a tearoom can be busy pretty much all day, especially in those times between breakfast and lunch and lunch and dinner when most other restaurants are nearly empty.

Teavana offers yet another model.

The Teavana Model

When Starbucks purchased Teavana, it was primarily a retailer of packaged teas.

All outlets enable passersby to sample a couple of Teavana's teas without actually entering the store. And some offer tea to go.

With no seating, each Teavana outlet is a relatively small place with therefore (again, relatively) a low rent.

Howard Schultz's promise to "do for tea what we did for coffee" implied that Teavana would follow the Starbucks model of a café/restaurant.

And sure enough, on 24 October 2013, Teavana opened the first of a projected one thousand[8] "tea bars," in New York.[9] Two years later, Teavana had six tea bars, three in New York, and one each in Seattle, Beverly Hills, and Chicago.

However, with the exception of the Seattle outlet, they were all shut down in January 2016.*

Teavana reverted to its original model. At least, in the United States.

Does this mean Starbucks is retreating from the tea space?

The answer is a helpful yes—and no.

What Tea Means for Starbucks

Tea is important to Starbucks.

In some markets, especially China and India, tea can outsell coffee in Starbucks stores.

As the company's rebranding of "Starbucks Coffee" to just plain "Starbucks" indicates, you're invited to come to its "third place" for coffee, tea, a snack, or any other reason you like. Including (in the United States) free Wi-Fi.

---

*One possible reason for the failure of Teavana's tea bars: unlike most other tea cafés, no coffee.

Tazo Tea, purchased by Starbucks in 1999 for $8.1 million, is, today, a billion-dollar brand, selling packaged and ready-to-drink teas through Starbucks and grocery outlets.

When Starbucks added Teavana to its tea portfolio, its announced intention was to make Teavana one of "the largest global brands" by achieving "$2 billion in sales" within the next five years.[10]

By the end of 2015, Teavana was halfway to that goal. It had expanded to a total of 411 outlets: 327 in the United States, 61 in Canada, 16 in Mexico, and 7 across the Middle East.

But most of Teavana's growth (so far) has come from offering Teavana teas in Starbucks and elsewhere, rather than from expanding Teavana's retail footprint. And cannibalizing Starbucks' Tazo Tea brand.

Nevertheless, according to Howard Schultz, Teavana is the fastest-growing segment within Starbucks, and that "I've never been more passionate, more enthused about what we're doing and what I think is possible. . . . We believe that Teavana stand-alone stores will be a big idea not only in the U.S. . . . but a much bigger idea in Asia over time."[11]

In 2016, Starbucks rolled out its Teavana brand across Asia with heavy in-store promotions, starting with China in August, and ending with India and Japan in December.

This suggests Teavana's future will follow the path of most other Starbucks acquisitions.

Over the years of its existence, Starbucks has purchased a wide variety of other companies and brands in addition to Tazo Tea and Teavana. Evolution Fresh (water), La Boulange (bakery), and Seattle's Best, among others.

Of all the brands it has acquired, only one other than Teavana—Seattle's Best—survives as a stand-alone brand.

It bought La Boulange to acquire its baking expertise. Soon thereafter, all La Boulange stores were closed, despite the original intention of keeping them going.

When it purchased the manufacturer of the Clover coffeemaker, production was reserved for Starbucks stores, and service to preexisting customers was discontinued.

Seattle's Best, a competitor Starbucks acquired in 2003, continues as a separate but *subsidiary* operation. Relegated to small outlets in gas stations and similar places catering to the takeout trade. As well as selling its own brand of lower-priced packaged coffees through groceries and other outlets, including Burger King, which now features Seattle's Best coffee on its menu.

Seattle's Best is a way for Starbucks to leverage and extend its range of coffee sales while preserving the Starbucks brand as *the* third place—and premium coffee brand.

In sum, Starbucks has acquired companies solely to enhance the Starbucks brand. This unrelenting focus on Starbucks suggests that Teavana's future path is primarily as a Starbucks adjunct brand. And as a packaged-tea retailer along its original model—a model not competitive with Starbucks itself.

This implies that the tea bar niche is potentially wide open—and that any entrant does not need to worry about a competitor with Starbucks-like financial resources.

Second, though Teavana appears to be the world's largest chain specializing in packaged-tea retail outlets, on a worldwide scale its footprint is tiny. Suggesting there is plenty of room for Teavana copycats to succeed.

Teavana's main competitors in the United States are online. Companies such as Talbott Teas, owned by the Jamba Juice smoothie chain, and Stash Tea, primarily a wholesale tea brand sold in grocery stores and online, as well as supplying food-service outlets around the United States. Plus specialty stores such as Harney & Sons[12] and Bellocq (both New York stores with an online presence), and just about every other tea brand and tea packager, from TWG to Twinings—not to mention other online retailers such as Amazon and Walmart.

But the entry of the Unilever-backed T2 brand into New York suggests the competition in this space is about to heat up.

Bubble Tea

Bubble tea chains currently appear to be the fastest-growing segment of the retail tea market.

The original bubble tea, invented in Taichung, Taiwan, in the 1980s, was a hot black tea mixed with condensed milk, syrup or honey, and tapioca pearls. Which is why it's also known as pearl tea.

Today, these chains offer a wide variety of mixed drinks, hot or (mostly) cold, ranging from the original bubble tea to juices and smoothies, with all sorts of unusual combinations in between.

Having sampled a few bubble teas, my reaction is similar to my attitude to Louis Vuitton handbags: I certainly understand *that* people buy them; but I can't emotionally relate to the why.

So I asked a number of regular customers of these chains what the attraction was. "Variety" was a common answer. The range of their offerings extend from the pedestrian to all manner of weird combinations. A few examples: milk tea with caramel and sea salt on top, brown rice green milk tea, and taro milk tea (though the

Call me old-fashioned, but I'll definitely pass on this combo.

teenage customers I've spoken to disagree; "Not weird at all," they say, looking at me as if *I'm* the one that's weird).

Price was another important attraction, especially in countries such as Taiwan and the Philippines, where competition is fierce.

"A nice change" was a reaction from a Starbucks regular.

The primary market is takeout, and most of these chains offer drinks only. Though some of those drinks come with ingredients that make them more like desserts. The cost of establishing a bubble tea store with no seating is relatively low.

Those bubble tea outlets with seating are often teenage hangouts. "Sometimes you see an old person. Thirties or so. But mostly young," one teenager told me.

In all cases, the service is usually quick. So the attraction boils down to a combination of speed, price, variety, convenience, and something different.

Tea Cafés, Tea Bars, Tearooms—and Teahouses

What *is* the difference between a tea café, a tea bar, a tearoom, and a teahouse?

Two of these names conjure up distinct images. A tearoom is the upscale British concept, typified by Bettys. A teahouse is the traditional Chinese model.

Yet, Chatime, Happy Lemon, and the myriad other bubble tea vendors are called teahouses. All they have in common with the traditional Chinese teahouse is that they are Chinese in origin and serve tea, among other things.

One thing you *can't* buy at a bubble teahouse is the *central* USP of the traditional version: a pot of green tea.

Compare Happy Lemon (left), one of the largest bubble tea chains, with the renowned Hong Kong traditional teahouse, Lok Cha (right).

"Tea bar" is a marketing concept (and a good one). But there's no difference between a tea bar and a tea café.

We need a more *meaningful* way to segment the retail tea market.

The key distinctions are:

- *Price:* luxury, midmarket, or down-market.

- *Type:* the café/restaurant or the packaged-tea vendor.

Using these distinctions gives us a better handle on the possibilities in this market niche.

Packaged Teas

The dedicated packaged-tea retailer is a small part of this market, Teavana and T2 being the leading examples.

Though they are not alone. The "Teavana model" of a small, low-rent space focusing on packaged teas is also offered by café/restaurants such as TWG and Argo.

This space has only two price segments: luxury (TWG and T2) and midmarket (Teavana and Argo).

The key element to success is to offer a wide range of teas (and "nontea" teas).

Café/Restaurant

Bettys is the prime example of the upscale British tearoom. But this segment of the market is mainly dominated by hotels offering the "British afternoon/high tea," especially in Britain. While the midmarket space is essentially competitive with Starbucks and other coffeehouses.

Indeed, the primary difference between a coffee shop and a tea café is that in one you can buy coffee beans (and also get a cup of tea), while the other has wall-to-wall teas (and you can also get a cup of coffee).

Some bubble tea chains occupy the down-market segment, mainly in countries where competition is fierce. In most countries, they're in the midmarket price range. A quick summary of the companies we've mentioned so far:

	Packaged-tea retailer	Café/restaurant
Luxury	T2, TWG*	Bettys, Dammann Frères, Kusmi Tea, Mariage Frères, Palais des Thés, TWG, Yauatcha
Midmarket	Teavana, Argo*	DavidsTea, Argo, Boston Tea Party, Tea At Sea, bubble tea chains**
Down-market		Bubble tea chains**

*Kiosks, offering packaged teas and (Argo) tea to go.
**Bubble tea chains span both mid- and down-market price categories; and a chain's price category can vary from one country to another.

Luxury Tea

With TWG, Teavana/T2, Bettys, and bubble tea, we've identified four different markets within the tea space.

TWG and T2 represent the high-end, luxury retailer of a wide range of high-quality loose-leaf teas. As luxury retailers, they benefit from conspicuous consumption: the purchase of products for the purpose of impressing other people.

Teavana, Argos, and Davids are midmarket equivalents of TWG, offering a smaller range, with many of the "teas" flavored in such a way as to have little relation to tea in the traditional sense of the word.

The endorsements of Howard Schultz, Bernard Arnault, and Unilever are clear evidence of an enormous business opportunity in this niche.

The Bettys Tearoom Model

Bettys is based around the specifically British tradition of afternoon tea mixed with high tea (a minimeal, with tea), and Devonshire tea (an afternoon tea combination of a pot of tea accompanied by scones, jam, and whipped or clotted cream; not the wimpish, American low-fat version of cream, either). Champagne is optional.

The Bettys experience is exportable *as is*. Indeed, it *has* been exported; you can enjoy the "British afternoon tea experience" in the Pierre Hotel (New York), the Tea Cosy (Sydney, Australia), or the Marriott Hotel (Singapore), and hundreds of other places around the world.[13]

Clearly, the appeal of Bettys' underlying USP of (let's not beat around the bush) beautifully presented "sugar shock and fat overload," combined with superb service, is universal.

While far from an empty space, a Bettys-style chain is a possibility. Alternatively, existing upscale restaurants could expand their customer base and utilize those empty morning and afternoon hours by offering a Bettys-style experience.

The Tea "Café"

Several companies are already in this space. A few examples:

Argo Tea, one-tenth the size of Teavana, has an interesting combination of tea cafés and TEAosks: small, attractively designed kiosks offering a range of packaged teas and teas and pastries to go.

DavidsTea, the Canadian tea café chain with 187 outlets in Canada and the United States, with plans to expand to 500 in the next few years.

And from Britain, a chain that could be a big hit in the American market— just from its name:

Boston Tea Party. A café chain that looks similar to Davids. And, indeed, to Starbucks—with coffee replaced by tea.

Unlike Teavana's tea bar, some of these chains serve coffee as well as tea, thus competing with the Starbucks experience.

But given the small size of these chains, a market leader has yet to emerge, so the business opportunities (plus a wide variety of franchise and country-franchise options) appear to be legion. While DavidsTea, as the largest, is currently the leading candidate, a now small or even totally new company could be the winner here.

We can come to a similar conclusion about the prospects in the bubble tea market. With the difference that, as this concept appears to be most popular in Asia, unless a China- or India-based chain arises, one of the existing Taiwanese chains is likely to be the Starbucks equivalent in this niche.

Investment Options

The investment opportunities seem limited, as the majority of the retail tea brands are submerged in much larger companies. For example, if the T2 brand were to multiply its profits ten or even a hundred times, Unilever's share price would hardly move. And Teavana's prospects, even if fulfilled, are not reason enough to invest in Starbucks. Though it may add to the attraction.

Just three publicly traded companies focusing on the tea retail sector remain: Canada's DavidsTea, and two Taiwanese companies, La Kaffa International (owner of Chatime) and Ten Ren Tea.

However, the financial information available on the Taiwanese companies is minimal. Even if you're fluent in Chinese.

As I write these words, DavidsTea remains the primary investment possibility.

On the surface, the *business* prospects for the company seem bright, and the company's stated mission and vision are clear and appealing.* Customer comments are positive,[14] suggesting the company offers a good customer experience.

But several question marks hover over the company. Its expansion into the American market is not paying off as projected. And in March 2016, the cofounder and visionary behind the company, David Segal, resigned.

Bad signs, to say the least. But the company is possibly worth keeping an eye on for future reference (see appendix 3, "DavidsTea," page 278, for a detailed analysis).

Meanwhile, alternative investment

Publicly Traded Tea Companies and Tea Brands

Canada:
  DavidsTea (DTEA, Toronto and Nasdaq)
Hong Kong:
  Longrun Tea (2898.HK, Hong Kong)
India:
  Tata Global Beverages (TATAGLOBAL.BO, India)
Japan:
  Ito En Ltd. (ITOEF, Japan)
  Tea Life Co. Ltd. (TEALF, Japan)
Singapore:
  TWG (via Osim, O23.SI, Singapore)
Taiwan:
  Chatime (La Kaffa International, 2732.TWO, Taiwan)
  Ten Ren Tea Co. Ltd. (1233.TW, Taiwan)
USA:
  Farmer Brothers Co. (FARM, Nasdaq)
  Teavana and Tazo (via Starbucks, SBUX, Nasdaq)

---

*For example, see this company-produced video: https://www.youtube.com/watch?v=OLr68UBhw0o.

opportunities could appear if other specialized tea retailers such as the Boston Tea Party, Argo, or Tea At Sea go public.

Fast Casual

"Fast casual" is a fast-food category that arose in the United States in the late 1990s.

It occupies a space between fast food (McDonald's, KFC, Pizza Hut, and so on) and sit-down restaurants with table service (TGI Fridays, Applebee's).

The primary differences between fast food and fast casual are:

1. *Price,* ranging from $9 to $13 compared to around $5 for fast food.

2. *Preparation.* Fast food is usually prepared in advance; fast casual is made to order.

While the wait time is longer for fast casual, a limited menu ensures that it is short. Other differences include a focus on fresh, healthy ingredients, and table service, with an average of around 50 percent of orders being for takeout.

While people disagree over the precise definition of *fast casual* (for example, Euromonitor includes Buffalo Wild Wings, Technomic does not, while the industry Web site, fastcasual.com, includes Starbucks!), it is generally agreed that the category was kicked off by Fuddruckers and Au Bon Pain in the nineties, and that the leading fast casual brand today is Chipotle Mexican Grill.

That the growth in this niche is far from over is demonstrated by the entry of McDonald's into this space with its touch-screen ordering system, which enables customers to personalize their order just as they do in Chipotle.

Let's apply the five clues to the market leader to see how it stands up.

"Fast Fine" Dining— a New Category?

Fast casual has spawned what could be a new category called fast fine dining.

These are quick-service restaurants started (so far) by full-priced fine-dining restaurant owners, with a limited menu of the same high-quality ingredients.

Examples include seven Larkburger stores in Colorado (larkburger.com), opened by Thomas Salamunovich, a classically trained chef, proprietor of the Larkspur Restaurant in Vail; 'Wichcraft sandwich chain in New York (wichcraft.com); and Farm Burger (www.farmburger.net), based in Atlanta.

It remains to be seen whether this will become a widespread category. One potential limitation: most (though not all) of these quick-service restaurants ride on the back of a full-service restaurant. The advantage: the smaller restaurants can entice new customers into the main one. Though that has not prevented Farm Burger from expanding into California and North Carolina. Watch this space!*

*www. qsrmagazine.com/competition/great-spin.

Chipotle Mexican Grill

1. They Permanently Change People's Habits

Although not the originator of the concept, Chipotle's success led to fast casual's dramatic growth from next to nothing to 5 percent of restaurant sales in the United States—or $35 billion!

To put that in perspective, that's a growth of—

> 550% percent since 1999, more than ten times the growth seen in the fast food industry over the same period, according to data from market research firm Euromonitor. Chipotle . . . has seen its sales more than quadruple during that time; Panera, another oft-used example, has watched its sales more than triple.[15]

2. They're Copycats

Chipotle founder Steve Ells credits the taquerias he had seen in California as the inspiration for his business idea.

However, he did not set out with the aim of starting a nationwide chain. A classically trained chef, he saw the first Chipotle (opened in 1993) as a way of learning the *business* side of the restaurant trade at a low investment cost.

His intention was to then step away from it to achieve his primary aim: setting up a full-service restaurant.

But when his first store was selling 1,000 burritos a day, compared to his break-even projection of 117, he recalls, "It was making much more money than I had ever anticipated. In my heart I was ready to start thinking about a fine-dining restaurant. A few people said, 'Steve, you should open another one of these.' So I called my dad, and he's, like, 'Really? Do you think Denver could have two of them?'"[16]

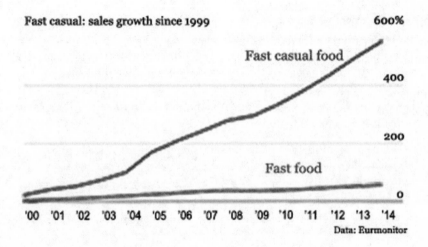

Fast casual: sales growth since 1999

Fast casual food

Fast food

600%
400
200
0

'00 '01 '02 '03 '04 '05 '06 '07 '08 '09 '10 '11 '12 '13 '14

Data: Euromonitor

Eventually Ells realized he was fulfilling his original passion through using only fresh, and then organic, ingredients, and he dropped the idea of starting a full-service restaurant.

In 1998, McDonald's invested in Chipotle, which enabled the company to expand from 13 to 489 outlets at the time McDonald's divested its stake in January 2006. For Chipotle, the association was a powerful learning experience, as it had inside access to the entire McDonald's *system*.

Although very different companies—for example, the only ingredient Chipotle and McDonald's have in common is Coca-Cola—Chipotle moved rapidly along the learning curve thanks to McDonald's input—and capital.

3. Their Success Is *Validated* by Competition

Chipotle's success has inspired two kinds of copycats:

Direct copycats. For example, Qdoba Mexican Eats (www.qdoba.com), founded two years after Chipotle, offers a similar menu and customer experience. Qdoba has grown to 641 stores compared to Chipotle's 1,700, proving that there's a wide market for this concept in the United States.

Concept copycats. Chipotle itself is a concept copycat, to the extent it copied the initiators of the fast casual trend, Panda Express and Panera Bread.

Companies such as Wingstop (1994), Shake Shack (2004), and especially Blaze Pizza (2012) are a few examples of the concept copycats that are expanding the fast casual category to almost every possible cuisine.

4. They're Driven by the Founder's Vision and Passion

Founder Steve Ells's original vision was diverted by the success of the first Chipotle into a quick-service restaurant serving food of fine-dining quality.

> "[People] thought I was crazy," Ells said, "but I had a very strong vision for the way Chipotle was going to look and taste and feel, and I knew it wasn't going to be a typical fast-food restaurant.
>
> "The idea was simple: demonstrate that food served fast didn't have to be a 'fast-food' experience. We use high-quality raw ingredients, classic cooking methods, and a distinctive interior design and have friendly people to take care of each customer—features that are more frequently found in the world of fine dining."[17]

Eventually, Chipotle's vision and mission were summarized into *Food with Integrity*. Ells explains:

> While using a variety of fresh ingredients remains the foundation of our menu, we believe that 'fresh is not enough anymore.' Now we want to know where all of our ingredients come from, so that we can be sure they are as flavorful as possible while understanding the environmental and societal impact of our business. We call this idea *Food with Integrity*, and it guides how we run our business.[18]

In 2015–16, this slogan lost much of its credibility as a series of salmonella, *E. coli,* and other infections hit Chipotle's customers and led to a dramatic fall in the company's sales and reputation.

We'll address Chipotle's reaction to this crisis in "Reputational Risk," below.

5. They Have Superb Management and Execution

Steve Ells's aim is to provide food "that is prepared in front of customers with a perfectionism that would defeat fancy sit-down establishments."

Business Excellence agrees:

> Even the company's growth strategy challenged orthodoxy: founder Steve Ells took a $360 million investment from McDonald's and used it to fund the rapid expansion, which led to an IPO. That success allowed him to buy out McDonald's, which exited with a handsome profit.
>
> Obsession over details is a hallmark of Ells's leadership; it took him four years of research and development before he approved the company's custom-designed tortilla warmers.
>
> "We hire for talents you can't teach," Ells told me. "Things like work ethic and honesty. We want people who are curious and capable of infectious enthusiasm. You can't teach this—but you can teach them how to run a Chipotle Grill."[19]

What Steve Ells looks for in applicants also relates to clue number four. Having curious and enthusiastic people on your team makes the job of transmitting the founder's vision and passion easier, ultimately leading to the unique customer experience that's the company's "trademark."*

Reputational Risk: Is Chipotle Hazardous to Your Health?

Clearly, Chipotle's otherwise excellent management had one rather large hole: food safety.

The possibility of serving contaminated food comes with the territory. Restaurant and grocery chains from McDonald's to Whole Foods have unwittingly sold food products that have infected their customers.

Indeed, 4,163 food-borne illness outbreaks were reported in the United States between 2010 and 2014, according to the Centers for Disease Control and Prevention.[20]

> It takes twenty years to build a reputation and five minutes to ruin it.
>
> —Warren Buffett

---

*For more, see this video from Bloomberg: www.youtube.com/watch?v=uERmpNGgaJA; and this interview with Steve Ells: www.youtube.com/watch?v=wmH73Diqf5Q.

When, like Chipotle, a company makes a point of using a wide variety of local suppliers, the result can be a monitoring nightmare. As a friend of mine put it, "If a mom-and-pop outfit is one of your suppliers, you may never know when the cows have been shitting in the vegetable patch."

An exaggeration perhaps, but it highlights the problem rather vividly.

For Chipotle, this was not a one-off problem, but a whole series:

- *August 2015:* "Sixty-four customers in Minnesota were infected with salmonella and about one hundred people were struck by norovirus in Southern California."[21]

- *October and November 2015:* An *E. coli* outbreak affected fifty-three people in nine states.[22]

- *December 2015:* Around 140 students at a Boston college were infected with norovirus; another incidence of *E. coli* hit five people in three states.[23]

The Vultures Gather

- *6 January 2016:* Chipotle revealed it had been served a federal grand jury subpoena related to a criminal investigation over its norovirus outbreak in Boston.[24]

- *8 January 2016:* A class-action lawsuit is filed against the company and certain of its officers by shareholders alleging they were deceived about the company's food-safety practices.[25]

Unsurprisingly, Chipotle's same store sales fell 14.9 percent, and its share price followed suit.

Does this mean we should write off Chipotle as an investment candidate—or leap in and scoop up shares at bargain prices?

A little history will help.

Remember what happened to Jack in the Box in 1993? And Taco Bell in 2006? Few people do.

In 1993, 732 Jack in the Box customers were infected with *E. coli*. Forty-five children required hospitalization and four of them died.

The company's initial reaction was denial. But eventually they admitted that they had *ignored* new Washington State regulations that would have prevented the infections.[26]

It took over a year for Jack in the Box's sales to recover—and by 1997 they were "considered the leader in food safety in the fast-food industry"!

In 2006, seventy-one Taco Bell customers were infected with *E. coli,* shredded lettuce being the most likely culprit.[27]

Chipotle

It was eighteen months before Taco Bell's same store sales recovered.

For Chipotle, solving its food-safety issues is a matter of *survival*. And solving them is doable.

So there's every reason to assume Chipotle's sales (and share price) will follow the same trajectory.

The Downside

Most likely, the vultures suing Chipotle will have to be paid to go away. Whether through a settlement or by fighting and losing the various lawsuits, Chipotle will probably end up paying out several million or tens of millions of dollars that will come straight off the bottom line.

And if the criminal investigation results in a charge, and Chipotle loses that, too, it will presumably have to pay a pretty hefty fine.

In addition, solving its food-safety problems will incur additional costs and may increase the company's cost base over the long term.

The net effect: a onetime financial event resulting in a onetime charge against profits, as happened when Starbucks lost its case with Kraft.

Ultimately, though, the strength of the Chipotle brand is demonstrated by the growth of earnings per share in 2015:

EPS Growth Rate Year on Year			
2015	2014	2013	2012
10.2%	35.6%	20.0%	28.0%

Ten percent is a dramatic decline from the 20 to 35 percent increases in the previous years. But in a year when everything went wrong for the company, it *still* increased earnings per share. And 10.2 percent is a number a majority of companies would be happy to have.

The Customer Experience

Ultimately, the health of *every* business depends on the customer experience. The higher its quality, the higher will be customer loyalty and repeat business. Repeat business that comes with zero marketing cost.

Doing it yourself is indubitably the best way to evaluate a company's customer experience. That way, you can get a personal feel for the quality and consistency of service across different locations.

But if you can't, you must rely on other people's comments. And if you don't have friends or relatives you can turn to, then what?

Here, the Internet is invaluable. While nothing beats being there yourself, sites such as yelp.com provide an incredible *variety* of customer reactions. More than you're ever likely to get by relying on people you know.

Chipotle's financial results are evidence of a good customer experience, but precisely *how good* is something they can't and won't tell us.

Skimming various yelp.com reviews, I came up with the following conclusions about Chipotle's customer experience:

1. Chipotle is receiving five-star write-ups even *after* the *E. coli* outbreaks. For example, this review posted on 10 January 2016 about a Chipotle store in San Jose, California:

   > With the recent outbreak of E. coli related news I was a little skeptical to revisit my all time favorite chain: Chipotle. However, everyone has to die from something and if I'm going to be living in constant fear of sickness then I'll be missing out big time.
   >
   > Burrito bowl with double meat, brown rice, black beans, and tons of lettuce is definitely the best post workout meal you can get so quickly and at such an affordable price. Also the plus side is that Chipotle lines are now shorter.[28]

2. Many negative reviews come from people who just don't like Chipotle's food. Not their cup of tea, so to speak.

   This shouldn't come as a surprise. Not *everybody* loves Chipotle. And not everybody will love your business, either.

3. Service issues that should not be happening. One example:

   > This one [Champaign, Illinois] *is always running out of stuff. The beans always look like*

they have been there all day. That being said, it's Chipotle! It's awesome anyway. I love Chipotle, Chipotle is my life! [Even so, this customer gave Chipotle four stars—on 7 January 2016. Emphasis added.][29]

"Always running out of stuff" suggests a supply-chain problem. A (one-star) comment about the same store from a year earlier:

Worst Chipotle experience I've ever had, which sucked, because I love Chipotle. Poor / lethargic / disinterested customer service. No chips or fajita veggies. Skimped portions served. Wish I had a better experience because I inevitably feel guilty for being so harsh, but maybe it'll kickstart a more enthusiastic team?

Another one-star review (6 May 2015) of a Chipotle in Hawthorne, California, suggests this may not be an isolated problem:

Worst Chipotle I have seen.

The first thing you notice is the line. And it never moves because at the end of it are the slowest, laziest, chattiest group of employees you've ever seen. . . .

Today I waited 20 min before they advised everyone that they had failed to cook enough beef, chicken or steak, and that it would be "veggies only" or face another 15-20 min wait. . . .

Move on. Time to find another burrito joint. Lazy, slow staff who spend more time chatting amongst themselves than they do making food.

Seriously—2pm on a Saturday afternoon and this clown of a manager has no food.[30]

A four-star review (4 January 2016) from the same store tells an opposite story:

I've visited this Chipotle a few times. Frankly, this is one of the better Chipotles I've visited for many reasons. . . .

Very friendly and fast. They got my order correctly, and precisely.

This is also one of the locations with the friendliest staff, and they never repeat or ask the same questions what you'd like in your order. . . .

I really don't have complaints for this location, as it tastes fresh, and always delicious.

Overall grade: A.

This is beginning to paint a picture of serious inconsistencies between different Chipotle outlets, and even at the same outlets at different times. Suggesting that while management has established procedures and goals, it has failed to monitor whether they are being *regularly* achieved.

Even some of those critical reviews come from people who tell us they just *love* Chipotle. Which is evidence of high customer loyalty. Indeed, some Chipotle customers go so far as to say, "We're totally willing to throw up a little."*

---

*See this article from the *Washington Post:* "E. coli? The Chipotle Cult Scoffs: 'We're Totally Willing to Throw up a Little.'"

I'll be the first to admit that I am far more intolerant and hypercritical of such outrageous lapses in quality and service than anyone else I know.

Clearly, as Chipotle's rapid expansion and 20 percent–plus growth rate in owner earnings demonstrate (numbers that are tough to argue with), plenty of Chipotle's customers are willing to give it a free pass when the quality of service is nowhere near the company's expressed standards.

Nevertheless, to me this is a red flag, which—subject to further research—suggests that were Chipotle's management to address this issue, it could grow even faster by retaining customers it is currently losing.

Or, it could represent a deeper problem. For example, Chipotle has grown too rapidly, with the result that management is spread too thin. Similar, perhaps, to the deterioration of the Starbucks experience from 2000 to 2008.

Whatever the actual cause, it seems I am not alone in coming to this conclusion. As this four-star review (Escondido, California, 20 November 2015) affirms:

> I am a big Chipotle Fan. My gripe with the missing star is INCONSISTENCY. From service to portions—especially portions, you just don't know what you're going to get. I have to blame management—or lack thereof, which is too bad because I love to eat here.[31]

Chipotle International

A big driver of growth for most American fast-food chains has been international expansion. Chipotle is following this model—but slowly and without (yet) dramatic success.

At the end of 2015, Canada had 7 Chipotles, the UK 7, France 3, and Germany 1. This compares to 1,755 in the United States.

Given that the first Canadian Chipotle was opened in Toronto in August 2008 and London was entered in May 2010, the rate of international expansion is not impressive.

But how to judge?

As Chipotle does not break out its international operations in its annual reports, we must find some way of estimating its international performance.

First, we can compare Chipotle with Taco Bell. Both offer Mexican food. Though not according to Mexicans: you won't find either of these chains in Mexico itself. It's more accurate to describe Chipotle's and Taco Bell's offerings as Mexican food adapted to American tastes. Or Tex-Mex.

Taco Bell, along with Kentucky Fried Chicken and Pizza Hut, is part of Yum! Brands. So comparing Taco Bell's international footprint to that of its two "sister" brands is one way of evaluating Chipotle's worldwide expansion possibilities:

	KFC	Percentage	Pizza Hut	Percentage	Taco Bell	Percentage
Total stores	19,420		15,605		6,206	
US*	4,393	22.6%	7,941	50.9%	5,987	96.5%
Rest of world	15,027	**77.4%**	7,664	**49.1%**	219	**3.5%**

*Including stores on US military bases abroad. Source: Yum! Brands, as of 2Q 2015 (www.yum.com/investors/restcounts.asp).

Relative to KFC and Pizza Hut, Taco Bell has close to zero international presence. And not, surely, from want of trying. As a multifranchisor, Yum! Brands has the buying power to "carry" Taco Bell on the back of KFC and Pizza Hut. If they've tried that, it clearly hasn't worked.

That's one indication that Americanized Mexican food doesn't travel too well. Does this mean Chipotle International will follow Taco Bell's path?

On the surface, it could. My initial impression was that American tourists could be a major factor in keeping these outlets afloat.*

Boots on the Ground

But . . . such initial impressions are just that. Impressions. Subject to research and verification. And at the end of the day there's no substitute for walking around.

So while my daughter, Natasha, was in London, I asked her to "walk around" on my behalf. Her report:

> Chipotle is really good. Especially the meat. In a couple of taquerias I went to in Australia the meat seemed to have been sitting around for a while and then they'd just reheat it. In Chipotle it was always fresh, hot, and really nice.
>
> Both Chipotles I visited were pretty busy, mostly Londoners with just a scattering of American and European accents.
>
> I also went to Chipotle's competition in London: Chilango. It seemed to me that wherever there's a Chipotle there's a Chilango somewhere nearby.
>
> Chilango is almost exactly the same as Chipotle. The setup very similar. Both have a conveyor-like production line, and you can see everything being prepared right in front of you.
>
> Chipotle's décor is pretty basic. But in Chilango most everything is colorful, so it's much nicer inside. More welcoming.
>
> My friend Kris says there's a bit more flavor in Chipotle's food than Chilango's. But I thought both are very good.
>
> Chilango seemed a bit more innovative. When I went they'd just added dishes

---

*For example, see this article from *Bloomberg Business:* http://www.bloomberg.com/bw/articles/2013-02-26/why-chipotle-sales-are-low-in-london.

like chili con carne burritos and taco soups. An experiment, the counter staff told me.

Both Chilangos I visited had proper seating areas. While in the Chipotle at Moorgate you could hardly turn around. Just six seats. Not somewhere to sit down and eat lunch, unless you just want to eat and run. Didn't feel friendly. Aimed at the takeout trade.

"There Was a Chilango Near Every Chipotle I Visited"

This was an unexpected discovery that ran counter to my first impression!

Chilango is a UK-based Chipotle clone. With ten outlets to date, it's expanding faster than Chipotle.

It turns out, thanks to a quick Google search, that Chilango is not alone. Other British Mexican fast casual chains include Tortilla (twenty-seven locations, eighteen in London) and Barburrito (twelve locations, three in London). Plus many others in the fast casual space serving different kinds of food: Byron (burgers), Leon (various fresh fast food), Rosa's (Thai), and Tossed (healthy salads), to name just a few.

Clearly, in London fast casual food is taking off. But Chipotle is not the prime beneficiary of this trend.

What's Driving Fast Casual

It's interesting to note that while some of these chains are in "everyday" spaces such as burgers and pizzas, many offer cuisines that are far from widely popular, such as Vietnamese, Thai, Greek, and South Asian.

Chilango in London.

To make sense of the underlying forces that are driving the dramatic expansion of the fast casual concept, it helps to understand how we acquire our tastes for unusual foods.

Some Like It Hot

For example, what's your tolerance for chili? And other spicy-hot foods?

Unless you grew up in India, the Szechuan or Hunan Provinces of China, Korea, Mexico, or Thailand, probably not high. Chili is a taste you acquire in adulthood. If at all.

Which is decidedly *not* the case in Thailand.

Once, while in Bangkok, I saw a mother introducing her two- or three-year-old daughter to chili. Extra-mild, to start with. But by the time she was six, she'd be calmly eating dishes that would blow off the top of your head (and mine).

If you're Thai, then Thai food is your daily diet. If you're not, it's an occasional treat (and light on the chili, please).

In the same way, we all grow up with some favorite foods. Especially the ones that Mother made. But also with certain other cuisines that are popular. In my case, Chinese and to a lesser extent Indian restaurants were everywhere when I was a kid. But I have no idea if there was a Mexican restaurant anywhere in Australia back then.

Most Americans, on the other hand, grow up with Mexican (or Tex-Mex) food all around them. For them it's nothing out of the box.

Elsewhere (except Mexico) Mexican is a taste acquired in adulthood. Or, as in my case, *not* acquired.

We all acquire our tastes in food in three stages.

Stage one. As kids, we eat pretty much anything our parents serve us. We have our favorites (usually McDonald's ☺), but we aren't picky.

Stage two. The majority of teenagers are the most finicky and hard-to-please eaters of any age. It's not just broccoli we wouldn't eat unless it was forced down our throats. In our teenage years we tended to avoid anything unusual, thus reinforcing basic lifetime preferences for a limited range of cuisines that we'll happily eat every day of the week.

Stage three. From our late teens onward, we start hanging out with friends from other backgrounds and begin to experiment with other styles of food. Eventually we add a wide range of other food flavors to our palate. But as a general rule these are occasional treats rather than dishes we would like to eat daily.

Beef-based Big Macs and Whoppers fit right into our daily diet. Indeed, except for Hindus and vegetarians, everyone eats beef. Hamburgers are simply a convenient way to do so.

This explains the popularity of fast casual chains such as Chipotle and Panda Express: unusual, good-quality food at a reasonable (though not cheap) price that could be classed as an occasional treat. Like having the occasional Godiva chocolate instead of your regular Hershey's bar.

This also explains the difference between Taco Bell and Chipotle/Chilango.

Taco Bell's appeal is primarily in the United States, where Tex-Mex is a taste acquired in childhood.

The higher-quality Mexican food served by Chipotle, Chilango, and their clones appeals to the *adult* stage of taste acquisition.

Hence Taco Bell's low penetration outside the United States, while Chipotle, Chilango, and their various copycats are in a different, upmarket space.

Chipotle: To Buy or Not to Buy?

Returning to Chipotle, how do its financials compare to the criteria we outlined in chapter 9?

It's hard to tell from its annual report whether Chipotle is minimizing taxes or overreserving. However, on the other measures Chipotle comes out exceptionally well:

Conservative debt management. Very conservative. Other than accounts payable and similar short-term liabilities, Chipotle has no debt at all!

A manageable ratio of profits to interest payments. With no debt, there are no interest payments.

As a result, the quick and current ratios of the company's ability to repay its short-term liabilities are, as you can see, amazingly healthy:

	2015	2014	2013	2012	2011
Quick ratio	4.01	3.33	4.86	5.18	6.15
Current ratio	3.97	3.58	3.34	2.93	3.18

A pile of cash. Chipotle is sitting on almost a billion dollars in cash and cash equivalents. Almost double its annual after-tax profits.

What's more, this ratio has remained reasonably constant over the past few years:

$ 000s	2015	2014	2013	2012	2011
Cash & cash equivalents	$977,573	$830,465	$578,203	$472,553	$456,243
After-tax profits	$495,583	$445,374	$327,438	$278,000	$214,945
Cash/profits ratio	197.3%	186.5%	176.6%	170.0%	212.3%

By every measure, Chipotle's cash management is highly conservative.

Dividends. Chipotle does not pay any dividends.

But the company is returning excess cash to the shareholders through share buybacks.

On our financial measures, Chipotle is looking better and better.

Owner earnings and intrinsic value. Chipotle's owner earnings have been rising consistently, almost doubling between 2011 and 2015:

Owner earnings				
2015	2014	2013	2012	2011
$599,642	$415,549	$375,150	$395,038	$281,045
Owner earnings per share (diluted)				
$19.03	$13.28	$11.80	$12.43	$8.86

Indeed, the compounded annual growth rate (CAGR) for owner earnings was an exceptionally healthy 20.86 percent.

Thanks to share buybacks, owner earnings per share have compounded a little faster: 21.05 percent per year. As you would expect, Chipotle's intrinsic value per share has risen in step with owner earnings:

INTRINSIC VALUE PER SHARE DISCOUNTED AT 4.27% (AAA CORPORATE BOND RATE)					
Growth rate	2015	2014	2013	2012	2011
10%	$464.20	$421.43	$310.71	$259.02	$202.34
15%	$627.08	$569.30	$419.73	$349.91	$273.34
20%	$789.96	$717.16	$528.75	$440.79	$344.34

INTRINSIC VALUE PER SHARE DISCOUNTED AT 8%					
10%	$247.77	$224.94	$165.84	$138.25	$108.00
15%	$334.71	$303.86	$224.03	$186.76	$145.90
20%	$421.64	$382.79	$282.22	$235.27	$183.79

Our numbers are similar (though not identical) to those from Old School Value, shown in the following chart:

Chipotle
Price vs Intrinsic Value

★ Buy when the stock's price is under intrinsic value less your margin of safety

Source: oldschoolvalue.com

Does this make Chipotle a long-term-investment candidate?

Quite likely, subject to three yardsticks:

1. Chipotle solves its food-safety problems.

2. The company continues to follow its conservative debt strategy, financing expansion from profits and cash flow rather than debt and equity.

3. The price is right—below intrinsic value with, given the reservations outlined above, a rather hefty margin of safety.

Or if you take the view that solving its food-safety problems is not only doable but a matter of survival, and that eventually Chipotle's current issues will go away, the time to buy would be when the price is right.

Chipotle's Footprint. Local . . .

A company that is increasing owner earnings 20 percent or more a year with zero leverage is, clearly, an outstanding business and an outstanding investment opportunity (at the right price).

To date, however, that growth has been almost entirely limited to the United States. Chipotle's growth in its home market will slow as it nears saturation.

To guesstimate what that saturation point might be, consider Chipotle's footprint in its hometown of Denver: thirty-four stores in a city with a population of about 650,000. Around 19,000 people per location.

If that same ratio is applied to the whole country, the saturation point would be something like 16,500 stores.

Even if only a half or a quarter of that number can be reached, Chipotle could still double or quadruple its existing size without leaving home.

. . . and International

And if it can add the international icing to the American cake . . . ?

Successful international expansion for Chipotle depends on two related factors:

1. Will the fast casual concept travel?

Given the number of American fast casual chains franchising worldwide, not to mention foreign copycats, the answer to the first question is a definite *yes!* As this table shows:

AMERICAN FAST CASUAL CHAINS EXPANDING ABROAD

Chain	Countries
BurgerFi	Mexico
Five Guys Burgers and Fries	Canada, Scotland
Jamba Juice	Philippines, Taiwan
Maui Wowi Hawaiian Coffees & Smoothies	Mexico, Saudi Arabia, UAE
MOOYAH Burgers, Fries & Shakes	Kuwait
Panda Express	Dubai
Smashburger	Panama
Zoup! Fresh Soup Company	Canada

Source: "2015 Fast Casual Top 100 Movers & Shakers," www.fastcasual.com, plus company Web sites.

2. Will non-Tex-Mex markets go for a Chipotle-style menu?

The answer to this question is harder to judge.

The success of Chipotle's British clones is definitely encouraging. But small potatoes compared to the US market—so far.

One back-of-the-envelope way to guesstimate international possibilities is to project from Chipotle's domestic penetration, related to the popularity of Mexican restaurants in other countries.

For example, according to yelp.com, Chipotle's hometown of Denver has 229 (non-Chipotle) Mexican restaurants. With 34 locations, Chipotle has 14.85 percent of the Mexican market.

In New York, Chipotle's share is far lower: 41 stores out of 1,264 Mexican restaurants. For a penetration of just 3.24 percent.

Using the lower New York figure to be conservative, we can project Chipotle's possible footprint in other cities and countries:

	Toronto	Melbourne	London
Mexican restaurants*	293	209	922
Chipotle projection	9	6	29

The London projection of twenty-nine stores is surprisingly similar to the existing total of Chipotle-style restaurants:

MEXICAN FAST CASUAL OUTLETS

Chain in London		In UK
Tortilla	18	27
Barburrito	3	12
Chilango	10	10
Chipotle	7	7
Total	**38**	**56**

*Note: the figures, from yelp.com, are not necessarily complete and may over- (or under-) estimate the actual numbers.

It looks as though we're on the right track. So let's take those London numbers and project them across the UK and the European Union to get some idea of the number of locations the Mexican fast casual space could potentially reach:

	Population (million)	Projected outlets
London	8.5	38
United Kingdom	64.1	287
European Union	508.2	2,272

And while we're at it, let's get a "second opinion":

Australia's Mexican Restaurant Chains	
Zambrero	103
Guzman y Gomez Mexican Taqueria	67
Salsa's Fresh Mex	54
Mad Mex Fresh Mexican Grill	51
Total	**275**

With a total of 275 outlets, these four chains have a penetration rate of one store per 84,110 people. And they're far from the only Mexican restaurants in the country.

That's a *big* change since I was a kid!

Vaguely Right Rather Than Precisely Wrong

As I mentioned, these numbers are *very* back-of-the-envelope calculations.

Are they accurate?

Of course not.

Indeed, that's not the main question. Which is:

Are they *indicative*?

Damn right they are.

These quick projections certainly do not tell us that this space can support 287 stores in the UK.

We could do a more accurate estimate. Several of them. And we should—if we're thinking of putting money on the table in this space.

But no matter how finely tuned a projection we can come up with, it remains a projection. And so subject to all manner of uncertainties.

Ultimately, though, we're not interested in a precise number. Rather, the questions we want answers to are:

1. Can this space support *more* outlets?

2. If yes, (a) a few more? Or (b) a helluva lot?

We can tentatively conclude that the answer is 2b, a helluva lot. Certainly compared to the size of the existing UK chains.

For instance, with close to two thousand stores, if Chipotle can add ten or twenty more outlets in the UK, the results will hardly nudge its stock price.

But if Chilango can add those ten or twenty outlets, we're looking at a double or triple.

Furthermore, these numbers tell us that this space is expanding in the UK—and Chipotle is at the bottom of the list. So while the potential exists for a thousand or two thousand stores across Europe, that prize seems more likely to go to one of these smaller, and *hungrier,* chains than to Chipotle.

Either way, any profit from international expansion will be gravy for Chipotle shareholders. But chateaubriand and champagne for any of these smaller UK chains, or other European competitors.

So long as we're happy to be vaguely right, the best way to profit from the international possibilities in this space is to ignore Chipotle and look at small, non-American Chipotle clones such as Chilango.

Chipotle or Chilango?

From this exercise, I have come to several conclusions:

1. Chipotle represents an outstanding investment—at the right price.

2. Fast casual, including Mexican, is taking off in London and could easily take off in other international markets.

3. Any international expansion by Chipotle is potentially icing on the main cake (but may turn out to be an annoying distraction, producing not much return).

4. Best case: Chipotle International could increase the company's current earnings somewhere between 50 percent and a double.

5. If the Mexican fast casual space can support just one hundred outlets in the UK, and five hundred to a thousand in the European Union, that represents an easy double or even quintuple for Chilango or one of its UK competitors.

6. However, an investment in Chilango et al. requires more investigation. Just to start with, these companies' financial returns, to the extent the information is available at all, are not on a par with Chipotle's annual returns.

And a reminder:

I've yet to visit Chipotle, Chilango, or any of their clones myself.

Yet, starting out from scratch, with the help of Google and people I know around the world, I have (I believe) spotted one definite, and possibly two or more, buy-and-pretty-much-forget investments. Without leaving home.

What's Next

Starting a business or investing in one are two sides of the same coin.

The underlying nuts and bolts are identical. A major difference is the *perspective.*

For example, imagine that one of your friends—let's call him Sam—comes to you with what sounds like a great business idea. So you're considering whether to finance him.

While your focus is on the business's *start-up* phase, you're concerned with questions like:

- Does Sam's *concept* make financial sense? Is it marketable?

- Can Sam create a compelling customer experience?

- Is Sam the kind of person who can *inspire* customers and employees?

- Can he build a *team*? Or is he likely to be a one-man band?

- And the other criteria we've identified that define a start-up that is *likely* to succeed.

Assume that Sam has all his ducks lined up in a row. But the financial requirements are a bit more than you can afford. So you decide to spread the risk by inviting others to put in some money.

All of a sudden, you've assumed the role of a *stock promoter.*

Your perspective has changed: to promote a stock successfully should you sell—

The Sizzle or the Steak?

A Vancouver stock promoter I met many years ago had noticed that some newly listed companies took off, while others with pretty much the same balance sheet and profit-and-loss statement stagnated or even fell.

By analyzing pairs of such companies, he discovered that what set one apart from the other was the *story*.

The company with the sexy sizzle caught the attention of the media, got brokers and investors hot under their collars and excited enough to open their wallets.

When he promoted companies like this—even when they had more story than substance—he could bank a handsome profit.

The boring, stodgy company that made bricks or industrial parts no one had ever heard of went nowhere. Even when it was the better *investment*.

Fact is, we all love stories. Fiction tops nonfiction on the bestseller lists—and bestselling nonfiction books are full of stories. TV is dominated by dramas and comedies. And when was the last time you went to the movies to watch a documentary?

The Big Short is the only recent one that comes to my mind. More "faction" than documentary, it has all the hallmarks of a classic drama. Ordinary and not-so-ordinary people skating on the edge of total failure as they confront, and eventually overcome, world-shaking events. While the supposed guardians of right and wrong are either asleep—or corrupt.

Turn to *Forbes, Fortune, Businessweek,* or your favorite investment adviser or Wall Street analyst and what will you find?

Stories.

We're *all* suckers for a good story.

Marketers and salesmen take advantage of this, spinning an entertaining yarn that (at its best) is the truth, and nothing but the truth.

But rarely the *whole* truth.

How often, in your experience, did the steak you just bought fail to live up to its sizzle?

I hate to think. I was a callow youth of nineteen when I made my first investment. I bought the story—hook, line, and sinker. Turned out there was no steak. That, sad to say, wasn't the last story I bought.

Did I say "investment"? I thought I was investing. In reality, I was *speculating.* And didn't know the difference. Didn't know there *is* a difference.

It took me a long time—and way too much money—to focus on the steak. Yet, I must admit, I'm still tempted by a great story.*

Cutting Through the Sizzle to the Steak

Buy the story and you're speculating.

To be an *investor,* you must cut through the sizzle and only buy the steak.

In a start-up, it's even more important to focus on the steak.

---

*Full disclosure: this book, in case you haven't noticed, is full of *stories.*

Buy a story on Wall Street and you can sell at any time.

There's no market whatsoever for your interest in a start-up. So if the steak never materializes, your money will disappear.

And in a truly great business, *the steak is better than the sizzle.*

So let's be realistic.

Cutting through the story to get to the nuts and bolts of the next Starbucks, Whole Foods, Walmart, or McDonald's *before* its shares explode, or starting your own, takes time and effort.

But—as a friend who read an earlier draft told me:

"I Don't Have the Time . . ."

"I don't have the time to do all that traveling and walking around you've been talking about. I'd rather just pay you five thousand dollars to *tell* me when *you've* spotted the 'next Starbucks.'"

Years ago when I was in the "investment-guru business" (as editor of the *World Money Analyst*), I might have taken him up on his offer.

But frankly, $5,000 is not enough. No, I'm not trying to raise his offer. I just want to point out that when *you* discover the next Starbucks, you're sitting on a gold mine.

Back in the days of the California gold rush, do you think a prospector who came across a mother lode shouted his discovery from the rooftops?

Hell, no!

He kept his mouth shut, registered his claim, and (maybe) only then gloated about it.

That's what you should do. Keep *your* mouth shut, buy as much as you can—and only then (maybe) talk about it.

> ● On Wall Street, what everybody knows is basically useless information. *What nobody (else) knows* is the yellow brick road to investment success.

Yes, finding what nobody else knows does take time. But quite possibly, less time than you might think.

Starting a business. The same principle, keep your mouth shut, applies when starting a business. The hard part is not the concept. It's the execution.

Quite likely, some people out there are far better at executing than you are. (Certainly true in my case!) If any of them get wind of what you're up to, they may get out of the gate before you can.

Much harder to achieve than keeping your purchase of a stock a secret. But not impossible. New ventures can even stay under the radar while in plain view. Which Walmart achieved by, fortuitously, opening for business in America's boondocks.

Become a critical customer. You frequent a host of businesses pretty much every day. Whether in shopping centers or online. You're *always* "walking around." From now on, walk around with your eyes wide open. *Evaluate* your customer experience. You'll soon discover how imperfect most businesses are.

When you come across a business with a *superb* customer experience, it will stand right out.

If your customer experience is the same the *next* time you buy from that business, and consistently good at the other branch(es) across town, you could be onto something.

In business, creative copycatting is a major key to success.

The process is the same: Walk around with your eyes open. Evaluate your customer experiences. With the aim of copying anything you find that will improve *your* customers' experience—and *your* profits.

It worked for Sam Walton and Walmart. It will work for you, too.

Decode the company's financial statements to see if they back up your estimate of the customer experience.

As we've seen with DavidsTea, a company can have loyal customers—without having (yet) *enough* customers to be profitable.

Or reverse the process. On Google or Yahoo! Finance you can screen stocks by EPS, return on capital, return on equity, or just about any other financial criterion you like.

When you find a company with outstanding financials, then check out the customer experience and other metrics we've been discussing to see if this business may qualify as the next Starbucks.

When You've Found a Great Company . . .

Then what?

Wait. You want more than a great company. You want a great *investment.*

A great investment is a great company *at the right price.*

The right price for a long-term, buy-and-pretty-much-forget investment is below intrinsic value, minus an extra margin of safety.

Which means you have to—

Be patient. Patience is the primary virtue of the successful *investor.* As George Soros put it: "When there's nothing to do, do nothing."

Too many people think that they're not investing unless they're buying and selling.

The truth is the opposite. *More activity* correlates with *lower returns*—partly due to higher transaction costs.[1]

Warren Buffett says he's happy to come across a good investment idea once or twice a year. Placing one or two buy orders a year takes just *minutes* of his time.

You just need to look at the *Forbes* list of the world's billionaires to see the result of such "masterly inactivity."

Of course, the world's greatest investors are not sitting around twiddling their thumbs in those many days, weeks, or months between their brief bouts of buying and selling.

On the contrary, the majority of their time is devoted to *searching* for investments that meet their criteria. The balance of their time is spent *monitoring* the investments they've already made.

Searching. The reality is, *no one* is going to find another Starbucks (or a hot copycat) every day of the week. Maybe not even once a year.

The times you can buy great companies at bargain prices are just as infrequent.

So the secret to profiting from the investment strategies we've outlined here is to identify great companies and figure out the price you are willing to pay so that when the time comes, you'll be ready to act.

Indeed, when that time does come, you may have more investment candidates than you have capital to invest.

And After You've Bought the Next Starbucks . . . Monitor

This does not mean checking the stock price every day. Indeed, when an investment meets all our criteria, price is the last thing we need to worry about.

What's far more important is to monitor whether the company is continuing to practice the five clues.

Any lapse—especially in the customer experience—is cause for concern; a possible time to sell.

What I'm Doing Right Now

As I write these words in early 2017, I'm sitting mostly in cash.

Collecting that magnificent 0.01 percent interest.

This is clearly *not* a strategy that will maintain the after-inflation purchasing power of my capital *in the short term.*

In other words, I'm *waiting.*

Waiting for the inevitable crash that always follows a boom. A rerun of 2008. When I expect to pick up dozens of truly great companies at fire-sale prices.

Am I suggesting you do the same?

Not necessarily.

You're a different person from me.

That sounds like a statement so obvious that even mentioning it seems pointless.

But *that* is one of the most crucial things to understand if you want to be a successful investor.

You're not me, I'm not you—and *neither* of us is Warren Buffett, George Soros, Benjamin Graham, Carl Icahn, Bernard Baruch, Peter Lynch, Peter Thiel, or any of the other members of the "investment hall of fame."

We can learn from them. And should.

But if you're familiar with those names, one thing is crystal clear when you think about it:

> ● *No two of those investors have followed exactly the same investment strategy.*

Each developed his own strategy to fit his unique personality, preferences, circumstances—and his particular skills, talents, and knowledge. As does every successful entrepreneur.

When you develop your own investment or business strategy, one unexpected result is peace of mind.

People who buy stories step onto an emotional roller coaster. They soar to euphoria and sink to panic as the market goes up and down.

When your investment or business approach is consonant with your personality, you are immune to Mr. Market's manic-depressive perturbations. And with sound financial management, you can even be immune to the economic cycle of boom followed by bust.

It is said, and truly, that the best time to buy is when everyone around you is panicking.

Which is only possible if your mind is clear when everyone else is losing his or hers.

And, yes, it is possible to achieve wealth and fame by marrying it, inheriting it, stealing it—or otherwise riding on someone else's coattails.

But nothing is more satisfying in life than discovering your own star and following it—to the exclusion of all others.

APPENDIX I: "From Poverty to Poverty in Three Generations"— What to Do When the Founder Departs the Scene

Remember the saying "from poverty to poverty in three generations"? With a few minor amendments we can apply it to the future course of corporations.

The meaning of the saying: a new fortune is created by the *founder,* who usually starts out with nothing. His children maintain and even expand that wealth. The grandchildren (or sometimes the children) squander it.

But let's consider *why* there is truth in this saying.

As we've seen with Howard Schultz, John Mackey, Sam Walton, and Ray Kroc, the founder is a person with a unique vision, mission, and combination of talents including superb, inspirational management.

People with this unique combination of traits are few and far between.

The founder's children grow up surrounded, so to speak, by the unique culture their (usually) father created. They absorb that culture. So when the founder dies or retires, the children take over and perpetuate that culture to some greater or lesser degree.

Not always. Ray Kroc's successor was Fred Turner, who joined McDonald's as a kid and rose through the ranks. He and many of his various associates absorbed the company culture that Kroc had created.

Turner was a worthy successor, expanding McDonald's beyond even Kroc's expectations.

So a corporation has two sources of continuity: the founder's children, and the company's managers and employees who were heavily influenced by the founder.

But there's a problem. *Collectively* the children and/or successor managers may have all the talents and abilities of the founder. Individually, none of them does.

We can state this categorically for one obvious reason: *not one of them has started anything from nothing.* Even a son or a daughter who has gone off to start his or her own business doesn't count as an exception—if Daddy gave them a helping hand.

A crucial moment in the life of every new corporation comes—

When the Founder Dies

Even when, like Ray Kroc and Sam Walton in their later years, the founder has stepped back from being the hands-on, day-to-day source of leadership and inspiration, he remains a source of wisdom, advice—and guidance.

What's more, despite his best intentions, he can't usually completely divorce himself from the business. Both Kroc and Walton were still focused on their "babies" long after they'd supposedly delegated everything to others.

As News Corporation CEO Rupert Murdoch said when asked what he'd do if he retired: "Die pretty quickly."

When the founder dies, what's left is his *memory*. For example, my mother died twelve years ago—yet I still carry on conversations with her in my head. Indeed, with my father, too, even though he is still alive.

In the same way, the founders' successors retain a similar mental replica, its strength depending on how fully they absorbed the founder's mentality.*

However, this mental replica is not identical to the original: it's a subconsciously created "mental construct," filtered through and colored by each person's own experiences, memories, and mental processes. The closer a person was to the founder, the more "real" the replica will be—but it's never exactly the same. Nevertheless, it still serves as a guide.

But when the *third* generation have direct experience of the founder, it's as young grandchildren or lowly beginning employees. So to the extent they imbibe the founder's culture, it's mostly second- or thirdhand.

Our focus here is on first-generation companies—while the founder is still in the saddle. Clearly Walmart and McDonald's are now into their third, fourth, or fifth generation of management. It's clear, especially with McDonald's, that some of the founding culture has gone.

By comparison, Walmart continues to follow Sam Walton's vision relentlessly, mainly because succeeding managements have kept Walton's focus and Walmart's USP (Unique Selling Proposition) of the lowest possible prices every day. A focus that relative to others such as Ray Kroc's QSCV (Quality, Service, Cleanliness, and Value) is exceptionally simple. That Ray Kroc, when visiting a McDonald's store, often cleaned the parking lot before going inside indicates that the *C* of QSCV didn't get all the way down.

A Company's Culture: Conscious or Unconscious?

Just as understanding a company's culture—that is, the combination of mission, vision, and operational methodology—is the key to identifying the next Starbucks, so determining how deeply the founding culture is embedded in a company is the key to forecasting its future after the founder departs.

The two simplest measures for an outsider to observe are:

1. Whether the culture's rationale has been fully outlined.

2. How effectively that culture is transmitted at the customer interface.

A third factor may be difficult for the outsider to establish:

3. Whether the company has a succession plan.

---

*To anyone acquainted with psychology, this is a familiar concept, termed subpersonalities. Each of us carries mental replicas of the most important people in our lives. Almost always that includes one's mother and father—who time and again rule someone's behavior long after they have passed away. Often, other significant people, too: a grandparent, aunt, or uncle, and/or someone who was a major inspiration, a "guru figure" of some kind. Such as those people, children or employees, who grew up following an inspirational leader like Howard Schultz, John Mackey, Sam Walton, or Ray Kroc.

1. Is the Company's Culture Clearly Defined?

When you can easily understand a company's underlying values and processes, the culture has been made conscious.

Intellectually understandable principles help transmit the culture from one generation to another by making it clear *why* the company does what it does. The absence of the specific *rationale* behind a company's culture is an inevitable source of problems when the founder departs the scene.

Consider the family of a self-made man. Normally, the father is so busy building his business that he has little time to spend with his children. The result: the extent to which his children inherit their father's outlook on life is a result of unconscious copying.

If the father has explained how and why he does what he does, his children will have the intellectual understanding *in addition to* the unconscious copying. Thus, it is far more likely that this second set of children will perpetuate their father's heritage than the first set.

So it is in a company.

Consider the difference between Walmart and McDonald's. Walmart's simple USP made it easy for successive generations to follow it faithfully. Ray Kroc, acting primarily from gut feel, did not *consciously* institutionalize the culture he created.

To appreciate how fragile a company's culture can be, consider what happened to Starbucks when Howard Schultz stepped back in 2000 (see page 83).

2. At the Customer Interface

Second, we can easily estimate whether a company's culture is embedded all the way down by analyzing our experience with it as a customer.

Does that experience communicate to us what the company says it stands for?

Answering that question is far easier when the principles behind the company's culture have been made fully conscious.

3. Is There a Succession Plan?

A third consideration is the nuts and bolts.

If the company's CEO is run over by a bus, are there designated candidates for succession trained and ready to step into his shoes?

"It's My Baby"

The relationship between a company's founder and his company can be, emotionally, as close as that between a mother and her favorite child.

James McLamore—cofounder (in 1954) and first CEO of Burger King—unwittingly demonstrates the truth of this proposition as he tells his and the company's story in his book *The Burger King.*

In 1967, Burger King merged with Pillsbury. McLamore remained CEO of Burger King until resigning in May 1972.

He also joined the Pillsbury board as a director, an indirect link with Burger King that ended in January 1989, when Pillsbury was taken over by Grand Metropolitan.

Nevertheless, as he tells Burger King's story from 1972 to 1998, when the book was completed, he always uses the word we, as if he were still part of the Burger King team.

What's more, especially after Grand Metropolitan took control, he was invited to become actively involved as a source of advice and inspiration to get Burger King back on track. A role he eagerly accepted—with no financial compensation.

His only motivation—and only reward—was to see his baby thrive.

While our focus has been the period when the founder remains in the saddle, it's important to understand generational transitions, especially the first one. As an example, let's apply this analysis to Warren Buffett's Berkshire Hathaway to determine the gold standard of succession planning.

Tap-Dancing to Work

Now in his eighties, Buffett remains firmly in the saddle of his creation: Berkshire Hathaway.

After he assumed control of Berkshire in 1965, the company became a vehicle for his investments. Both in the stock market and, with the purchase of National Indemnity in 1967, into insurance and later into buying whole companies.

Whether purchasing a portion of a company on the stock market or 80 percent to 100 percent of one, both are, from Buffett's perspective, *investments.* Requiring an answer to the question "Do I want to buy this company *with the existing management in place?*"

In most takeovers, the purchasing managers are sure they can do better than the incumbents, so more often than not the target's management is gutted.

Buffett's approach is the opposite. He'll only buy a company when the existing managers commit to stay on and continue to run the company *after* they've sold out.

The result: a conglomeration of businesses that have nothing to do with one another. No synergies are imposed by the head office—even when, as with Berkshire Hathaway subsidiaries Borsheims Fine Jewelry and Helzberg Diamonds, or Nebraska Furniture Mart, Jordan's Furniture, RC Willey Home Furnishings, and Star Furniture, they're all in the same business space.

And Buffett has often paid a *lower* price for many of these businesses than the sellers could have achieved elsewhere. Why? Because he guarantees that the seller's baby will continue to exist as is, *forever:* he promises to never sell it, a major attraction to businesses' creators who wish to see their legacy survive intact, long after they themselves have passed away.

The result is a unique company. A conglomerate of different businesses that actually works. Very different from ITT, LTV, Gulf+Western, and the other conglomerate "darlings of the market" in Wall Street's go-go years (page 63).

A major reason it works is that Berkshire is *more* than a conglomerate of companies. It's also a conglomerate of *cultures.*

Berkshire's Two-Way Culture Flow

Each Berkshire subsidiary, when acquired, came with its own culture—a combination of mission, vision, and operational methodology. That culture—when embedded all the way down—was perpetuated, regardless of Warren Buffett's or other Berkshire subsidiaries' preferred practices.

The result is a two-way culture flow. From bottom up, *and* from top down.

However, Buffett required new subsidiaries to make two major exceptions, two changes:

1. *Capital allocation* was reserved for the head office. Thus, each subsidiary acquired, on top of its original culture, Buffett's top-down capital discipline. Projects requiring capital injections had to meet Buffett's standards to go ahead. This restriction—*not* a real restriction if you're a rational manager—was quickly embedded into the subsidiaries' cultures.

2. *Succession:* a subsidiary's CEO had to nominate his successor. Which implies that one (or more) of his managers is *trained* to be ready to step into his shoes.

So the post-Buffett question now becomes, which part(s) of which culture(s) are likely to be disrupted by his passing on?

Buffett's Roles

Before addressing that question, we need to consider Buffett's roles as Berkshire's CEO.

He has reserved two functions for himself (everything else being delegated):

1. *Capital allocation:* investing Berkshire's continually growing pile of cash.

This consists of two parts:

    1a. Purchasing whole businesses as investments *with management in place.*

    1b. Purchasing portions of businesses via the stock market and related investment activities.

2. *Inspiring entrepreneurs* who've just received a large check or oodles of Berkshire stock to show up for work every day as if nothing had changed.

These roles are, naturally enough, directly related to Berkshire primary sources of income:

1. Earnings from the company's diverse range of subsidiaries.

2. Insurance, which generates float that can be used for investment.

3. Profits and dividends from Berkshire's investment portfolio.

Buffett's involvement ranges from minimal (#1) to medium (#2) and intense (#3).

So let's consider them in order in relation to Buffett's roles.

Earnings: Going Concerns That Keep on Going

As noted, Buffett's acquisition criteria ("with management in place—we can't supply it") ensure that postacquisition, there is no disruption of the new subsidiaries' operations.

While Warren Buffett will be sorely missed, as these subsidiaries are effectively separate operations from the head office, his absence should have little immediate impact on their sales, profitability, or operations.

> If Warren asked me to do anything, I would do it.
>
> —Richard Santulli, former CEO, Executive Jet Inc.

After all, the CEOs of those businesses are still there because they love what they do (see "It's My Baby"). Buffett's passing won't change that. And while they'll no longer be able to call Buffett for advice (which most of them don't), when in doubt they'll be able to answer the question "What would Warren do or say?" themselves with reasonable accuracy from their mental replica.

So we can also be reasonably certain that Berkshire's *existing* businesses will continue to operate in the same way. Not just in the short term but for as long as each subsidiary's culture continues to be passed on from one management generation to the next.

The current performance of Berkshire's earlier acquisitions—See's Candies, Nebraska Furniture Mart, Borsheims, and GEICO, to name just a few—suggests that forever is an achievable time perspective for their continued successful operations.

> Buffett's respectful treatment of his managers has instilled in them an ambition to "make Warren proud," as one puts it.
>
> —Businessweek

The major effect in the medium term may be in the *acquisition* of new businesses.

Warren Buffett is a superb judge of character. As Buffett's friend and fellow Benjamin Graham "alumnus" Walter Schloss put it:

> Warren is an unusual guy because he's not only a good analyst, he's a good salesman, *and he's a very good judge of people.* That's an unusual combination. If I were to [acquire] somebody with a business, I'm sure he would quit the very next day. I would misjudge his character or something—or I wouldn't understand that he really didn't like the business and really wanted to sell it and get out. *Warren's people knock themselves out after he buys the business,* so that's an unusual trait. [Emphasis added.][1]

This is arguably the Buffett talent that will be hardest to replace.

Should Berkshire's post-Buffett management be more in the Walter Schloss mold, the success rate of post-Buffett acquisitions may inevitably decline.

Overall, given the enormous cash-generating power of Berkshire's *existing* subsidiaries, it will be many years (if not longer) before any such effects will have a significant impact on the company's bottom line.

That said, Berkshire HQ is not the only source of acquisitions. Many of the company's subsidiaries are, in a sense, "mini-Berkshires," making what Buffett calls "bolt-on" acquisitions. Acquiring companies that fit or extend *their* business model, that are too small to be on Buffett's radar. Collectively, they continually have a significantly positive impact on Berkshire's total earnings.

Finally, given the institutionalization of Buffett's capital-allocation role, we can confidently assume that all subsidiaries' surplus cash will continue to be forwarded to the head office for investment purposes.

4. Insurance: Positive Float

Similarly, all Berkshire's insurance subsidiaries have absorbed the Buffett culture of walking away from any insurance deal that is not favorably priced.

"Favorably priced" means a manageable risk of loss combined with a price that will generate an underwriting profit. As Buffett puts it:

> The nature of our insurance contracts is such that we can never be subject to immediate demands for sums that are large compared to our cash resources. This strength is a key pillar in Berkshire's economic fortress.
>
> If our premiums exceed the total of our expenses and eventual losses, we register an underwriting profit that adds to the investment income our float produces. When such a profit is earned, we enjoy the use of free money—and, better yet, get paid for holding it.[2]

From Buffett's point of view, the beauty of insurance (provided it is correctly priced) is that premiums are received up front while claims are paid later—often, *many* years later.

The result is "float": premiums received that can be invested until claims must be paid. Here, from Buffett's 2014 "Letter to Shareholders," is the growth of Berkshire's float for the previous forty-four years:

Year	Float[3] ($ millions)
1970	$39
1980	$237
1990	$1,632
2000	$27,871
2010	$65,832
2014	$83,921

As with Berkshire's other subsidiaries, there is every reason to assume that the ingrained culture of underwriting discipline will continue to generate increasing float for the foreseeable future. Subject to payouts of long-standing claims (such as asbestos) that will soon come due.

5. Investments

Buffett's investment ability has been the driving force for Berkshire's success since he assumed control in 1965.

Aside from Lou Simpson, who managed GEICO's investment portfolio until he retired in 2010, all investment decisions were made by Warren Buffett.

Until recently.

Most people (including me) have assumed that Warren Buffett's talents in this field were irreplaceable.

But as Buffett himself implies in his essay "The Superinvestors of Graham-and-Doddsville,"[4] this is far from the case.

His essay profiles eight investors who were all influenced by Benjamin Graham's investment methods. All outperformed the S&P 500 over different time periods.

Buffett tapped Todd Combs (who joined Berkshire in 2010) and Ted Weschler (2011) as investment managers. They have since proved their worth—as Buffett reported in his 2013 "Letter to Shareholders":[5]

> In a year in which most equity managers found it impossible to outperform the S&P 500, both Todd Combs and Ted Weschler handily did so. Each now runs a portfolio exceeding $7 billion. They've earned it.

I must again confess that their investments outperformed mine. (Charlie says I should add "by a lot.")[6]

Intriguingly, when the value of Berkshire's fifteen largest stock holdings is subtracted from its total stock investments (of $117.47 billion), the balance (listed as "Others") is $15.7 billion. Which suggests Combs and Weschler may be managing close to all of Berkshire's "other" stock holdings.

Either way, Buffett clearly hired these two because they were already "graduates of Graham-and-Doddsville," with records as hedge fund managers to prove it.

So in the investment field, as with Berkshire's subsidiaries and its insurance operations, we can assume with reasonable safety that post-Buffett, Berkshire's investment returns will continue to exceed those of the S&P 500 for many years to come.

Indeed, having spent four years (so far) working under the Master, it is highly probable that both Todd Combs and Ted Weschler will have a highly accurate mental replica of Buffett's investment approach.

Structure

Perhaps more than any other CEO in the history of business, Warren Buffett has established various controls to ensure, as best as anyone can, that not only management operations but Berkshire's unique culture will continue after his departure.

Via his "Letters to Shareholders" he has assured his coinvestors that he and the board have developed a detailed succession plan, though he has not revealed all the details:

> Essentially my job will be split into two parts. One executive will become CEO and responsible for operations. The responsibility for investments will be given to one or more executives. If the acquisition of new businesses is in prospect, these executives will cooperate in making the decisions needed, subject, of course, to board approval. We will continue to have an extraordinarily shareholder-minded board, one whose interests are solidly aligned with yours.
>
> Were we to need the management structure I have just described on an immediate basis, our directors know my recommendations for both posts. All candidates currently work for or are available to Berkshire and are people in whom I have total confidence. Our managerial roster has never been stronger.[7]

Possible candidates include Ajit Jain (BH Reinsurance CEO) and Greg Abel (Mid-American), who are, says Berkshire vice chairman Charlie Munger, "proven performers who would probably be under-described as 'world-class.' 'World-leading' would be the description I would choose. In some important ways, each is a better business executive than Buffett."[8]

Buffett also suggests that his successor as chairman will be his son Howard Buffett:

My only reason for this wish is to make change easier if the wrong CEO should ever be employed and there occurs a need for the Chairman to move forcefully. . . . In my service on the boards of nineteen public companies, however, I've seen how hard it is to replace a mediocre CEO if that person is also Chairman. (The deed usually gets done, but almost always very late.)[9]

This division of chairman from CEO is a safeguard that is rarely found in listed companies anywhere in the world.

On the Downside

Another unique feature of Berkshire Hathaway is that it's the only listed stock in the world that has a guaranteed downside.

Buffett has indicated that Berkshire will repurchase shares if the price ever falls to 120 percent of book value.

There is every reason to assume that in at least the medium term, the post-Buffett management will follow that rule.

A "Buffett Premium"?

In the days following Warren Buffett's departure, absolutely nothing in terms of operations, profits, or earnings at Berkshire Hathaway will change.

What may change is the market's *perception* of Berkshire Hathaway's future.

If, as seems highly likely, Berkshire's stock price has a "Buffett premium" that disappears on his departure, given our analysis, it should be an excellent time to load up on Berkshire Hathaway stock.

In the longer term, Berkshire will face the same problem it faces now, except on a larger scale.

Long gone are the days when a See's Candy (purchase price, $25 million) or Nebraska Furniture Mart (purchase price, $55 million) can impact Berkshire's bottom line.

Today, Buffett repeatedly points out that only "elephants," such as Burlington Northern or MidAmerican, will suffice.

Should Berkshire's cash pile continue to grow, even elephants will not be enough. The post-Buffett management may have to find mammoths or mastodons instead.

In sum, with minor exceptions, most of Berkshire's sales, revenues, and profits for *this* year are the result of processes initiated and decisions made and executed in the preceding several years, if not decades.

The main *short-term* difference might be that Berkshire would miss out on a few "elephant" opportunities that Buffett would have purchased had he been on the spot. But as the results of a new purchase don't have a material effect on Berkshire's bottom line *immediately*, there would be little change in Berkshire's profits for that year.

To put it another way, Berkshire is a cash-generating machine that will certainly go on generating cash for many years after Buffett departs.

Inevitably, there will come a time, due to its size, when Berkshire can no longer outperform the market by any significant amount. Or certain crucial aspects of its culture may fade away.

That's a long-term rather than medium-term possibility. In the meantime, we can confidently conclude that Berkshire Hathaway, post-Buffett, will continue to follow its current growth path.

Berkshire's Corporate Gold Standard

Berkshire's succession plans provide another corporate gold standard we can use to evaluate the likely course of other companies when their founder departs.

Here are a few questions to determine whether a company has a clear succession plan.

IS there a succession plan?

If not, and if no one has been groomed to fill the founder's shoes, the company may go through several CEOs before finding its feet again.

An easy way to find out? Go to an annual meeting and ask the CEO, "If you were to walk out the door at the end of this meeting and be run over by a bus, what would happen to the company?"

If the CEO stutters, you know there's no succession plan in place.

Is someone groomed to step into the CEO's shoes?

If so, the chances of a smooth transition are higher than if the new CEO comes from outside the company.

Is the company's mission and vision really clear, and simple to understand?

The simpler the company's USP, the easier it is for everyone to follow.

For example, Walmart's "lowest everyday prices" makes it clear to everyone, from the CEO to the greeter at the store entrance, what the company aims to achieve.

To put it another way, the simpler the vision, the harder it is for anyone, including an incompetent CEO, to screw it up.

How deeply is the company's culture embedded?

If not deeply embedded, the company may go through several CEOs before finding its feet again.

Similarly, if the company's culture has been made conscious, it is more likely to endure after the founder departs.

APPENDIX II: A Quick Guide to Making Money in the Franchising Business

A franchisor has four ways of making money:

1. *Sell franchises* for cash up front.

2. *Sell supplies* to the franchisees.

3. *License* franchises for a percentage of sales.

4. *Be a banker,* financing franchisees, or building stores and leasing them.

Or, as is the case with the majority of franchisors, all of the above.

Even then, one of these ways tends to become the franchisor's primary focus, which is a major determinant of the company's ultimate success or failure.

1. Sell Franchises

When Harry Axene began franchising Dairy Queen his prime focus was on selling territorial franchises for $25,000 to $50,000.

His success spurred dozens of new franchisors attracted by the easy up-front money to be made from selling territories.

Minnie Pearl (page 63) is the extreme example of focusing on selling franchises: fast profits. But once all territories are sold, that revenue stream ends.

When the franchisor's primary focus is up-front sales, he has little or no interest in ensuring a uniform customer experience across all stores—and may not even care whether the franchisees ever make a dime. Which was certainly the case with Minnie Pearl.

In his sales visits to restaurant kitchens across the United States, Ray Kroc had seen the almost total *in*consistency between different stores of the same franchise chain. Dairy Queen was one of them. Some Dairy Queen franchisees stuck to the basic soft-serve menu, while most added an array of other products, from hamburgers and hot dogs to enchiladas and tacos.

One reason Kroc vowed to focus on maintaining control of the quality of *all* McDonald's outlets.

Nevertheless, territorial sales are a recipe for faster growth—the strategy that put

Burger Chef within shooting distance of overtaking McDonald's in 1971; one that also lifted Wendy's to the number two slot in the American market, passing Burger King, in 2013. Though Burger King regained the number two spot in 2015.[1]

Selling territorial franchises is a strategy used by almost all franchisors, including Burger King and McDonald's.

But Ray Kroc added a twist: territorial franchisees had to get *permission* to open another store. A franchisee who failed to meet Kroc's operating standards was denied that permission. So in Dallas for many years there was just *one* McDonald's store.

Thanks to the twist, McDonald's avoided the downside of territorial sales: large franchisees with enough clout to go their own, independent way, ignoring the standards set by the franchisor.

Internationally, *all* restaurant chains, from McDonald's to Starbucks, must follow the territorial sales strategy in countries that prohibit foreigners from owning retailers.

And even in countries that invite foreign investors, it is often more efficient to team up with a local partner.

2. Supplying Franchisees

A second source of revenue is supplying franchisees with equipment and menu items.

As the subsidiary of an equipment maker, Burger Chef's franchise agreements *required* franchisees to equip their restaurants exclusively with SaniServe machines.

From its beginning, Burger King centralized the sourcing of food and equipment. Initially, all its stores were company owned, but the sourcing continued when Burger King began franchising. As it grew, it, too, began manufacturing kitchen equipment.

The commissary and equipment manufacturer—two separate subsidiaries—became significant profit centers. But the impetus behind both was to better serve the franchisees, the reverse of Burger Chef.

When Burger King began expanding nationwide, supplies for new stores were delivered from a variety of manufacturers in different parts of the country. It could take three or more weeks to equip a new store once the building was completed. McLamore and Edgerton found that by centralizing all supplies in Miami, they could deliver everything a new store required—from cooking equipment to pencils and paper—in two truckloads. A new restaurant could now be up and running in just three *days*—at a lower cost to the franchisee.

Burger King then created a construction subsidiary in partnership with a Miami contractor. Specialization further reduced the franchisee's cost, and the needed construction time to sixty days from breaking ground—or less.[2]

Burger King franchisees—unlike Burger Chef's—were not required to buy from Burger King HQ. Most did though, since in its early years sources of specialized equipment were scarce, compared to the situation today. And franchisees appreciated Burger King HQ's aim of making everything easier for them.

Division of Focus

When the same management team owns *and runs* two or more businesses, a fundamental question arises: Which one has first priority?

And related: Are you willing to sacrifice the profits of one business to boost the profits of another?

In the case of Burger Chef, the answer to that second question was no, which caused some tension between franchisees and the management. When SaniServ began producing a french fryer, franchisees had to buy it. Previously, they had been using the same one as McDonald's, one they felt was superior to the SaniServ model.

Burger King's primary focus in supplying franchisees was to serve them. Initially, profits from supplying franchisees were secondary to expanding the chain. Later, all three subsidiaries were sold.

This approach became a significant source of positive cash flow for both Burger Chef and Burger King. Kroc adopted it, too—but with a crucial difference.

Like Burger Chef, Kroc's initial interest in McDonald's was equipment sales: the vision of selling eight MultiMixers at a time to restaurants spreading from Los Angeles to New York and Miami.

But thanks to his restrictive agreement with the McDonald brothers, even if he'd wanted to (which he didn't), Kroc had neither the cash flow nor the capital to consider going into the equipment or commissary businesses.

Aside from selling two or three MultiMixers (rather than the expected eight) to each new McDonald's, *all* supplies were sourced from unrelated third parties.

But their selection was not random; nor was it left to the franchisees' discretion. McDonald's suppliers were chosen by Kroc, based on whether they were willing and able to produce according to Kroc's tight specifications. But they sold direct to franchisees.

In the short run, Burger Chef and Burger King benefited from the additional profit source. But in the long run McDonald's reaped the rewards of the intense focus on a single source of revenue.

3. Percent of Sales

Both unable and unwilling to profit from territorial sales or supplying franchisees, Kroc was left with just one source of income: percentage of sales.

Sonneborn's real estate financing strategy enabled Kroc to get around his restrictive agreement with the McDonald brothers—and put Kroc and the franchisees firmly in the same camp.

4. The Starbucks Model

The ultimate key to franchising success is ensuring a consistent customer experience across all outlets and cultures. And despite the advantages of Kroc's approach, his method is not the only way.

Chains such as Pret A Manger and Chipotle achieve this by owning all the outlets.

Starbucks' approach is in between these two extremes. Worldwide, the company owns just over half of all outlets (in the United States, company stores are 61 percent of the total), the remainder being franchised.

Yet, wherever you go, you'll see that the key ingredients of Starbucks' products—especially coffee and tea—are supplied by the company.

Indeed, competing chains such as Coffee Bean & Tea Leaf follow the same practice. If each outlet did its own sourcing for these key ingredients, the result would be chaos, with different tea and coffee flavors at every store.

Any of these four franchising models (singly or in combination) can result in a successful business—*provided* the primary focus of the company, its suppliers, its partners, and its franchisees is the customer experience.

APPENDIX III: DavidsTea

As the primary investment candidate in the retail tea sector, DavidsTea is worthy of investigation, even though on most of our criteria it turns out to be negative.

Unfortunately, in searching for the next buy-and-pretty-much-forget investment, we're going to reject far more companies than we will accept. Including companies such as DavidsTea that on first impression appear promising, but on further investigation fail on too many of our criteria.

Still in the Start-up Phase

Financially, DavidsTea is still in the start-up phase, even though founded in 2008 and despite having 193 stores.

On the positive side, gross sales have been increasing.

On the negative side, while same store sales are rising at around 6 percent annually, the *rate* of same store sales has been declining from a peak of 17.8 percent in 2013.

The primary cause of this decline is Davids' expansion into the US market. Its American stores' gross sales are, at best, *half* the gross of its Canadian stores.[1] Which strongly suggests that Davids chose the wrong market for expansion beyond Canada.

Continuity of management. But the major question mark over DavidsTea's future is continuity of management.

A primary factor in the long-term success of Starbucks, Whole Foods, Walmart, McDonald's, and other high-growth companies is that the founder and his management team stay in place essentially till "death (or senility) do us part."

But in the year following DavidsTea's 2015 IPO, an almost complete turnover occurred at the top, including the resignation of the company's founder and visionary, David Segal.

Whether this new team is an improvement remains to be seen. As we have no way of judging the new management without a sufficient period of data, DavidsTea *cannot,* currently, be a candidate for a long-term investment.

DavidsTea's financials. Though the company was founded in 2008, financial data is only available from 2013. So we have insufficient data to infer long-term judgments of the management's financial behaviors.

Nevertheless, on certain measures the company's financial behavior looks highly promising:

Conservative debt management? Following its 2015 IPO, Davids paid off its long-term debt of C$4.29 million, ending the year with zero long-term debt.

In addition, at the IPO preferred shares were converted to common stock, so eliminating the dividend on these shares.

Thus, the only interest payments are on short-term liabilities. For example, the company has a revolving credit facility of C$20 million.

However, since prior to the IPO the company did make extensive use of debt financing, we cannot assume that the management has a long-term commitment to a debt-free or low-debt company.

A manageable ratio of profits to interest payments? The company's ratio of profits to interest payments is not meaningful. Nevertheless, with no long-term debt, in the worst-case scenario of a deep recession, DavidsTea will not be burdened with interest payments.

The quick and current ratios are also positive:

As of 30 January	2016	2015	2014
Quick ratio	4.46	1.32	1.14
Current ratio	5.41	1.96	1.80

A pile of cash? As of 31 January 2016, DavidsTea had C$72.5 million in its cash kitty. The increasing cash from the previous years is, however, the result of the IPO rather than accumulated profits.

C$ 000s	2016	2015	2014
Cash & cash equivalents	$72,514	$19,784	$15,350
After-tax profits	$13,360*	$8,309	$2,705
Cash/profits ratio	542.77%	238.10%	567.47%

*Not counting a noncash charge of $140.9 million related to the conversion of preferred shares to common stock at the IPO.

Dividends? Unsurprisingly, DavidsTea does not currently pay any dividends and doesn't expect to do so for the foreseeable future. We don't know whether that is company policy or just a reflection of the reality that until 2016, there were no profits to distribute.

Despite these positive signs, the rest of the financial news, while potentially promising, is not too good.

Marginally profitable. In the years leading up to 2014, the company made an operating loss.

While it achieved profitability in 2015, that record is not a good sign for an eight-year-old chain with so many outlets!

A major reason for that change from loss to profitability is that the IPO, by enabling the company to pay off all its long-term debts, has eliminated over a million dollars in annual interest charges.

Return on equity and return on capital are both negative.

Growth in gross sales and same store sales are both positive at 27.35 percent and 6.9 percent respectively.

But, as noted above, same store sales growth has been declining. The high growth in same store sales appears to be coming from its home market, while Davids' expansion into the United States is sending the growth rate down.

Unfortunately, the company provides no breakdown of results in the two different markets. And this is not the only omission in the company's financials.

In summary, with insufficient data to project *owner earnings* and *intrinsic value,* and serious question marks over the potential of its US expansion, not to mention the management changes, it's impossible to make a realistic forecast of DavidsTea's future earnings.

The best case we can make for DavidsTea is that it may continue to expand profitably. But not at a sufficiently high rate of growth to warrant considering it as a candidate for a long-term investment.

APPENDIX IV: Resources

A wealth of information is available that can extend and add to your knowledge of the subject we've covered in these pages.

What follows is a selection of books, Web sites, and other sources I think you'll find most useful.

On my Web site you'll find a number of articles and other resources on general investment topics. From time to time (on no fixed schedule) I'll add new posts on my Money Markets & Mischief blog. You can sign up for either all posts or money and investment topics only.

Plus a complimentary eBook: *How to Make More Money by Sitting on Your Butt.*

That's just one of the many contrarian conclusions I've usually come to from a lifetime in the markets. Usually the hard way: by losing money or missing out on a slam dunk opportunity.

Check it out here: marktier.com/sitting.

And also, two questionnaires that can help improve your investment returns:

What's Your Investment Personality?

The simplest way to become a better investor—and make more money more easily—is to discover, focus on, and *act from* the investment style that suits you best.

In my book *The Winning Investment Habits of Warren Buffett & George Soros* I identify three major "investor archetypes":

The Analyst, personified by Warren Buffett.

The Trader, epitomized by George Soros, who acts decisively, often on incomplete information, trusting his gut feel, supremely confident that he can always beat a hasty retreat.

The Actuary deals in numbers and probabilities. Like an insurance company he is focused on the overall outcome, totally unconcerned with any single event. The actuarial investment strategy is, perhaps, best characterized by the legendary investor Benjamin Graham. It's also the basis of most successful commodity trading systems.

Each of us has a natural affinity with one of the three archetypes.

What's yours? Knowing the answer is essential if you want to develop an investment style that you know is going to work for you.

Find out what kind of investor you are by completing my "Investor Personality Profile."

Discover Your Investment IQ

A second questionnaire will give you a detailed report on your investment habits and strategies.

You will discover how you, as an investor, compare to Warren Buffett, Carl Icahn, and George Soros.

Plus you'll also receive a detailed report highlighting your investment weaknesses—and strengths.

And exactly what steps you need to take to make more money more easily.

You'll find it at marktier.com/iq.

Let's now turn to other topics, beginning with general investment resources, before turning to resources specific to the various topics we've been discussing here.

Investment Resources (General)

Unsurprisingly, I highly recommend my own *The Winning Investment Habits of Warren Buffett & George Soros.*

This book is not about investing per se, but about the *mental habits* Warren Buffett, George Soros, and other successful investors including Carl Icahn, Sir John Templeton, Benjamin Graham, and Bernard Baruch have all practiced religiously.

Whatever your investment style, you'll improve your investment returns by adopting the mental habits of the world's greatest investors.

Essential reading for any investor taking a long-term view is Benjamin Graham's *The Intelligent Investor* and *Security Analysis,* plus Warren Buffett's "Letters to Shareholders."

Believing you have to be able to predict the market to be a successful investor is one of what I call the Seven Deadly Investment Sins.*

The antidote is *The Fortune Sellers: The Big Business of Buying and Selling Predictions,* by William A. Sherden.

He shows that only one class of forecasters beats the naïve forecast (the weather / the market / the dollar / etc., will be / do the same today as it did yesterday) with any regularity: weather forecasters. But only for forecasts for up to four days in the future. And even then, by only a small margin.

So next time you're tempted to listen to some guru's market prediction, remember that you can beat any guru—on average—by simply "predicting" that the market will do tomorrow what it did today.

Finally, *Finding the Next Starbucks,* by Michael Moe, takes a "top-down" approach to searching for the next high-growth company. An excellent companion to the "bottom-up" perspective you've been reading here.

Old School Value

While many financial indicators are readily available on Yahoo! Finance and Google Finance, oldschoolvalue.com goes dozens of steps farther by crunching those numbers for you on any US-listed company, in more ways than you've ever thought of before.

OSV is an invaluable aid to making informed buy or sell decisions, even when (or *especially* when) number crunching is not your forte.

Try it out for yourself: oldschoolvalue.com.

---

*This topic is the subject of chapter 2 of *The Winning Investment Habits of Warren Buffett & George Soros.*

Management and Company Culture

Both *Onward,* by Howard Schultz, and *Who Says Elephants Can't Dance?,* by Louis Gerstner, demonstrate the importance of restoring (Starbucks) or reinventing (IBM) a company's *culture* to ensure its future profitability.

John Mackey outlines a primary reason behind Whole Foods' success in *Conscious Capitalism*—the creation of a unique company culture.

Good to Great and *Built to Last,* both by Jim Collins, are essential guides to appreciate the components that go into creating a great and lasting business.

In *Friend and Foe,* Adam Galinsky and Maurice Schweitzer apply the results of scientific research to creating the atmosphere of trust and managing the tension between cooperation and competition.

Building a successful brand is one of the more powerful marketing tools available to any business. *Brand Royalty,* by Matt Haig, is a fascinating and highly useful survey of the world's top one hundred brands—and what made them successful.

Starting Your Own Business

Robert Kiyosaki's *Cashflow Quadrant* makes the fundamental differences between a real business and a one-man band crystal clear.

One essential difference between the two is *system.* And Michael Gerber's *The E-Myth,* and its companion, *E-Myth Workbook,* are essential guides to developing a business *system.**

After writing that when planning a business you should "begin at the end rather than the beginning" (page 134), I was pleased to have my view powerfully reinforced when I came across *Start at the End,* by David Lavinsky. He's an entrepreneur who, today, advises business owners on how they can improve their results by focusing on their ultimate goals and working backward to the establishment and running of a business, rather than the other way around.

The $100 Startup, by Chris Guillebeau, is based on hundreds of interviews with people from all around the world who have retired from the corporate rat race and created a business so they can do their own thing—and get paid for it.

While Guillebeau's focus is on starting a small business rather than the next Starbucks, the key takeaway is how easy it really is to start a profitable business on a shoestring. Whatever your ultimate aim.

Zero to One, from PayPal founder Peter Thiel, is based on a course about start-ups he gave at Stanford University in 2012. His focus is on building a business that will offer something new, and potentially revolutionary.

While not a how-to book, *Zero to One* offers a set of guidelines based on Thiel's extensive experience in the high-tech and venture capital fields.

Finally, here are three information sources I find particularly helpful. Each offers a regular e-mail news update:

Fast Casual, fastcasual.com/.

Nation's Restaurant News: nrn.com/.

And *CBInsights,* which covers a wide range of industries, including high-tech: cbinsights.com.

---

*For more on these two books see "Running (or Starting) a Business? Here Are Two Must-Have 'Guide Books.'" http://marktier.com/running-or-starting-a-business-here-are-two-must-have-guide-books.

Franchising

An enormous amount of information and advice on franchising is freely available thanks to the Internet.

A good place to start is the *Franchise Business Review,* www.franchisebusinessreview .com, and its article "5 Reliable Resources for Your Franchise Research": http://www .fbr50.com/5-reliable-resources-franchise-research/.

Another source: the International Franchise Association (www.franchise.org), which, despite its name, is primarily US oriented.

Similar organizations in other countries can help you with the local franchising rules, regulations—and opportunities. Country-specific Google searches on *franchising* will bring up organizations similar to the International Franchise Association, and other resources that will help you get started.

Venture Capital / Angel Investing

Here are three links that offer crucial input for anyone thinking of starting a business. Big or small.

In this TED Talk, Idealab founder Bill Gross discusses the single biggest reason why start-ups succeed: https://www.ted.com/talks/bill_gross_the_single_biggest_reason_why_startups_succeed?language=en.

Negative feedback is often more useful than praise. Better to get it *before* you start. "5 Signs Your Startup Is Screwed" highlights five important factors you must avoid if you want to succeed: http://www.infoworld.com/article/3017681/it-careers/5-signs-your-startup-is-screwed.html.

Indian VC Mahesh Murthy's sixteen-point checklist helps him decide whether to invest in a start-up. Highly useful: https://www.quora.com/Seedfund-What-does-Mahesh-Murthy-look-for-in-a-company-before-investing-in-it-at-seed-level.

Finding venture capital. In the last twenty-five years, tens if not hundreds of thousands of venture capital funds have come into existence all over the world.

So much money is chasing so many business ideas this is probably the best time in history to be an entrepreneur.

If you're looking for venture capital, here are some directories and other sources of information:

> http://www.boogar.com/resources/venturecapital/index.htm
> https://www.angelinvestmentnetwork.us/
> http://angelnetwork.com/
> https://gust.com/

"Top 10 Angel Investor Groups," according to *Entrepreneur* magazine: https://www. entrepreneur.com/article/220149.

Equity crowdfunding is another source of capital:

> https://www.dealmarket.com
> http://www.icapitalnetwork.com/
> https://roundvip.com/
> http://www.palico.com/
> http://www.moneycrashers.com/equity-crowdfunding-sites-investors-entrepreneurs/
> https://angel.co/

https://circleup.com/
https://www.fundable.com/
https://www.crowdfunder.com/
https://www.equitynet.com/
https://wefunder.com/
https://localstake.com/
https://www.seedinvest.com/
https://www.techcoastangels.com/
http://www.investorscircle.net/
http://www.goldenseeds.com/
http://www.northcoastangelfund.com/
https://www.bandangels.com

Crowdfunding is another source of risk capital:
http://www.crowdsourcing.org/
http://crowdfundchampion.com/directory/
http://crowdexpert.com/investment-crowdfunding-platform-directory/
http://chilango.co.uk/

UK Company Credit Checks

If you want to run a credit check on a company in the United Kingdom, as we did in chapter 12 on Bettys, Henry Newrick is ready to help. You can contact him at henry@ teamgroupuk.com.

Bibliography

Bianco, Anthony. "The Warren Buffett You Don't Know." *Businessweek,* 5 July 1999.

Buffett, Warren. "Berkshire Hathaway Acquisition Criteria." *Berkshire Hathaway Annual Report,* 2003.

_____. "Letter to Shareholders." *Berkshire Hathaway Annual Report,* 2009.

Correa, Cristiane. *Dream Big.* Brazil: Sextante, 2014.

Faris, Stephan. "Ground Zero: A Starbucks-Free Italy." *Businessweek,* 9 February 2012.

Gerstner, Louis V., Jr. *Who Says Elephants Can't Dance?* New York: Harper, 2003.

Graham, Benjamin, and David Dodd. *Security Analysis.* New York: McGraw-Hill, 1934.

Hogue, Joseph. *Sector Report: Organic Food.* Toronto: High Alert Institutional Research, 2014.

Jackson, Tim. *Virgin King.* London: HarperCollinsPublishers, 1995.

Kaufman, Michael T. *Soros: The Life and Times of a Messianic Billionaire.* New York: Knopf, 2002.

Kroc, Ray, with Robert Anderson. *Grinding It Out: The Making of McDonald's.* New York: St. Martin's Press, 1987.

Leonard, Devin. "Burger King Is Run by Children." *Bloomberg Businessweek,* 24 July 2014. http://www.bloomberg.com/news/articles/2014-07-24/burger-king-is-run-by-children.

Love, John F. *McDonald's: Behind the Arches.* New York: Bantam Books, 1995.

Lowe, Janet. *Warren Buffett Speaks: Wit and Wisdom from the World's Greatest Investor.* New York: Wiley, 1997.

Mackey, John, and Raj Sisodia. *Conscious Capitalism: Liberating the Heroic Spirit of Business.* Boston: Harvard Business Review Press, 2013.

McDonald, John P. *Flameout: The Rise and Fall of Burger Chef.* Lost Enterprises Publishing, 2011.

McLamore, James. *The Burger King: Jim McLamore and the Building of an Empire.* New York: McGraw-Hill, 1998.

Sanders, Scott R. *Burger Chef.* Chicago: Arcadia Publishing, 2009.

Schultz, Howard. *Onward: How Starbucks Fought for Its Life Without Losing Its Soul.* New York: Rodale Books, 2011.

_____. *Pour Your Heart into It: How Starbucks Built a Company One Cup at a Time.* New York: Hyperion, 1997.

Stone, Brad. *The Everything Store.* New York: Back Bay Books, 2014.

Walton, Sam, with John Huey. *Made in America: My Story.* New York: Bantam Books, 1993.

Ward, Steven D. *The Coffeeist Manifesto: No More Bad Coffee!* Seattle: Amazon Digital Services, 2012.

Notes

CHAPTER 1: WHY AREN'T THERE ANY STARBUCKS STORES IN ITALY?

1. Stephan Faris, "Grounds Zero: A Starbucks-Free Italy," *Bloomberg Businessweek*, 9 February 2012, http://www.businessweek.com/magazine/grounds-zero-a-starbucksfree-italy-02092012.html.

2. Howard Schultz, *Pour Your Heart into It: How Starbucks Built a Company One Cup at a Time* (New York: Hyperion, 1997), 51.

3. Ibid., 51–52.

4. "Starbucks Set to Rock Italy's Cafe Culture," *ABC News,* http://abcnews.go.com/Business/story?id=88256&page=1#.UX2jECv89uB.

5. John F. Love, *McDonald's: Behind the Arches* (New York: Bantam Books, 1995), 15.

6. Ibid., 39.

7. Joseph Hogue, *Sector Report: Organic Food* (Toronto: High Alert Institutional Research, 2014), 6.

CHAPTER 2: "MOST EVERYTHING I'VE DONE I COPIED FROM SOMEBODY ELSE"

1. Sam Walton with John Huey, *Made in America: My Story* (New York: Bantam Books, 1993), 47.

2. Ibid., 53.

3. Brad Stone, *The Everything Store* (New York: Back Bay Books, 2014), 124.

4. http://phx.corporate-ir.net/phoenix.zhtml?c=83830&p=irol-reportsannual.

5. Ray Kroc with Robert Anderson, *Grinding It Out: The Making of McDonald's* (New York: St. Martin's Press, 1987), 11.

6. Ibid., 9–10.

7. Ibid., 11–12.

8. http://en.wikipedia.org/wiki/Burger_King.

CHAPTER 3: WHEN THE COPYCAT GETS COPIED

1. "US Coffee Shops Still Simply Too Hot to Handle," *Market Research World*, http://www.marketresearchworld.net/index.php?option=com_content&task=view&id=566.

2. Steven D. Ward, *The Coffeeist Manifesto: No More Bad Coffee!* (Seattle: Amazon Digital Services, 2012), 116.

3. http://www.slate.com/articles/news_and_politics/hey_wait_a_minute/2007/12/dont_fear_starbucks.single.html.

4. "Facing off with McDonald's," *Forbes Asia*, February 2013, 64.

5. Information from "Coffee Shop Revolution Continues to Stimulate the High Street," *Guardian*, 22 June 2012, http://www.guardian.co.uk/business/2012/jun/22/coffee-shop-revolution-continues.

6. Conal Urquhart, "While Last Orders Ring for Struggling Pubs, Coffee Shops Are Booming," *Guardian*, 22 December 2012, http://www.guardian.co.uk/lifeand-style/2012/dec/22/pubs-coffee-shops.

7. *Whitbread Annual Report*, 2011–12, 2, http://www.whitbread.co.uk/content/dam/whitbread/siteimages/investors/results-reports/annual-report-2011-12.pdf.

8. Mitu Jayashankar, "V. G. Siddhartha Is Branching Out," 29 June 2011, http://forbesindia.com/article/big-bet/vg-siddhartha-is-branching-out/26282/0?id=26282&pg=0.

9. As of 28 March 2016. A "meter" on the company's Web site (http://www.cafecoffeeday.com/—scroll down to the bottom) tracks the current total.

10. http://www.referenceforbusiness.com/history2/83/Tchibo-GmbH.html.

11. As of 2012: http://www.thisisitaly-panorama.com/business-news/this-mccafe-is-mcgood/.

12. Faris, "Grounds Zero."

13. http://en.wikipedia.org/wiki/Tesco.

14. http://www.carrefour.net/en/articles.html?t=29.

15. http://www.carrefour.net/en/articles.html?a=22274.

16. http://stock.walmart.com/.

17. http://corporate.walmart.com/our-story/our-stores.

18. http://www.mckinseychina.com/wp-content/uploads/2012/05/Inside_Chinas_Hypermarkets.pdf.

19. Barbara Farfan, "2010 World's Largest Hypermarkets—Complete List of Biggest Hypermarkets Chains," 26 October 2015, http://retailindustry.about.com/od/famousretailers/a/worlds_largest_retail_hypermarket_supercenter_superstore_chains_world_rankings_list.htm.

CHAPTER 4: HOW JOHN MACKEY'S *VISION* SAVED WHOLE FOODS FROM DROWNING

1. John Mackey and Raj Sisodia, *Conscious Capitalism: Liberating the Heroic Spirit of Business* (Boston: Harvard Business Review Press, 2013), 5.

2. Ibid.

3. Ibid., 6.

4. Ibid., 3.

5. Ibid.

6. Ibid., 5.

7. Ibid., 7.

8. Ibid.

9. Milton Friedman, John Mackey, and T. J. Rodgers, "Rethinking the Social Responsibility of Business," October 2005, http://reason.com/archives/2005/10/01/rethinking-the-social-responsi.

10. Howard Schultz, *Onward: How Starbucks Fought for Its Life Without Losing Its Soul*, (New York: Rodale Books,) 2011, 35.

11. Ibid.

12. Ibid., 90.

13. Ibid., 34.

14. Ibid., 9.

15. Much to Schultz's annoyance, this memo was quickly leaked. You can read it here: http://www.businessweek.com/stories/2008-01-07/howard-schultzs-memobusinessweek-business-news-stock-market-and-financial-advice.

16. Schultz, *Onward*, 41.

17. Ibid., 65–66.

18. Ibid., 5.

19. Ibid., 193.

20. Ibid., 196.

21. Ibid., 195.

CHAPTER 5: HOW RAY KROC'S MCDONALD'S TRUMPED BURGER KING WITH SUPERIOR *ENTREPRENEURIAL* MANAGEMENT AND EXECUTION

1. As of 18 July 2013: http://www.theguardian.com/news/datablog/2013/jul/17/mcdonalds-restaurants-where-are-they.

2. James McLamore, *The Burger King: Jim McLamore and the Building of an Empire* (New York: McGraw-Hill, 1998), xxix.

3. Ibid., 3.

4. Ibid., 9.

5. Ibid., 46.

6. John P. McDonald, *Flameout: The Rise and Fall of Burger Chef* (Lost Enterprises Publishing, 2011), 6.

7. Scott R. Sanders, *Burger Chef* (Chicago: Arcadia Publishing, 2009), 8.

8. McDonald, *Flameout*, 65.

9. Sanders, *Burger Chef*, Frank Thomas Jr.'s preface, 6.

10. McDonald, *Flameout*, 107.

11. Kroc with Anderson, *Grinding It Out*, 71.

12. Ibid., 81.

13. Daniel Gross, *Forbes Greatest Business Stories of All Time* (Hoboken, NJ: Wiley, 1996), 184.

14. McLamore, *Burger King*, 101.

15. Ibid., 36.

16. Ibid., 33.

17. Ibid., 67.

18. Ibid., 104.

19. McDonald, *Flameout*, 118.

20. Ibid., 126.

21. Ibid., 124.

22. Ibid., 146.

23. Love, *McDonald's*, 168.

24. Kroc with Anderson, *Grinding It Out*, 84.

25. Ibid., 137.

26. Love, *McDonald's*, 227.

27. Jiji, "McDonald's Japan Logs ¥14.594 Billion Loss After Challenging Quarter," *Japan Times,* http://www.japantimes.co.jp/news/2015/05/01/business/corporate-business/mcdonalds-japan-logs-%C2%A514-594-billion-loss-after-challenging-quarter/#.VURSKyGqqkp.

28. "Best and Worst Fast-Food Restaurants in America," July 2014, http://www.consumerreports.org/cro/magazine/2014/08/best-and-worst-fast-food-restaurants-in-america/index.htm.

29. https://finance.yahoo.com/news/mcdonalds-broken-franchisees-furious-133644537.html.

30. Cristiane Correa, *Dream Big* (Brazil: Sextante, 2014).

31. Ibid.

32. Ibid.

33. Ibid.

34. Devin Leonard, "Burger King Is Run by Children," *Bloomberg Businessweek,* 24 July 2014, http://www.businessweek.com/printer/articles/214894-burger-king-is-run-by-children.

CHAPTER 6: FINDING THE NEXT STARBUCKS "BY WALKING AROUND"

1. Sue Mitchell, "Pie Face Goes into Administration," *The Sydney Morning Herald,* 24 November, 2014. http://www.smh.com.au/business/retail/pie-face-goes-into-administration-20141124-11suzv.html.

2. Heather Holland, "Pie Face Suddenly Closes Nearly All Its NYC Locations," 17 October 2014, https://www.dnainfo.com/new-york/20141016/union-square/pie-face-suddenly-closes-nearly-all-its-nyc-locations.

3. *Berkshire Hathaway Annual Report,* 1998, 10.

4. *Berkshire Hathaway Annual Report,* 2002, 8.

5. Leonard, "Burger King Is Run by Children."

6. Louis V. Gerstner Jr., *Who Says Elephants Can't Dance?* (New York: HarperCollins, 2003), 44.

7. Ibid., 15.

8. http://www.nytimes.com/2016/04/20/technology/intel-earnings-job-cuts.html.

9. http://www.infoworld.com/article/3104389/microsoft-windows/the-case-against-windows-10-anniversary-update-grows.html.

CHAPTER 7: DREAM BIG: START YOUR OWN

1. Gerstner, *Who Says Elephants Can't Dance?*, 182.

2. https://www.quora.com/What-is-the-perfect-startup-team.

3. Love, *McDonald's*, 50.

4. Ibid.

5. Ibid., 21–22.

6. Michael T. Kaufman, *Soros: The Life and Times of a Messianic Billionire* (New York: Knopf, 2002), 127.

7. Personal conversation.

8. Ryan Mac, "The Mad Billionaire Behind GoPro: The World's Hottest Camera Company," *Forbes*, 4 March 2013, http://www.forbes.com/sites/ryanmac/2013/03/04/the-mad-billionaire-behind-gopro-the-worlds-hottest-camera-company/.

9. Ibid.

10. Mike Shatzkin, "Three Points Worth Adding to the Excellent Account of the Amazon Story in the Everything Store," *Idea Logical Company* (blog), 4 November 2013, http://www.idealog.com/blog/three-points-worth-adding-excellent-account-amazon-story-everything-store/.

11. Warren Buffett, "Letter to Shareholders," *Berkshire Hathaway Annual Report*, 2009, 6, http://www.berkshirehathaway.com/letters/2009ltr.pdf.

12. https://en.wikipedia.org/wiki/Pebble_(watch).

13. M3D LLC, "The Micro: The First Truly Consumer 3D Printer," *Kickstarter*, 7 April 2014, https://www.kickstarter.com/projects/m3d/the-micro-the-first-truly-consumer-3d-printer.

14. Adrianne Jeffries, "If You Back a Kickstarter Project That Sells for $2 Billion, Do You Deserve to Get Rich?," *Verge*, 28 March 2014, http://www.theverge.com/2014/3/28/5557120/what-if-oculus-rift-kickstarter-backers-had-gotten-equity.

15. Leonard, "Burger King Is Run by Children."

CHAPTER 8: THE FRANCHISE APPROACH

1. https://www.sba.gov/sites/default/files/FAQ_March_2014_0.pdf.

2. http://www.entrepreneur.com/franchises/fastestgrowing/index.html.

3. John Samuel Raja D and Chaitali Chakravarty, "Vikram Bakshi and Amit Jatia: A tale of McDonald's Two Franchise Partners in India," *Economic Times*, 24 September 2013, http://articles.economictimes.indiatimes.com/2013-09-24/news/42361242_1_india-wazir-advisors-countries.

4. Sarah Treleaven, "How a Canadian Burger Outlet Made Its Way to the Middle East," *Financial Post,* 31 March 2014, http://business.financialpost.com/entrepreneur/franchise-focus/how-a-canadian-burger-outlet-made-its-way-to-the-middle-east.

5. Louella D. Desiderio, "Potato Corner to Open 60 Stores Here, 10 in Indonesia," *Philippine Star,* 6 June 2015, www.abs-cbnnews.com/business/06/06/15/potato-corner-open-60-stores-here-10-indonesia.

6. www.pc-history.org/altair.htm.

CHAPTER 9: INVESTMENT STRATEGIES FROM BUFFETT TO THIEL

1. Gerstner, *Who Says Elephants Can't Dance?,* 5.

2. Benjamin Graham and David Dodd, *Security Analysis* (New York: McGraw-Hill, 1934), 17.

3. Ibid., 18–19.

4. Ibid., 158.

5. Ibid., 161.

6. "Berkshire Hathaway Inc.: An Owner's Manual," 1999, http://www.berkshirehathaway.com/owners.html.

7. Graham and Dodd, *Security Analysis,* 18–19.

CHAPTER 10: BUY THE "NEXT STARBUCKS" AT THE IPO—OR BEFORE

1. https://en.wikipedia.org/wiki/Initial_public_offering_of_Facebook#First_day.

2. Tim Loughran with Jay R. Ritter, "Why Has IPO Underpricing Changed over Time?," http://www.nd.edu/~tloughra/whynew.pdf.

3. Tim Loughran with Jay R. Ritter, "Why Don't Issuers Get Upset About Leaving Money on the Table in IPOs?," https://www3.nd.edu/~tloughra/moneyonthetable.pdf.

4. Claire Cain Miller, "The Next Mark Zuckerberg Is Not Who You Might Think," *New York Times,* 2 July 2015, http://www.nytimes.com/2015/07/02/upshot/the-next-mark-zuckerberg-is-not-who-you-might-think.html?pagewanted=all&_r=0.

5. Tucker Max, "Why I Stopped Angel Investing (and You Should Never Start)," *Observer Business & Tech,* 11 August 2015, http://observer.com/2015/08/why-i-stopped-angel-investing-and-you-should-never-start/.

6. Emilie Sandy and Adam Pescod, "Chilango Is Leading a Mexican Wave," *Elite Business,* 1 October 2015, http://elitebusinessmagazine.co.uk/interviews/item/chilango-is-leading-a-mexican-wave.

7. "Crowdfunding Project Creator Settles FTC Charges of Deception," *Federal Trade Commission,* 11 June 2015, https://www.ftc.gov/news-events/press-releases/2015/06/crowdfunding-project-creator-settles-ftc-charges-deception.

8. "Recapping a Round??," Gotham Gal (blog), http://gothamgal.com/2015/07/recapping-a-round/.

9. Max, "Why I Stopped Angel Investing."

CHAPTER 11: CATCH—OR CREATE—A TAILWIND

1. "History of Early American Automobile Industry," http://www.earlyamericanauto-mobiles.com/americanautomobiles25.htm.

2. Carren Jao, "How Companies Are Trying to Bring Marijuana Ads Online," *Entrepreneur,* July 2015, http://www.entrepreneur.com/article/246896.

CHAPTER 12: FINDING THE NEXT TAILWIND TO RIDE

1. Lauren Sieben, "American Council on Education and Pearson Will Redevelop GED as for-Profit Program," *Chronicle,* 15 March 2011, http://chronicle.com/article/American-Council-on-Education/126736.

2. http://www.boston.co.za/qualifications/career-qualifications/personal-development-occasional-study/ged-grade-12-equivalency/.

3. Jessica Tan, "TWG's Ritzy Tea," *Forbes,* 4 December 2009, http://www.forbes.com/global/2009/1214/life-singapore-murjani-bouqdib-twg-ritzy-tea.html.

4. OSIM Quarterly Report, 31 March 2016, 8, http://osim.listedcompany.com/newsroom/20160419_171506_O23_QMIJEEVNQXNE76MX.1.pdf

5. https://www.bettys.co.uk/about-us.

6. www.tripadvisor.com/Restaurant_Review-g187046-d1011681-Reviews-or90-Bettys_Cafe_Tea_Rooms_Harrogate-Harrogate_North_Yorkshire_England.html#REVIEWS.

7. https://www.bettyscookeryschool.co.uk/.

8. Dan Bolton, "Teavana Fine Tea + Tea Bar Opens in NYC," Tea Biz (blog), 23 October 2012, https://teabizblog.wordpress.com/2013/10/23/first-look-teavana-fine-tea-tea-bar-opens-in-nyc/.

9. Bruce Horovitz, "Starbucks Debuts Teavana Bar, and It's a Doozy," *USA Today,* 23 October 13, http://www.usatoday.com/story/money/business/2013/10/23/starbucks-teavana-fast-food-tea-tea-houses/3146149/.

10. Dan Bolton, "Teavana's Global Ambitions," *World Tea News,* 20 March 2015, http://worldteanews.com/news/teavanas-global-ambitions.

11. Dan Bolton, "Teavana Growth Could Be 'Quite Amazing,'" *World Tea News,* 1 June 2015, http://worldteanews.com/news/domestic-news/teavana-growth-could-be-quite-amazing.

12. https://www.harney.com/.

13. For more examples see the best tea shops around the world, the fifty best tearooms in London, or the eight best spots for afternoon tea in New York.

14. https://www.google.com/search?sourceid=chrome-psyapi2&ion=1&espv=2&ie=UTF-8&q=yelp+davids+tea&oq=yelp+davids+tea&aqs=chrome..69i57j0j69i64l2.3007j0j4&gws_rd=cr&ei=NB_RVqCEDMbsmAXfvb3YBA.

15. Roberto A. Ferdman, "The Chipotle Effect: Why America Is Obsessed with Fast Casual Food," *Washington Post,* 2 February 2015, https://www.washingtonpost.com/news/wonk/wp/2015/02/02/the-chipotle-effect-why-america-is-obsessed-with-fast-casual-food/.

16. Kyle Stock and Vanessa Wong, "Chipotle: The Definitive Oral History," *Bloomberg*

Business, 2 February 2015, http://www.bloomberg.com/graphics/2015-chipotle-oral-history/.

17. https://www.youtube.com/watch?v=wmH73Diqf5Q.

18. http://ir.chipotle.com/phoenix.zhtml?c=194775&p=irol-homeprofile&t=&id=&.

19. http://www.bus-ex.com/blog/chipotle-leadership.

20. Michael Smith, "CDC: Tainted Food Tied to Regular Illness Outbreaks," *Medpage Today,* 3 November 2015, http://www.medpagetoday.com/InfectiousDisease/PublicHealth/54473.

21. Ahiza Garcia, "Chipotle Subpoenaed over Norovirus Outbreak," *CNN Money,* 15 January 2016, http://money.cnn.com/2016/01/06/news/companies/chipotle-subpoena-norovirus/.

22. Ibid.

23. Ibid.

24. Ibid.

25. Thomson Reuters, "Chipotle Sued for Misleading Investors over Food Safety," *Business Insurance,* 8 January 2016, http://www.businessinsurance.com/article/20160108/NEWS06/160109832/chipotle-sued-for-misleading-investors-over-food-safety?tags=%7C329%7C302.

26. https://en.wikipedia.org/wiki/1993_Jack_in_the_Box_E._coli_outbreak.

27. Alison Griswold, "Taco Bell's 2006 *E. coli* Outbreak Is a Scary History Lesson for Chipotle," *Quartz,* 7 December 2015, http://qz.com/567567/taco-bells-2006-e-coli-outbreak-is-a-scary-history-lesson-for-chipotle/.

28. http://www.yelp.com/biz/chipotle-mexican-grill-san-jose-3.

29. http://en.yelp.com.ph/biz/chipotle-mexican-grill-champaign.

30. http://www.yelp.com/biz/chipotle-mexican-grill-hawthorne.

31. http://www.yelp.com/biz/chipotle-mexican-grill-escondido-2.

WHAT'S NEXT

1. Brad M. Barber and Terrance Odeon, "Trading Is Hazardous to Your Wealth: The Common Stock Investment Performance of Individual Investors," *Journal of Finance* 4, no. 2 (April 2000). The authors show that investors who traded stocks actively had, on average, a far lower return than investors who followed a buy-and-hold strategy.

APPENDIX I: "FROM POVERTY TO POVERTY IN THREE GENERATIONS"—WHAT TO DO WHEN THE FOUNDER DEPARTS THE SCENE

1. Lowe, *Warren Buffett Speaks,* 102–3.

2. *Berkshire Hathaway Annual Rport,* 2014, 8–9.

3. Ibid.

4. *Intelligent Investor.*

5. Berkshire Hathaway, "Letter to Shareholders," 2013, 5.

6. Berkshire Hathaway, "Letter to Shareholders," 2014, 37.

7. Lowe, *Warren Buffett Speaks,* 108.

8. "Letter," Berkshire Hathaway, 2014, 42.

9. Ibid., 36.

APPENDIX II: A QUICK GUIDE TO MAKING MONEY IN THE FRANCHISING BUSINESS

1. Leslie Patton, "Burger King Tops Wendy's to Regain No. 2 U.S. Hamburger Spot," *Bloomberg Business,* 27 May 2015, http://www.bloomberg.com/news/articles/2015-05-26/burger-king-tops-wendy-s-to-regain-no-2-u-s-hamburger-spot.

2. McLamore, *Burger King,* 92.

APPENDIX III: DAVIDSTEA

1. http://seekingalpha.com/article/3672616-davids-tea-toxic-brew-sweet-promises-overpowered-bitter-reality.

ACKNOWLEDGMENTS

Some projects are sprints. Writing this was a marathon. No question, without the help of many and varied people I'd still be puffing along, most likely a long way from the finish line.

To begin with, this book's very existence is directly attributable to my agent, Al Zuckerman. Believing in the concept, and that I could deliver on it, he sold the yet-to-be-completed manuscript to St. Martin's Press.

Now, with a deadline to meet, it was time to really get to work.

Writing can be a lonely process. Chuck de Castro and Patrick Gramaje both helped me to write faster.

Chuck kept me on the straight and narrow over the many months it took to reach THE END. His continual feedback, crits, and suggestions made the words flow way faster. Without Chuck's help, I would never have finished this project on time. While Patrick's comments, combined with his ability to analyze company financials, dig into the venture capital sector, fast casual, tea, and other sectors, to mention just a few, were invaluable.

Raquel Narca read (and reread!) each chapter "hot off the press," dramatically improving the flow and clarity, while Alexis Gotladera typed and retyped tens of thousands of words, not all of which appeared in the final manuscript, and prepared most of the tables and diagrams.

Kris Wadia's input was an immense help in refining my understanding of management. I first experienced his management abilities when he "cleaned up my business" some twenty-five years ago. He has since gone on to higher (and much higher-paying) positions—and deservedly so.

Larry Abrams guided me through the potential pitfalls, potholes—and profits—of venture capital.

I must also thank my daughter, Natasha, for being in the right place at the right time to investigate Bettys, Chilango, and the London branches of Chipotle and their competitors on my behalf.

But, sad to say, a first draft remains a first draft until several pairs of eagle eyes have gone through and (too often!) torn it to pieces.

Byron Callas and Eunice Rivero both gave me detailed and hardheaded crits, some requiring extensive rewriting. All of them dramatically improving my words.

Bay Butler, Ivy Choy, Anthony Dawson, Dale Haling, Don Hauptman, Jae Jung, Ellis Levine, Janice Matthews, Henry Newrick, Robert Nirkind, Dan Rosenthal, Tim Staermose, Jerome Summers, Anthony Wile, and Ellen Young all provided helpful information on a variety of different topics, in addition to useful feedback on the manuscript itself.

Finally, it's hard for me to thank the amazing team at St. Martins Press enough. Steven Henry Boldt did an incredible job of editing the manuscript, adding major improvements and refinements to my all-too-often awkward words. St. Martins' production team came up with a dramatic cover design, better than anything I had ever thought of. Their marketing and publicity team of Laura Clark, Paul Hochman, John Nicholas, and Sarah Becks helped place this copy in your hands, while Michael Homler and Lauren Jablonski made it all happen.

Thank you all.

Naturally, any remaining mistakes are mine. So if you happen to find one that slipped through the intensive editing process, or have bouquets rather than brickbats, I'd love to hear them either directly (www.marktier.com/contact) or in a review on the Web site of your choice.

Index